KW-361-061

FINDING WORK

Cross National Perspectives on Employment and Training

Edited by

Ray C. Rist

The Falmer Press

(A member of the Taylor & Francis Group)
London, New York and Philadelphia

923575 FP

UK The Falmer Press, Falmer House, Barcombe, Lewes, East Sussex, BN8 5DL

USA The Falmer Press, Taylor & Francis Inc., 242 Cherry Street, Philadelphia, PA 19106–1906

© 1986 Selection and editorial material copyright R. C. Rist

All rights reserved. No part of this publication may be reproduced, stored in a retrieval system, or transmitted in any form or by any means, electronic, mechanical, photocopying, recording or otherwise, without permission in writing from the Publisher.

First published in 1986

Library of Congress Cataloging in Publication Data

Finding work.

   Includes bibliographies and index.
   1. Youth—Employment.   2. Occupational training.
3. Employees, Training of.   I. Rist, Ray C.
HD6270.F53   1986   331.3′42592   86-8974
ISBN 1 85000 124 3
ISBN 1 85000 125 1 (pbk.)

Typeset in 10/12 Bembo by
Imago Publishing Ltd, Thame, Oxon

Printed in Great Britain by Taylor & Francis (Printers) Ltd, Basingstoke

2957
331.342592

A6069

FINDING WORK

ACOT

2 5 NOV 1986

LIBRARY

Contents

Contents

Introduction *Economic Growth and Job Creation: Just How Relevant Are Employment and Training Programs?*[1]

Ray C. Rist

Consider the following: Western Europe between 1973 and 1985 experienced thirteen straight years of rising unemployment; urban black youth in the United States have unemployment rates somewhere near 45 per cent; more than 6600 robots are in use in various sectors of West German industry; between 1970 and 1980, Western Europe lost some two million jobs while the United States created approximately twenty million new jobs; training expenditures in Sweden average approximately $450.00 (US) per year per worker while the average in the United States is approximately $100.00; one of eight French workers receives some job-related training each year at a total combined cost to the public and private sectors of more than 10 billion French francs; as its shipbuilding industry declined during the 1970s, Japan successfully retrained 50,000 shipyard workers for new jobs; and 1985 may be the first year since 1978 in which no Western European nation suffers a decline in economic growth.

While many more examples of the kind noted here could be provided, the implications are clear. Unemployment, structural changes in the economy and in the work place, retraining of dislocated workers, and finding strategies that are successful in assisting youth to make the transition from school to work are common challenges confronting industrialized societies. While the emphasis (or crisis) might be different from one country to another, the central fact remains — each industrial country is undergoing rapid shifts in its various economic sectors and these shifts are having ripple effects across the society. It is to how the various countries are responding with policy and program initiatives that this present volume is addressed.

As the collected chapters here make clear, the responses are not simply on the margin. Sustained periods with little or no job creation, with declines in economic growth, and with some groups pressing for greater participation in the labor force (for example, youth, women, minorities and refugees), have meant that the policy apparatus has not been able to respond with a 'business as usual' approach. Rather, the emergence of a worldwide shortage of jobs, coupled with a basic restructuring of the industrial division of labor across nations, has meant that each country has had to re-examine and rethink basic policies and programs that may have been in place for decades. As but one example, consider this comment by Eizenstat and Spring on the current unemployment insurance program in the United States: 'Unemployment insurance in America has gone largely unchanged since its exactment in 1935 at the depth of the Depression as a program to provide the unemployed with income during periods of temporary unemployment'.[2] They and others have called for a basic restructuring of this program to better respond to the current economic conditions of the country.

The Bottom Line

While hinted at in some places, and made quite explicit in others, the bottom line that keeps emerging in the articles to follow is an absolute insistence that central to any efforts at dealing with the current economics dislocations and upheavals is a primary focus on economic growth. Economic growth is seen as the key ingredient to stimulate demand — and it is demand that will generate job creation. Western Europe will not reverse thirteen straight years of increasing unemployment with still better apprenticeship programs nor will the United States increase employment opportunities for urban minority youth through more sophisticated career awareness programs. Indeed, one could argue that with high demand driving greater job creation, many of the presumed barriers to employment would quickly disappear. The addition of a million new jobs in England, France or West Germany could do wondrous things in terms of reshaping existing assumptions regarding employment and training programs. Presumed deficiencies in youth and dislocated workers might be thought less constraining if there was a consistent demand for their labor.

Two other aspects of the central theme in this collection also bear mention. First, there is not much expectation that technology is going to be the saviour for present economic problems. Indeed, there are several writers here who are not at all sanguine that 'high-tech' is going to result in any real job growth at all, once one takes into account the displacement, the automation, and the skill (rather than labor) intensive nature of the work. While the statistic is not presented in any of the papers, it is interesting here to note that taken together, the five most rapidly growing high-tech areas (computers, lasers, etc.) in the United States are projected to generate fewer new jobs in total between 1985 and 1995 than will the projected demand in the same time frame for 900,000 new janitorial positions. Second, it also should be noted that none of the authors take the position of espousing 'no growth' as a national policy. While something of a trend (fad?) just a few years ago, each of the authors here sees the various countries taking vigorous and active steps to generate economic growth.

New and perhaps unconventional responses are needed to the persistent problem of unemployment and dislocation, but one unconventional response that does not get serious attention is to argue for no growth and to instead restructure economic activities within the parameters of existing systems.

The Bottom Bottom Line

Stated simply, economic growth is a necessary but not sufficient condition for ensuring employment opportunities. Coupled with job creation is the need for a coherent employment and training policy. As can be seen in the United States, economic growth alone has not solved a number of employment problems, be they those of the 245,000 displaced steel workers, unemployed youth, or those 2.3 million workers who lost manufacturing jobs since 1980 because of automation and foreign competition. What a thoughtful employment and training policy provides is the systematic application and allocation of resources targeted in such a manner as to achieve maximum benefits for those most in need. To argue that growth alone will solve the problems of those who wish to be employed, but who are not, is to argue for a large measure of randomness in the labor markets. It can be supposed that in the absence of sustained and targeted efforts, most unemployed persons would find some work somewhere. But the social and emotional costs, the lost economic contributions, and the frequent mismatches between the individual job-slot and the individual worker are all negative aspects of this strategy.

It can also be argued that none of the industrialized countries are totally without some form of employment and training policy, ergo the point above that growth alone is a viable strategy is rendered moot. I agree with this contention. Consequently, it is my view that the concern must necessarily shift to an examination of the appropriateness and adequacy of existing policies and programs. More precisely, and to a concern of this present volume, an examination is needed of the ways in which existing efforts are (or are not) synchronized to simultaneously maximize high employment and adapt to changes in the employment structure. The challenge for each of the countries discussed here is to formulate employment and training policies that contribute to both concerns: maintain a strong demand for employment and concurrently train individuals for the seemingly ever-changing labor market.

What complicates and often inhibits effective employment and training policy is that such policy cannot be created and implemented in a vacuum. There are any number of other political, social, and economic forces that can either complement or conflict with employment and training policies. Stated broadly, employment and training policies have to be considered in the context of existing constraints — both national and international, of wage policies, of tariffs and protectionism policies, of the financial stability of the national currency, of the viability of different industrial and service sectors, and of the demographic characteristics of those in and those about to enter the labor market. While such a list (and I am sure this is not exhaustive) can be intimidating at first glance, it is nonetheless the case that each of the countries represented here (with the possible exception of China) are all conducting their employment and training efforts within this context. The issue is not whether it can be done, but rather how successfully can such policy and program initiatives be conducted.

Programs and Policies: Sorting Through the Trends

While it is admittedly a risky proposition to try and tie together strands of analysis from such diverse countries as are represented in this volume, there are nonetheless insights to be gained in specifically addressing what trends appear at present to be in place. Specifically, there are at least four 'knowns' that highlight our understanding of the role of employment and training efforts in industrial countries. They are:

(a) More is known about measuring the outcomes of programs than is known about the processes and dynamics that created such outcomes.

(b) More is known about the conditions and forces that generate program failure than is known on how to generate and sustain program success.

(c) More is known about the ways in which national or federal initiatives are created and instigated than how they are received at the local level.

(d) More is known about how to respond to those seeking employment and training services through treating them as 'clients' than is known about how to respond and equip individuals to be co-participant in making decisions on their future.

While this short list is not exhaustive, taking it as a whole does generate certain implications that reflect the trends in employment and training practices and policies now in place. The first is that both the knowledge base and the actual participants have frequently suffered from the view that 'good' employment and training programs are those that come close to being 'actor proof'. This view has had wide popularity, positing that good programs do not depend upon the particular competencies or values of those who either operate or participate in such programs, but that a system can be so constructed that persons are able to move through and receive skills without the vulnerabilities that come from a reliance on individual participants or trainer. Perhaps the highwater mark of this approach was in embracing of computer-based, individualized learning units that could be completed entirely alone. The notion was that skills could be programmed and individually learned without traditional modes of teacher-student interaction or classroom participation. But what has been recognized recently is that such an approach ignores a key ingredient for success — the inspired and competent efforts of staff. True, poor staff and low morale can hinder a program, but positive outcomes seem most apparent when good staff with high morale and motivation give their best efforts. In addition, the actor proof strategy is simply not viable in many countries. When one considers the training needs in China or the on-the-job training strategies used in Japan, the man-machine strategy has to give way to a concern for developing effective close-in person-to-person training strategies.

Second, for a person to opt for an employment and training program is frequently a complex decision. There are considerations not only of future occupational opportunities, but of working through the present costs and benefits as well. Employment and training programs frequently mean during some period of time the near or complete absence from the labor market, thus loss of income and perhaps even seniority. Joining a training program may also mean changing living arrangements, moving from one city to another, finding oneself again in the role of student, and others. The point in stressing the web of considerations facing a person who is interested in training is that the intrinsic value of the training itself may not be sufficient to persuade the individual to join. Day care, low cost loans or stipends, transportation, moving allowances, and non-conventional hours may all be possible responses to help make possible the decision to opt for training.

Third, and related to the first, is that the evidence is persuasive that the one 'treatment' that appears to be predictive of program success, especially for youth, is individualized attention. The persons who are enrolling in employment and training programs are frequently persons who have not experienced much success, and may not have been in a conventional school or classroom for years. They have accumulated a list of unmet technical, academic, and social needs. Responding well tends not to be possible in large-scale, mass-training programs. Taking the time to carefully assess strengths and needs of individuals, and tailoring a program to build on strengths and address needs seems to have positive payoffs. Treating the individual as a 'whole person' is essential.

Finally, there is the distressing matter of the conventional wisdom that there is not really much one country has to learn from another. There seems to be a general consensus that each country has to discover its own wheel. The examples are multiple. Consider this description of the May 1985 meeting in Milan of 600 European trade unions:

> The fact is that today, the unions are having a rough time. 'Radical neo-liberalism' and 'radical neo-conservatism' are spreading as one delegate complained after another. New technologies are creating more and more unemployment. No one had any advice to give except to say that it was no use trying to transfer the American attempts to

solve the problem to Europe, with its totally different social and political tradition, as the socialist Italian premier Bettino Craxi said in his speech of welcome.[3]

While the America-to-Europe transfer of job creation strategies can be debated (as the Europe-to-America transfer of the apprenticeship model is also debated), the point is that some aspects of particular programs may well have applicability. It is the task of analysts and policy-makers to sort these out and see what can be done to learn from one another. Comparative work is time-consuming and can be costly. But to see the industrial countries *a priori* shutting down the discussion on the grounds that each is so unique and so distinct that there are no points of common interest is unfortunate. While the forces that are shaping the economies of the various countries cut across national boundaries with impunity, the responses seem to be predicated on a nation-by-nation basis. The looming worldwide job shortage — of literally millions of jobs — is not one that can be satisfactorily solved exclusively within various nation-state boundaries. Recognizing common strategies or learning from differences seems an eminently sensible approach. It is one that this book would nurture explicitly.

On the Present Volume

The chapters presented here are all original contributions, save one. They have taken as their point of departure some aspect of the employment and training policy/program strategy in various industrialized countries. Several of the authors have chosen to focus in-depth on an individual country; others take as their task the development of cross-national perspectives and comparisons. Further, there are chapters that address what is being done for youth and others that deal with the situation of adults. There are also variations among chapters in that some provide greater attention to programmatic initiatives and others focus on the policy considerations and formulations. The sum total of this collection is something of a mosaic — patterns and forms might vary, but the sum total of the effort is a rather unique perspective on how different industrial countries are developing and implementing their employment and training strategies.

A note to readers: While the message traditionally of a book goes in one direction, from author to reader, there is every justification in the present instance to try and make the linkage in both directions. To learn of work in different countries and to know of one or more persons who has an interest or expertise in that country can make an important contribution to further research and writing. Networking in comparative research is extremely critical. Consequently, the addresses of all contributors are listed at the end of this present volume. It is hoped that readers will feel free to write the respective authors, probe points in more detail, or provide additional information. Such an exchange is welcomed and to be encouraged.

Notes

1 The views expressed here are those of the author and no endorsement by the United States General Accounting Office is intended or should be inferred.
2 *The Washington Post*, 9 September 1984.
3 *Frankfurter Allgemeine Zeitung*, 20 May 1985.

Part One
Policy Directions For Youth

Introduction

Attempting to generalize across national employment and training policies is risky and the necessary caveats are many. But based on the studies included in this volume, the following are tentative generalizations that appear to reflect the major directions in which select industrialized countries are moving with their employment and training policies for youths.

First, there appears to be consensus that it is important to address the problems that impact on youth employment earlier than when the unemployment actually appears. The strategy is one of working to keep the youth in a school or training program. The transition from school to work appears more successful if, in fact, that student is in school when the transition is made. Stated differently, when the student loses the institutional support of the school or a training program, the difficulties multiply and the opportunities diminish for a successful job placement.

Second, there is considerable benefit in combining school and work, rather than thinking in 'either-or' terms. While a number of employment programs in the various countries are oriented towards those who have left school, evidence is mounting that a combination of employment opportunities is a particularly effective strategy for facilitating the transition into full-time work. The emphasis here is especially important to school-based programs where traditionally the student is given information about jobs, filling out applications, how to dress for a job interview, etc., but where the student never has the opportunity to actually experience holding a job. Articles here from Denmark, Australia, and the United Kingdom are particularly instructive on this point.

Increased efforts are being made to target resources and programs so as to concentrate the possibility for demonstrated impacts. This third policy direction indicates a movement away from the dominant view of the past two decades — that comprehensive services to large populations were necessary for success. For a combination of reasons, including costs, lack of demonstrated success with the comprehensive strategy, and the seemingly intractable nature of some unemployment, there has been a shift towards particular programs for particular populations. This shift is reflected in the following chapters where there is a discussion of the targeting that is taking place in many of the countries analyzed here. In Denmark, the targeting is on those students still in school, hoping through increased services and development of job skills that the transition to employment will be facilitated and more successful. In Australia, the targeting appears to be centering on those school leavers with no certificate and no job training. In the United States, the emphasis appears to be on two quite distinct groups — those quite close to employability, and those some distance away.

The interesting policy shift reflected in increased emphasis on targeting is one away from scope to one of specificity. Further, what targeting implies in the current period of program cutbacks and loss of funding is that there will be some youth who will receive few or no services. If a young person now finds him or herself outside one of the designated target groups, there is a very real possibility that he or she will have no assistance at all. This shift is thus not simply theoretical, but one that will have real repercussions for youth. Decisions about who is most in need or who is most likely to benefit will result in the allocation of resources differently than has been generally the case in recent years. Targeting is fundamentally a form of social triage, and none of the countries discussed here have come easily to the policy criteria by which this decision is made.

Fourth, policies aimed at providing youth with employment and training opportunities while still in school have often found themselves at odds with policies established for other groups as well. For example, conflicts with unions, with school authorities, with government wage boards, with regulatory commissions establishing working ages, hours, and locations, and with other groups who want support in their efforts to find employment all coalesce to constrain the options for youth policies. From one vantage then, the resulting policies for youth all sub-optimize the potential strategies that could be put in place because no strategy is free from the conflicts noted above. Youth needs are just, but so are those of many others who seek access to the labor market and who want assistance through employment and training programs.

Having said this, there are also many areas where policies and constraints are in place that are counterproductive and do not need to be there. They are the result of tradition, of leaving unexamined policies in place long after they have outlived their usefulness, and of assumptions about youth and their abilities that are simply not the case. (As but one quick example, the calendar for school attendance in that United States is a historical artifact from the time in the nineteenth century when most youth were in small towns or rural areas and were involved with farming. The rationale no longer exists, the policy persists.) Other efforts could also be made with minimal intervention, for example, making sure that funding for in-school youth initiatives coincides with the school year so that students have the opportunity for joint education and training programs.

Finally, and this links back to the early comments on targeting, there is a growing recognition of the different needs of youth in different life circumstances. The answer to the question, 'What works best for whom?' is central to this differentiated strategy. Greater attention is being given to the match between the individual and the program. Parenthetically, one unanticipated benefit noted in the United States is that the programs have had to think more clearly about just who they serve best and what kinds of opportunities they can best provide. Shifting in this policy direction has resulted in a clearer division of labor among programs and an emphasis within programs on doing what they do best.

Taking together these five aspects of youth employment and training policy, there are several conclusions to be drawn. First, differentiation is a term that summarizes many of the current initiatives. Comprehensive programs are being replaced with more tightly conceived programs that provide only some services to some clients. Second, the rate of change within the economies of the countries, coupled with demographic shifts in the youth populations, means that no effort is likely to be satisfactory for very long. Continual adaptations and modifications are inevitable, discouraging as they may be to those who are entrusted with the day-to-day responsibilities for managing programs. Generalizations about who can most benefit from what and when are continually decaying. Finally, the constraints on trying new initiatives discussed earlier means that there will be few new efforts from which one can learn just how really effective a policy or program might be. The margin of error in presuming to know about what works when and for whom will continue to be high.

Vocational Preparation: Policy Issues in England and Western Europe

Dudley Plunkett

The Development of Vocational Preparation Programmes

The history of English education is filled with envy over how adeptly many continental nations have dealt with the training of their young workers and craftsmen. An inferiority complex is detectable in comments of English observers ever since the time of the Paris Exhibition of 1867.[1] The symptoms of feebleness in vocational education in England were identified early, but the disease eluded proper diagnosis. Always enamoured of Oxford, Cambridge and the public schools, English educationists failed in the main to appreciate adequately what Napoleon had done for French education, what Grundtvig had achieved through the folk high school movement in Denmark, or what lessons the Germans had learnt from the 1918 debacle.

More than fifty years after the Germans first provided part-time vocational training for all young people leaving full-time education England still hesitates. A British Government White Paper at the beginning of the 1980s explicitly differentiated those untrained school leavers who were unemployed from those who were in employment.[2] In giving the former priority for short-term political reasons, the authorities were none the less once more postponing the creation of a comprehensive education and training system to meet the needs of a modern community. This policy was questioned at the time by the Youth Task Group which advised the Government to move towards a system of training for young people up to the age of 18 which was comprehensive in terms of availability and access, as well as sufficiently broad-based in its scope to meet both young people's and employers' needs.[3]

The massive expansion of the lycee d'enseignement professionnel, and the lycee technique, the near-saturation enrolment of the Swedish gymnasium, the EFG and BGBJ (basic training year) courses in the vocational schools of Denmark and West Germany aimed at providing a foundation for vocational training, are all examples of a common thread to European education that it may be valuable to follow in greater detail. It is arguable that, while English education has been neglectful of mass vocational training of the traditional type, the country has responded more swiftly than many others to the new factor of widespread youth unemployment by pioneering an educational approach, now usually referred to as vocational preparation, or more recently in England pre-vocational education. It may be that different societies can learn from each other by observing more closely how they meet the particular priorities of their individual situations.[4]

The existence of the EEC and the persistent interest taken by the organization in the vocational training field have meant that it becomes yearly more difficult to interpret developments in the field of employment and education by treating countries in isolation. While the major focus of this chapter is upon England, it is illuminating to make reference to particular European countries and to the European Commission itself wherever there has been mutual influence or relevant comparison or comment made in the formulation of vocational training policies.[5] The scope of this paper is largely restricted to the education and training of young people who have just finished full-time compulsory schooling, and are in the phase to which the label 'vocational preparation' has been attached.[6] Developments within this phase obviously ought not to be disassociated from more advanced or continuing education and training, but they have been so numerous and complex in recent years that they need specific attention. After considering general policy issues in the field, therefore, I shall review the build-up of vocational preparation programmes in England and Western Europe, and then consider, in two separate sections of the chapter, current reappraisals of and further possible options in youth education and training policies.

Public Policies, Strategies and Administrative Structures for Youth Training

Related to the policy issues that have characterized the discussion of youth in transition from school to adult and working life in Western Europe are more profound theoretical and longer-term questions about social values and societal goals which remain equally contentious. In particular, there is no consensus about the value of education to society. Among the themes of discussion are such issues as:

(a) What contribution does education make to economic development?
(b) What kinds of learning are to be considered valuable?
(c) What social costs result from selective forms of education?
(d) What is the role of the education system in relation to employment and lifelong learning?

The ways these issues arise, or how they come to be resolved, necessarily vary from country to country, but there is a general sense that they force educational systems onto the defensive by their querying of some of the most widely held assumptions of the period from the end of World War II to the end of the 1960s.

It may be an exaggeration to say that in the early 1960s education was seen as an unmitigated good, but certainly the prominent economists of education of that time measured education by its length in the equations by which they calculated rates of return to financial investment in education. Now we are more aware of education as consumption, and, with their straitened budgets, governments are looking for more direct and perhaps simpler ways in which education can enrich the labour force and contribute directly to economic development, or 'wealth creation'. This does not necessarily mean that only forms of education that produce a measurable economic return are regarded as justified, but the arguments about how we are to value learning are much more polarized. In recent years many, and particularly those from the government or industrial sectors, have placed emphasis upon basic skills, job-related education and training, and retraining, others have argued the priority of cognitive development and intellectual versatility. Others again have given most importance to the values of personal development and the acquiring of life-skills that could lead to the maximizing of individual self-determination. The growth and strength of these arguments is to some extent plotted in this chapter.

A persistent preoccupation of the last few decades has been with the consequences for individuals and society of having stratified educational systems which offer disproportionate opportunities to the talented. It is apparent that the divisive functions of formal education risk becoming greater in the future than they have been in the past because the burdens of working life have previously always been able to serve as the levers of social and political control. As modern technology lifts these burdens, there is a need to temper the inequalities arising in societies divided between the employed and the unemployed in ways which are virtually unprecedented, at least in the Western world. The unemployed cannot be thought to forfeit their rights to education and training, and especially to those forms of learning that prepare for socially valued activities and lifestyles which are capable of being alternatives to the merely passive state of being unemployed. These are some of the issues that show up patently in the current situation of the unqualified, untrained and unemployed school leavers, who in Western Europe alone are numbered in the millions.[7]

Finally, there is the risk that the discussion focusses too narrowly upon formal education, and the school system is made the scapegoat for all the malaises and maladjustments of our social, and particularly our economic, systems. Some would cut back formal education, except for the intellectual elite, and introduce instead industry-led training to meet immediate economic requirements. Others look for a coherent education and training policy for youth that recognizes a continuing role for general education in schools, but are still uncertain how this may be linked to foundation training on publicly subsidized apprenticeship-type programmes and the practical involvement of industry in the delivery of training through sandwich and release arrangements.

Underlying the failure to develop a clear national policy for youth in this field has been the issue, which surfaces continually in political and professional discussions, as to whether an education or a training model should be adopted for post-school youth. Nor is this simply an academic argument, for the fact is that many industrially successful countries, including Japan and the United States, offer substantial general education programmes rather than industrial training to most 16–18 year olds. What is not in dispute is that English youth have less opportunity for either vocational training or general education once they have completed compulsory schooling than in most other industrialized countries. Therefore the debate continues: should meeting the criteria of employers and learning job-related skills be treated as more vital, because more immediately verifiable and usable, than learning that helps the young person to prepare for adult life and for participation in the civic community?

Related to these issues of principle are a far-from-resolved set of organizational questions about the delivery of education and training programmes. The control exercised by the schools over such programmes has long gone in West Germany, if it ever existed there, but is persistently strong in France, has recently been reasserted in Sweden[8], and is now being vigorously challenged in England. However, this is only a surface issue, for there is no obvious reason why a monopolistic education and training system should be *per se* either superior or inferior to one that is split into separate sectors. Both types exist in Western Europe at the present time. Sweden provides the clearest example of a system which has left youth education and training virtually entirely under the aegis of the school system. On the other hand, the German system, the so-called 'dual system', might be more accurately designated as an industry-based approach, given the strong role played by firms and by chambers of commerce and industry.

In most Western European societies there has been a strong rivalry between ministries of education and labour or employment over the control of vocational training, and the new programmes for unemployed youth, financed as they are on a virtually unprecedented scale, have become a particularly contentious area of public expenditure turned into a particularly choice shuttlecock. But this is only one of many fragmentations that can be found in the European systems in which, for example, separate institutions for compulsory and post-compulsory education frequently lack adequate liaison and provision for student progression, employers and teachers criticize each others' views and ways of operating, and there are competing guidance services and widely contrasting pedagogical practices.

The socio-economic context for this debate is, however, becoming increasingly homogeneous. While England may have led the way amongst the larger Western European nations in the scale of its youth unemployment, it has been the case throughout the European labour markets that young people have been forming an increasing proportion of the total unemployed in recent years. The record numbers of teenagers reaching school-leaving age in every country, and the common factor of technologically-induced gaps in the labour markets for unskilled or unqualified workers, have acted in conjunction in such a way that young school leavers are everywhere finding themselves subject to new and intense pressures as they seek to plan their preparation for working life. Not only is there severe competition among both qualified and unqualified job-seekers, but young people are often demotivated by structural changes in the labour market that can remove a desired job destination even while a school leaver is training hopefully for it.

It cannot be ignored that the problems in the transition from school to working life are much more severe in the case of the unqualified, the handicapped, ethnic minorities, children of migrant workers, inner-city or isolated rural poor and, in some societies, for girls as a sex. Where these factors coincide, long-term exclusion from the labour force can result. This marginalization of the young becomes an extreme form of social stratification, since many such social factors are mutually reinforcing.[9] Moreover, young people who are economically marginalized tend to experience exclusion from a variety of social, cultural and political activities. For example, they lack the socialization experiences of belonging to the workforce, they remain segregated at home or in age-homogeneous groups, or they are debarred from activities that cost money or require substantial travel. The social and political costs of coping with such groups in society have led to the designation of certain categories of school students as 'risk groups', and this has considerably broadened the terms of the education and training debate. It is one matter to calculate returns to investment in training on an individual basis, but this approach provides no adequate rationale for evaluating counter-marginalizing education and training programmes. It may be, however, that it is precisely in this area that our social policies are least developed and most uncertain.

Responding to the Youth Employment Crisis

England

Youth unemployment levels began to soar in England from 1974 onwards, but it was only in the later 1970s that there was a major national programme designed to meet the needs of jobless youngsters. The initiator of the programme was the Manpower Services Commission (MSC) which comes under the authority of the Secretary of State for Employment. The Youth Opportunities Scheme, which included a variety of provisions for courses, work projects, workshops and industrial placements, was originally seen principally as a vehicle for expediting a job placement. In practice, this concept gave way before rising jobless rates, and it became necessary to think more radically about how school leavers could be most effectively helped to get a foothold in the labour market. The MSC Youth Training Scheme (YTS), which then came into operation early in 1983, aimed 'to provide ... a better start in working and adult life through an integrated programme ... which can serve as a foundation for subsequent employment or continued training or relevant further education'.[10]

Although originally seen as a basic training scheme for all young people starting work who did not have a formal training course available to them, the YTS has mainly recruited the unemployed. It provides a one-year programme which, although offered independently by a large number of local managing agents, is intended to conform to centrally laid down design criteria. Currently, the main features of the YTS are that it should provide broad learning opportunities in personal and vocational skills through a number of specified design elements. The design elements are:

(a)   an induction programme to inform trainees about the YTS, its purposes and organization, as well as the specific training plan to be provided by the particular local agent;
(b)   occupationally-based training;
(c)   thirteen weeks off-the-job training/education planned as an integral part of the whole scheme;
(d)   work experience planned to provide skill learning;
(e)   learning in the core areas of number and its application, communication, problem-solving and planning, practical skills, and computer literacy/information technology;
(f)   guidance and support under the responsibility of a named person;
(g)   assessment of needs and attainments at regular intervals;
(h)   review and recording of progress, including trainee participation and awarding of a YTS certificate.[11]

The design of the YTS has been built up from the experience of the Youth Opportunities Programme. Its delivery is monitored by the MSC Quality Branch, who are responsible for its continued development. While the involvement of so many agents adds variety and potential to the scope of the Scheme, there have been difficulties in ensuring an adequate understanding of its provisions, not only by trainees but also by the managing agents themselves.[12]

As the atmosphere of concern over the transition of young people from school to adult and working life has grown, there has also been a major impact upon the curriculum of full-time education in schools. The Technical and Vocational Education Initiative (TVEI) is an MSC pilot programme, very hurriedly launched in 1983, to 'explore and test methods of organizing, managing and resourcing replicable programmes of general, technical and vocational education', for 14–18 year olds, across the ability range and on a voluntary and non-sex discriminatory basis.[13] The underlying philosophy of the TVEI is vocational through its emphasis upon applications of science and technology, though the programme leaves open options to include traditional academic courses and examinations, and its objectives include 'the encouragement of initiative, problem-solving and other aspects of personal development'.[14]

A third major new element in the system has been the introduction of a full-time, one-year course of pre-vocational education, the Certificate of Pre-vocational Education (CPVE), for 16–17 year olds immediately following the compulsory education period. This course represents a rationalization and extension of a variety of pre-vocational courses already certificated by such bodies as the Business and Technician Education Council, the Royal Society of Arts, and the City and Guilds of the London Institute. It has been widely regarded as an education-based alternative to the YTS, with a strongly contrasting philosophical foundation. Stemming from a significant report entitled *A Basis for Choice*[15], this pre-vocational curriculum proposal has gradually taken shape around a set of key aims, as follows:

(a)   to assist the transition from school to adulthood by further equip-ping young people with the basic skills, experiences, attitudes, knowledge and personal and social competencies required for suc-cess in adult life including work;
(b)   to provide personally/individually relevant educational experience which encourages learning and achievement;
(c)   to provide young people with recognition for their attainments by acquiring a qualification embodying national standards;
(d)   to provide an accepted basis for progression to continued education, training and/or work.[16]

The course has three major components. First, there is a common core comprising about two-thirds of the total programme, and including the ten areas of: personal and career development; communication; numeracy; science and technology; industrial, social and economic studies; information technol-ogy; skills for learning, decision-making and adaptability; practical skills; social skills; and creative development. Secondly, there are vocational studies which are based upon broad occupational areas which should be organized to enable young people to distinguish between and compare a range of activities and contexts. Thirdly, there are optional additional studies which are to reflect the personal interests and needs of the students.

All of these schemes represent a radical departure from current practice in education and training in England, both in their specified content and in the training or pedagogical approaches involved. The particular features that challenge more traditional practice have been their common emphasis upon experiential learning, and the close association of academic institutions with industrial agencies in sandwich schemes and work experience. More concern than hitherto has been accorded to guidance of young people through the maze of new courses and the problems of job-finding, and to profile assessment, which forms a key element of each of the new programmes.

Dudley Plunkett

Western Europe

While it is beyond the scope of this chapter to do justice to the developments in the vocational preparation field that have been occurring simultaneously in continental systems and in the European Commission, it is important to attempt to make at least a summary appraisal. Since 1976 the Commission has taken a close interest in member states' policies for youth. In December of that year, a Resolution of the Council of Ministers established the Community Action Programme on Transition from Education to Working Life, and the Commission has since actively pursued pilot projects to develop new work in this area, concentrating especially on the compulsory education phase.[17] Twenty-nine projects, jointly financed with national governments in nine member states, experimented over the four years from 1978–82 with various practical remedies for problems and dislocations in the education and training of young people.

The European Community has experienced severe problems of youth unemployment in nearly every region. The number of jobless young under 25 stood at over four million in 1982, when the Council and Ministers for Education, citing these and other factors, recognized the 'certain prospect of continuing high youth unemployment'[18], the relatively diminished occupational opportunities for disadvantaged categories, the problems of sex and race discrimination, the existence of low level jobs without opportunities for training, and the neglect of information to help create less traditional forms of employment. As a result of these conclusions, the Council decided to relaunch the Action Programme for a second phase in 1983, reflecting a continued concern about the urgency of the problems and the value of the new and coordinated efforts that had been made to cope with them by the member states working with the European Commission.[19]

Substantial programmes of study and research have also been mounted in this area by the Council of Europe and by the OECD.[20] There is no space to review here the varied documentation of recent years, but it reflects debate over the same major policy issues as in the European Community, and has contributed to shaping a new concept of 'vocational preparation' in youth education and training. Effectively, there has been a general trend from academic to vocational emphases in education, and although much discussion has centred upon the need to balance the two, this has proved difficult in the context of rapidly rising youth unemployment. It is where attempts have been made to respond to the youth unemployment situation that the vocational preparation concept has emerged. According to the European Centre for the Development of Vocational Training (CEDEFOP), the basic notion of vocational preparation is of an 'integrated mixture of skill training, general and social education and personal counselling designed to help young people progress from school to working life'.[21]

In practice, we have long been accustomed to the critique of traditional academic education, most forcefully pursued by the de-schoolers. What has since developed has been a dual emphasis upon practical approaches to education and training, in both schools and in training agencies linked to the labour market. There has evolved a variety of strategies, representing a range of provision in the different countries of Western Europe. In France, reliance has mainly been placed upon the full-time educational system, in both the compulsory phase to 16, and in the colleges d'enseignement professionnel and the lycees techniques. Special programmes have been mounted for the young unemployed, but these have been seen as temporary, and for a minority, even though current statistics would seem to belie this.[22] In contrast to this education-based model, West Germany and Denmark have built traditions of industry-based or industry-influenced training for young people in transition to working life. Germany had accommodated to the growing problems of youth employment by instituting a vocational preparation year immediately following full-time compulsory education, and this model has also developed in the Danish EFG courses. Sweden, on the other hand, has fluctuated between the two models, for some time allocating young people leaving the school system to labour market training under the Labour Market Board, but now, following legislation in 1980 gathering all education and training into the upper secondary school, though with new efforts to develop mechanisms for linking education and the working world through short courses with indus-trial attachments and with employer involvement in curriculum policy-making.[23]

It will be apparent that uncertainty prevails over a number of philosophi-cal and design issues in approaches to vocational preparation. Implicit in the concept is a belief in the availability of jobs as a plausible objective of the preparation process. This belief is questionable, it hardly needs saying, in contemporary economic conditions, and especially in depressed urban areas or in the cases of particular sub-groups of young people, when the adverse significance for employment prospects of a range of social factors may alter monthly, as the extent of effective marginalization of young people reveals itself.

The Second Phase of Critical Reappraisal

England

After several years of searching for more adequate models for youth education and training, the different government departments and other agencies involved in England are little nearer to any consensus merely because the term vocational preparation has been in vogue. The ideological dimensions to the debate have been heightened by the recognition that, in practice, what is labelled vocational preparation may be a misrepresentation or a misnomer, since young people need preparation for personal survival, enforced leisure, and adult life in general, as much as for paid employment that may not even become available.

This same slippage in reality-labelling characterizes the 1984 White Paper of the British Government *Training for Jobs* which ignores job-creation but proposes a much more strictly employer-led approach to youth training.[24] The argument that favours relying upon market forces to guide youth training policies paradoxically produces tendencies that centralize decision-making in the state education system, and in England this is even leading to a displacement of both local and central educational authorities in favour of other departments of Government with closer links to industry, and especially the Departments of Employment and of Trade and Industry. The issue that arises is whether the new emphasis upon vocationalization of the curriculum and on new technologies subject matter has actually any relevance for the youth unemployment crisis, however much it meets the short-term needs of the functioning economy.

It is important to be clear about the philosophical issues involved, since they determine how programmes for young people are designed. For example, skill training in a broad vocational area can have short-term economic pay-offs, but if the skills learnt are of practical everyday use they also have survival value at the individual level. If young people recognize this bonus there is more chance that they will be motivated to acquire the skills, and thus be more confident to seek job opportunities associated with them. Much the same can be said about work experience components of training schemes. The worst characteristic of such attachments is where they have no longer-term value and consist merely in watching the working world or, worse still, providing underpaid labour for it. The broadening of experience through realistic vocational guidance, on the one hand, and through enhanced personal and social education, on the other, reflects a quite different philosophy which will carry through into the whole design of the support being offered to young people in transition.

In terms, however, of the young unemployed, what used to be thought of as a minority has become a majority of those leaving school to seek work. The effect of vocationalized curricula on such people may be to create ever more unbridgeable gulfs between strata of educated and uneducated groups, corresponding to employed and unemployed in a shrinking labour market in which it is the least skilled levels of work that are disappearing. For these reasons, there are a number of key aspects of the new education and training programmes that are attracting critical attention. The first is whether there is a streaming process operating, with different categories of young people being recruited according to explicit or implicit selection criteria. Thus, sex discrimination in occupationally based programmes is alleged, as where information technology is interpreted as electronics for males and word-processing for females.[25] A second major issue is that of progression, for if trainees on the YTS have no obvious training destination to follow their experience on the scheme they are effectively disadvantaged in relation to those who chose to follow more traditional lines of vocational training. Thirdly, adequate integration of job placements and off-the-job training has remained an unresolved problem of vocational preparation programmes. This is a matter in which there is no shortage of criticism and of statements of intent, but it continues to be cited as a critical need.[26] From work experience to experiential learning can be a longer step than might at first appear.

Stemming from the criticism that the new youth programmes have been too centred upon short-term job preparation, a further issue is the extent to which they are capable of preparing young people for the wide range of challenges that adult life confronts them with when their training ends. The implication is that the curriculum, personal relations and guidance provided in such programmes, and indeed throughout their formal schooling, must be broadly appraised. Closely related to this point is the factor in quality of schemes which is ascribable to the experience, skills, knowledge and attitudes of training staff. Staff development is recognized by almost all commentators as a crucial variable, a lever of change, and yet thinking about the processes involved in upgrading staff is still at a primitive level compared with the patent need.[27] In general terms, what appears to be lacking in current strategies is any real long-term view, not only of the potential social and political relevance and impact of the programmes that have been designed, but also of how the youth programmes are to articulate to possible developments in further training, continuing retraining, and job development and creation.[28]

Examining the balance-sheet of youth education and training in England, it is possible to recognize a number of positive features. First, there is now, as was not previously the case, a guarantee to all young school leavers of a year of work and/or education and training. This provision goes beyond the minimum prescribed by the European Community's Council of Ministers, in their Resolution of 1983,[29] though it falls short of the two year programme that is increasingly discussed in the Commission, as well as amongst opposition political parties and other groups in the United Kingdom. Attitudes are, however, changing, and the debate about youth policy is incomparably keener and better informed than when the special programmes for the young unemployed were instituted in the late 1970s.

Moreover, the response to the problems posed by youth unemployment has extended further into the formal educational system as a whole. Because the curriculum of so much of secondary education has reflected the concepts and scope of the knowledge recognized and purveyed in the higher education system, studies that aim to familiarize young people with the 'real world' as a preparation for adult life have either been neglected or else have been regarded as soft options for the academically less able. Recent attempts to alter this pattern, by developing courses of personal and social education, have so far been only partially successful. Their challenge to the traditional curriculum, however, is no less significant than that which they offer to the philosophy underlying many of the new forms of vocational preparation for young people in transition. In their very different ways, both academic and vocational education have been narrow, cloistered, and unresponsive to the needs of young people in contemporary social and economic conditions.

The potential of schools to resolve such problems unaided is very limited. Not only have they found it difficult to assimilate new curriculum models that threatened established views of the worthwhileness of knowledge and ways of teaching, but they have lacked resources for staffing and staff re-training to bring about even favoured developments. In the isolation of many schools from other agencies in the community, furthermore, little space was found for learning outside the classroom, especially in industrial and other work settings. There is vigorous work developing in these fields, with particular agencies providing closer liaison between the educational and the working worlds in particular, but this is only part of a major problem requiring much more investment than the TVEI Pilot Programme or the coordinating efforts of dynamic individuals working in scattered curriculum development projects.

One of the main criticisms of the House of Lords Select Committee report was that the education and training system in England was insufficiently coherent, and that it was not understandable to those who had to use it. The report drew further attention to familiar structural and administrative problems that have dogged the decentralized and multifarious arrangements, not only in youth training but in the educational system as a whole. Central/local rivalries hamper collaboration. Inter-ministerial conflicts of values and views, unresolved uncertainties about aspects of an overall strategy that would specify opportunities, motivate young people, and ensure a clearly defined social, material and vocational status for them, all undermine any efforts to remedy the shortcomings in the United Kingdom's youth training record, relative to those of other European countries. The Select Committee concluded: 'In the UK there is an urgent need to bring together the whole education, training and employment of young people in a coherent framework which can be understood by employers, parents, educators and trainers, and above all by young people themselves'.[30]

Western Europe

The European Community has shown an increasing commitment to meeting the needs of young people, especially those in risk situations and affected by unemployment. In one important development, a restructuring of the European Commission in 1981 brought together the previously independent Directorates of Education and of Vocational Training into a new Directorate of Education, Vocational Training and Youth Policy. The value of this change was shown when it finally became possible, in 1984, to begin formal Community-wide meetings of ministry of education and ministry of labour officials, so that they could exchange experience and work together.[31] Although, at the time of writing, it is too early to see the results of these meetings, which are expected to occur two or three times a year, they do follow the best recent practice in the individual countries, and are an indispensable part of any movement towards more coherent education and training policies, for example, through linking the work of the compulsory schooling phase to adult training and retraining.

The priority status to be given to the needs of the young was clearly indicated in the Council of Ministers 1983 Resolution on vocational training policies, which accepted the commitment 'to improve the quality and scope of vocational training for workers of all ages. Although priority should be given to young people and the long-term unemployed, constant attention should be paid to the training and re-training of other workers, especially those most at risk from changes in the labour market'.[32] Specifically, the member states resolved to follow the principle of the youth guarantee, by doing 'their utmost to ensure that all young people . . . can benefit over a period of at least six months and if possible one year following full-time compulsory education from a full-time programme involving basic training and/or an initial work experience to prepare them for an occupation'.[33]

The aspects of transition education for young people which were to be given major emphasis in the second phase of the Community Action Programme reflected the main findings from the first phase which were summarized above. They were: 'the interplay between schools and the outside world and . . . a broader form of social and vocational preparation for adult life'.[34] This represented a development beyond the 1979 Resolution of the Council of Ministers on alternance education policies, which gave strong approval to the effecting of closer links between industry and education or training establishments.[35] The continuing failure to achieve this in practice is cited by the CEDEFOP representative giving evidence to the House of Lords Select Committee.[36] The strategy adopted from 1983 has been to set up pilot projects based in areas or 'action districts' within which cooperation between educational and other services could be improved in relation to the particular needs of communities with high youth unemployment. The implicit assumption is that modes of cooperation must be worked out in the field and cannot be legislated from above. There are now thirty such projects in the ten member states. They are due to run until 1986, and to be followed by a year of organized efforts to report and disseminate the experience gained.[37]

It is widely held that the West German training system offers a model that should be imitated in England.[38] The particular features that have been identified are the universal requirement of part-time training for those leaving the compulsory education phase, the fully functioning alternance system, the level of cooperation between the training institutions and what are called the social partners in the private sector, and the overall quality and standards achieved in vocational training. Germans and others giving evidence to the Lords Select Committee, as well as commentators in other recent reports, question whether imitation is strictly possible in this case, for the German system has grown out of age-old traditions and builds upon entirely different attitudes and relationships than those which exist in English industrial life.[39]

Speculation on this matter will undoubtedly be assisted by the work focussing on the coordination of local agencies in the second phase of the Community Action Programme.

It is doubtful whether German secondary schools are any more successful than English ones in evolving a curriculum that can prepare effectively for adult life, and it is the vocational training schools (*Berufsschulen*) that will most repay the attention of British policy-makers. Significant weaknesses are also appearing in the German system, however, as youth unemployment grows and hits hard at members of minority groups, especially the children of migrant workers, and at the 18+ age group, among those who have completed their vocational training and have not been able to obtain a job in the firm in which they have had their training place.

The Swedish system presents the most rationally ordered structure and arrangements which, together with the recent legislation integrating all post-compulsory provision in the upper secondary school, and the thorough review of upper secondary education recently completed by a royal commission[40], now seeks to meet the needs of the 90 per cent of the age group who continue into post-compulsory education. The problems that remain lie with the 'residual' or 'risk' groups of youngsters who have rejected further schooling, without having any viable alternative, and who are materially and morally at risk through unemployment, drugs, criminal activity or social inadequacy. The measures to combat such problems by developing youth centres and elaborate systems of follow-up, which are possible in a society with a small population base with relatively greater resources,[41] will be a focus of interest in other European societies where a much greater proportion of cases are falling through the net of provision.

When the socialist government came to power in France it gave a high priority to dealing with the youth unemployment situation. The critical and creative Schwartz Report of 1981 had been commissioned by the government, and was substantially implemented.[42] The particular merit of the report was its holistic stance. The situation of young people was analyzed not only in labour market terms, but with respect to problems of incorporation into civic life, accommodation, leisure, access to the media and to health facilities, justice and other more strictly educational and pedagogic needs. The strategy proposed by Schwartz was close to that of the Community 'action district' idea. A number of local centres (missions locales) were designed to bring together in one locality the various agencies from both the educational system and the labour market whose activities needed greater coordination. The centres guide young people towards education and training measures available to them locally, as well as facilitating their social welfare.

Reports of the measures in practice are fragmented, but criticism has been made of high absentee rates and of the measures being concentrated on young people who are not those most in need. The major problem, however, as might be expected, has been the continuing conflict between the different agencies involved, each jealous of its territory and autonomy.[43] The problem particularly relates to the national educational system, which is vastly dominant in terms of its share of the administration of the special courses provided. The inflexibility of this system shows through in various ways. First, the traditional vocational education system is seen as the permanent fixture, with the special measures for the unemployed expected to be phased out within a matter of years. This means that there is an unwillingness to open up significant resources of permanent staff and accommodation in vocational schools where courses are held. An informal streaming system has emerged, which only reinforces the disadvantages of the vulnerable unemployed trainees. Secondly, Schwartz proposed that there should be a major development in the unitization of qualifications, so that young people on fragmented courses, moving backwards and forwards between jobs and training, could gradually build up towards major qualifications through 'unites capitalizables'. The concept of a pyramid of qualifications is not proving acceptable to vocational trainers, who regard the lower levels of units as threatening the standards to which they have traditionally worked.[44]

Current Options

This chapter has surveyed a period of very great changes in youth education and training policies in England and in Western Europe. Not only have I been forced to be far from comprehensive, but it is not possible to be in any way conclusive. These developments have occurred because of social and economic changes which are ongoing. Youth unemployment has shown a tendency to stabilize in England, largely because of massive intervention programmes, but it is very probable that all Western European societies will see further increases in jobless rates, and that these will continue to affect the less qualified youngsters disproportionately.

Any solutions introduced in line with current policies must be regarded as provisional, and it has been the argument of this chapter that the concept of vocational preparation, which arose as an attempt to reorientate post-compulsory education and training, is itself based upon assumptions that current social and economic conditions render questionable. Vocational preparation can only be a preliminary response. On the other hand, it has been valuable to examine the processes of policy development in the wider setting of Western Europe, rather than simply in England, because the various countries of that region do share many common characteristics and problems. This concluding review of current questioning and possible future developments will necessarily be somewhat more speculative, and will cover a wider conceptual canvas than education and training issues alone.

There has been a recognition throughout this discussion of vocational preparation measures that they could be seen either simply as an economic issue or as a wider social programme. Under the pressures of the recession many societies have tended to seek short-term answers both to the problem of meeting needs for skills in the labour force and to the needs of unemployed youth. This conflation of two problems, one a matter of economic efficiency and the other one of social control in the final instance, has led to the ignoring of more fundamental issues of equity in the treatment of different elements of the population. Concern with the quality of the labour force results in quite different education and training policies than does a sense of obligation to the socially vulnerable, or to risk groups. The needs of employers and of the industrial sector span a much narrower range than do the needs and wants of young people leaving compulsory schooling. A curriculum that attempted to answer these latter needs would not be solely vocational, but would be directed to goals of a social character and to meeting the requirements of individual members of society. The difference in fact is not merely in curriculum content but in philosophy, and even in the politics of knowledge. In other words, we are forced to admit the relevance of questions of value, and specifically the value of education and training to society conceived both as a socio-economic system and as the product of an implicit social contract between persons.

The distinction between needs and wants of young people is an important one. Social and economic analyses comparing the experience of different groups in society reveal contrasts, suggest trends, and may help us to define needs. To define wants, we simply have to ask the social groups or individuals in question. Needs are selected by authorities and officials; wants are identified by unique interests. Vocational preparation, I suggest, has primarily been conceived as a need of young school leavers and of employers. But even if it is agreed by all concerned that it is a need, this is not the same as identifying what is wanted. How far are young school leavers to be seen as self-determining, as having rights for example to non-discrimination, to social security and health and safety protection, to material and social status?[45] This is a serious question, since it is apparent that the young are regarded by many as a problem, as if they did not have equal rights, and the result of this is that they can sense society as impervious to their desires, which is equivalent to saying that their lives can tend to become socially meaningless, or marginalized. It cannot be said that the potential alienation of the young has yet been taken adequately into account in the formulation of education and training policies.

Future Policies

Future policies in the field of youth education and employment can only in part centre upon the provision of programmes of education and training. No less essential are a concerted economic policy for job development and a new social vision about the place of employment in people's lives, and in society. Each of these three points needs some elaboration as a conclusion to this chapter.

It is clear that in none of the Western European societies has the system of education and training for young people leaving compulsory schooling yet been adequately thought through, either philosophically or organizationally. If young people are not simply to be cynically manipulated into illusory hopes of traditional careers, the curriculum offered to them must transcend traditional vocational education, and also vocational preparation as it has been described here. Surely the minimum requirement is for a curriculum that balances its efforts between responding to individual developmental needs and leading young people to a preliminary state of preparedness for adulthood, in which meeting the criteria of employers can only be one element.[46] And such a programme, however vital to the most disadvantaged, or risk groups, is now really required as a common curriculum for all. This view of the curriculum cannot be wished into being, but a first step would be to articulate it, and to demonstrate as clearly as possible that there are contradictions needing to be resolved between the views of those who see education and training as means to an economic goal and of those whose concern is with social, moral and cultural values and standards.

The current philosophical impasse is mirrored in the fragmentation of the system. All seem to be agreed that there is a need for more contact, dialogue, clarification of aims and the seeking of greater consensus between the various sectors concerned with the education and training of young people. It may be useful to summarize some of the points on the agenda of such discussions. It has been argued here that there is a need for a coherent and flexible system of education and training that reconciles our needs for:

(a)   an immediate occupation and lifestyle for young people leaving compulsory schooling;

(b)   the upgrading of skills in the young workforce in ways that respond flexibly to personal and economic needs and provide links and progression between levels of education and training programmes;

(c)   the effective integration of on-the-job training and basic or conceptual learning;

(d)   engaging young people as participants in selecting and developing their own line of work and development;

(e)   organizational evaluation and control, and full collaboration between sectors, agencies and departments of government;

(f)   staff development to ensure education and training methods which motivate young people and make the best use of the potential of those working in youth programmes;

(g)   attention to the rights, needs and wants of the most disadvantaged groups, such as ethnic minorities, the handicapped, girls where they suffer from discrimination or stereotypes, and the many categories of socially inadequate young people who have become marginalized and alienated, for whatever reason;

(h)   the balancing of the interests of employers in industry and of young people seeking to join the labour market.

The societies that have been studied in this chapter are in various different ways progressing towards such developments in their education and training systems, but the diversity of viewpoints and practices needs greater resolution. The work of the European Community in the Action Programme on Transition from Education to Working Life has highlighted most of these concerns and, in its second phase, is taking direct initiatives to develop and exchange ideas and strategies to promote more coordinated action. In England, the pace of innovation in the education and training field has brought considerable confusion, especially to client groups, and it is increasingly recognized that some degree of rationalization is essential if young people are to follow the programme that will be most relevant to their needs, rather than that which they happen to have heard of by chance.

However, no amount of restructuring and publicizing of existing education and training opportunities can solve the problems caused by a shrinking labour market affected by the spread of new technologies. The scapegoating of education and training, which has been very common in England over the last decade, has simply ignored the need for job development and for investment to open up new job opportunities. And where these have been tried through public intervention, for example through the MSC special programmes in England, they have been far too short-term to attract the attention of their clientele until unemployment intervened. In fact, the MSC Community Programme, which is aimed at job creation, imposes unemployment as a condition of entry, and thus cannot realistically be a part of anyone's longer-term planning. The argument that longer-term policies cannot be afforded simply begs the question about the purposes of society and government. How meaningful is it to argue that we can afford economic development, but not increased quality of life?

We are driven by this survey of policies in the field of education and training to the recognition that centralized and inflexible arrangements are failing to meet the changing needs and wants of young school leavers. Where the underlying aims and strategies are narrowly focussed upon short-term job placement, or where employers fail to take adequate responsibility for opening up opportunities to the young, the conviction grows that the minimum task for policy-makers is to define a broader social programme, one that takes the education and training of young people beyond vocational preparation and places it in the context of integrated economic and social development measures which link together a whole series of job and further education and re-training opportunities. One cost of failing to develop such policies must be to drive a wedge between the employed and the unemployed, whereas the challenge is to increase the permeability of this divide, to reduce the stigma of unemployment which causes so much stress and despair, and fundamentally to separate employment and survival chances.[47] England is only one of the societies of Western Europe which needs critical review and development in this field, but its special characteristic is that, although among the first of the industrial societies, it has displayed a persistent and fundamentally unavailing tendency to survive without being renewed.

Notes

1 The early atmosphere of national self-criticism is described by ASHBY, E., (1958) *Technology and the Academics*, London, Macmillan, pp. 57–8.

2 Secretaries of State for Employment, Education and Science, Scotland, and Wales, (1981) *A New Training Initiative: A Programme for Action* (Cmnd 8455), London, HMSO.

3 Manpower Services Commission, (1982) *Youth Task Group Report*, MSC.

4 A useful compendium of recent relevant comparative information and data is provided by the House of Lords Select Committee on the European Communities, (1984) *Youth Training in the EEC*, London, HMSO.

5 An insider view of how such policy is formed is given by JONES, H., (1983) in *Education in the European Community*, Proceedings of the North of England Educational Conference, Liverpool.

6 The term was given national currency in England with the publication of Further Education Unit, (1981) *Vocational Preparation*, London, FEU, and in the wider European setting by HARRISON, J., (1982) *Planning Vocational Preparation Initiatives for Unemployed Young People*, Berlin, European Centre for the Development of Vocational Training — CEDEFOP.

7 Unemployed under 25s were 36.4 per cent of the total unemployed in the EEC in March, 1984 (38.9 per cent in the United Kingdom). See *Youth Training in the EEC*, table 3.

8 See PLUNKETT, D., (1982) 'The risk group: education and training policies for disadvantaged young people in Sweden and Denmark', *Comparative Education*, 18, 1, pp. 39–46.

9 A working party report in France indicated very effectively some of the social implications of the marginalization of young people. See Ministere du Travail et de la Participation (1978) *Processus de Marginalisation des Jeunes*, Paris, Ministere du Travail.

10 *Youth Task Group Report*, para. 4.3.

11 Although listed in many official Manpower Services Commission sources, this current update of YTS specifications was taken from PICKLES S., (1984) 'Quality in 1984', *Youth Training News*, March. The September issue of the same journal reported that recruitment to the YTS for 1983–84 reached 354,000.

12 Reported in Training Division, Manpower Services Commission, (1984) *Report on YTS Pilot Schemes*, MSC.

13 Manpower Services Commission, (1984) *Technical and Vocational Education Initiative Review 1984*, MSC, p. 3.

14 *Ibid.*

15 Further Education Unit, (1979) *A Basis for Choice: Report of a Study Group on Post-16 Pre-employment Courses*, London, FEU.

16 Joint Board for Pre-vocational Education, (1984) *The Certificate of Pre-vocational Education: Consultative Document*, Joint Board.

17 *Resolution* of the Council of the European Communities and of the Ministers for Education meeting within the Council, 13 December 1976.

18 Council and Ministers for Education, *Proceedings* of 24 May 1982, on the subject of Education and Training in the Context of the Employment Situation in the European Community, p. 7.

19   *Ibid.*, annex 2 to the annex.
20   In particular, there is the work of the Council for Cultural Cooperation of the Council of Europe, in Project no. 1 'Preparation for Life', and a series of reports from the OECD, such as (1977) *Education and Working Life*, Paris OECD; (1983) *The Future of Vocational Education and Training*, Paris, OECD; and (1983) *Education and Work: The Views of the Young*, Paris, OECD.
21   *Planning Vocational Preparation Initiatives* ..., p. 20.
22   PASQUIER, B. and NOEL, M., 'Vocational Training in France', memorandum in evidence to the House of Lords Select Committee, *op. cit.*, pp. 282–6.
23   'The Risk Group ...', *op. cit.*
24   Secretaries of State for Employment, Education and Science, Scotland, and Wales, (1984) *Training for Jobs* (Cmnd 9135), London, HMSO.
25   See, for example, the critical appraisal of the YTS by the Greater London Training Board, (1984) *Review of the New Training Initiative 1981–84*, GLTB, or that by Youthaid, (1984) *The Youth Training Scheme*, London, Youthaid.
26   *Ibid.*, and also in the official report of the first year of the YTS: Youth Training Board of the Manpower Services Commission, (1984) *Youth Training Scheme Review 1984*, MSC.
27   See the author's six country report on this subject: PLUNKETT, D., (1982) *Staff Training and Development for the New Youth Programmes: a Comparative Study of Policy and Practice in Western Europe*, Paris, European Institute of Education and Social Policy.
28   Policy Studies Institute, memorandum in evidence to the House of Lords Select Committee, *op. cit.*, pp. 147–9.
29   Council of the European Communities Resolution of 11 July 1983 on 'Vocational training policies in the European Community in the 1980s', *Official Journal of the European Communities*, 20 July.
30   *Youth Training in the EEC*, para. 84.
31   JONES, H.C., Director of Directorate-General V (Social Policy, Employment and Education) of the EEC, in evidence to the House of Lords Select Committee, *op. cit.*, pp. 248–61.
32   *Ibid.*, p. 3.
33   *Ibid.*, p. 4.
34   Council and Ministers for Education, Proceedings of 24 May 1982, *op. cit.*, p. 9.
35   Council of the European Communities, Resolution of 18 December 1979, on 'Linked work and training for young persons', *Official Journal of the European Communities*, 3 January 1980.
36   SELLIN, B., in evidence to the House of Lords Select Committee, *op. cit.*, pp. 234–46, but see also European Centre for the Development of Vocational Training — CEDEFOP, (1982) *Alternance Training for Young People: Guidelines for Action*, Berlin, CEDEFOP.
37   See the reports of the European Community Action Programme (1984) on the *Transition of Young People from Education to Working Life*; *Policies for Transition*; *Thirty Pilot Projects*; and *Education for Transition: The Curriculum Challenge*, Brussels, Community Action Programme.
38   For example, in Manpower Services Commission and the National Economic Development Council, (1984) *Competence and Competition: Training and Education in the Federal Republic of Germany, the United States and Japan*, London, National Economic Development Council.

39 LEMKE, H., of the German Federal Ministry of Education, memorandum in evidence to the House of Lords Select Committee, *pp. cit.*, pp. 309–13.
40 See (1981) 'Sweden: report of the Commission on the upper secondary school', *Bulletin of the Council of Europe*, 5, and (1984) 'Sweden: upper secondary schooling on the eve of a major period of reform', *Bulletin of the Council of Europe*, 2.
41 WENNAS, O., (1983) 'The Youth Guarantee of Gothenberg', Conference on Education, Youth and Employment, Jordanhill College, Glasgow.
42 SCHWARTZ, B., (1981) *L'Insertion Professionnelle et Sociale des Jeunes*, a report to the Prime Minister, Paris, La Documentation Francaise.
43 COHEN, P., (1984) 'Emploi des Jeunes: du Social a l'Economique,' *Le Monde de l'Education*, June.
44 *Ibid.*
45 KODITZ, V., (1981) *Youth Unemployment and Vocational Training: the Material and Social Standing of Young People during Transition from School to Working Life*, Berlin, CEDEFOP.
46 These issues are given an extended discussion by WATTS, A.G., (1983) *Education, Unemployment and the Future of Work*, Milton Keynes, Open University Press.
47 The close association of unemployment with severe stress, self-inflicted injury and even suicide is being suggested by a growing body of research. See PLATT, S. and KREITMAN, N., (1984) 'Trends in parasuicide and unemployment among men in Edinburgh, 1968–82', *British Medical Journal*, 289, 6451, 20 October.

Australia's Targeted Employment Subsidy: The Special Youth Employment Training Program[1]

Ralph E. Smith

Abstract

Employment subsidies have been supported by many economists as a means of reducing unemployment without worsening inflation or, at least, of achieving a given decrement in unemployment with less inflation than if it were achieved through general economic expansion. This is sometimes referred to as 'cheating the Phillips curve' or reducing the non-accelerating inflation rate of unemployment (NAIRU) or the natural rate of unemployment. Targeted employment subsidies also provide a means of redistributing jobs.

Australia, in fact, has had an employment subsidy scheme to encourage employers to hire long-duration unemployed youth since 1976. The Special Youth Employment Training Program (SYETP) provides firms with $75 per week for up to seventeen weeks as an inducement for them to hire persons under the age of 25 who have been unemployed for at least four of the preceding twelve months. A larger subsidy is available to firms for hiring youth who have been unemployed at least eight months.

Review of Australia's experience with SYETP illustrates many of the issues involved in converting the theory of employment subsidies into practice and in measuring their effectiveness. The immediate purpose of SYETP is to induce employers to hire a particular group and provide them with work experience that might help them to secure stable employment. Studies of the program participants indicate that this is being accomplished. The issues raised in this chapter have to do with the overall impacts of the subsidy scheme on the Australian labour market: Is it redistributing jobs? Is it permitting Australia to have more employment and less unemployment for a given level of inflation than could be achieved otherwise?

Analysis of the available information concerning the impact of SYETP on the Australian economy suggests:

The scheme has operated on a very small scale during most of its life. Even though over 300,000 jobs have been subsidized since SYETP began, there have never been more than 40,000 subsidized jobs at any one time; during most of its life, less than half this number have been subsidized. Most of these jobs have gone to teenagers and many of them probably would otherwise not have existed or would have been filled by more experienced workers. At no time has the program provided enough jobs to reduce the teenage unemployment rate by more than 1.5 percentage points and the total Australian unemployment rate by more than 0.2 percentage points.

The scheme has been successful in redistributing job opportunities in favour of long-term unemployed youth. Reduction in the unemployment rate of this group probably put less pressure on wages than would have resulted from an across-the-board reduction of similar magnitude. However, there is no direct evidence with which to test this assumption.

Employers have responded to the incentives provided by the terms of SYETP as economic theory and common sense say they should. Specifically, decisions about whom to hire have been influenced by the terms of the subsidy, as well as the eligibility criteria. The fact that it is a flat rate subsidy appears to have led employers to select from among the youngest of the eligible long-term unemployed youth. Moreover, the scale of the subsidy has influenced their decisions about whether to participate at all. A large reduction in the subsidy between 1978 and 1979 was associated with a sharp reduction in the number of subsidized workers hired.

I Introduction

Australia, in common with most modern economies, seems unable to return to the low unemployment rates to which it had grown accustomed without generating unacceptably high rates of inflation. This state of affairs has spawned a number of proposals to change the underlying structure of the economy such that more favourable unemployment–inflation combinations could be attained. One suggestion has been the use of employment subsidies targeted on groups who are having particularly severe problems in the labour market. They are supported by many economists as a means of 'cheating the Phillips curve' or shifting the natural rate of employment.[2]

Australia, in fact, has had subsidies to encourage employers to hire long-duration unemployed youth since 1976, through the Special Youth Employment Training Program (SYETP). From financial years 1976–77 through 1981–82, approximately 300,000 young people were approved for SYETP-subsidized employment, at a cost to the Commonwealth Government of over $250 million (Kirby (1981) and Minister for Employment and

Industrial Relations (1982b)). In this chapter the incentives provided by SYETP are described and the responses to these incentives analyzed. The policy issues addressed in this chapter involve the potential and actual roles of targeted employment subsidies in the Australian economy: Could they reduce national unemployment with less inflationary side-effects than other policies? Could they redistribute job opportunities toward disadvantaged job-seekers? What effect has the Commonwealth's current targeted employment subsidy scheme had on the Australian labour market?[3]

The next part of the chapter outlines the economics of targeted employ-ment subsidies, beginning with definitions of the various types of subsidies and the goals that one might seek to achieve through subsidies. The major part examines the use of targeted employment subsidies in Australia, including a description of the Special Youth Employment Training Program (SYETP) and a review of its impact on the Australian economy and employer behaviour. Evidence is presented that, although the number of people whose employment is subsidized each year is too small to have had any significant impact on aggregate employment and unemployment, it does appear to be influencing the hiring decisions of firms that have participated in the scheme. Conclusions are presented in the final part.

II The Role of Employment Subsidies in a Nation's Economic and Employment Policy Mix

'Employment subsidies' is a term that encompasses a variety of subsidy proposals and programs for a number of different purposes. The commonality is that each type of employment subsidy involves payment to employers to offset some or all of the costs of employing eligible workers. They can be intended and designed to achieve redistributional, efficiency, stabilization, or a combination of goals. The Australian subsidy examined in this chapter, SYETP, and its American counterpart, the Targeted Jobs Tax Credit (TJTC), are intended to achieve redistributional and efficiency objectives. This part of the chapter begins with a discussion of the major types of subsidies and their uses and then reviews the economics of targeted employment subsidies, the category that includes SYETP.

Types of Subsidies

The particular type of subsidy examined in this chapter is a targeted hiring, flat rate subsidy. Targeted means that only a particular class of worker qualifies. In the Australian SYETP, the class is delineated in terms of age and duration of unemployment during the preceding year.

The fact that a subsidy is a hiring subsidy means that no credit is given for otherwise-eligible workers already employed.[4] The distinction between a hiring subsidy and a regular employment subsidy blurs as the subsidized period lengthens, especially for types of workers and jobs that are normally high turnover. The standard SYETP subsidy period, four months, is clearly a hiring subsidy.

A flat rate, rather than percentage, subsidy is one in which the amount received by the employer per period does not depend on the amount paid to the eligible worker; that is, it is a per capita amount. The standard SYETP scheme provides employers with $75 per week of employment of an eligible worker, regardless of the wages actually paid.

Employment subsidies have been advocated for the achievement of all three of the standard goals of economic policy: equity, efficiency, and stabilization. Targeted subsidies obviously are thought of in the context of equity goals: if successful, they redistribute job opportunities in favor of the target group. But they also have the potential to expand total output under conditions to be discussed later in this section. Non-targeted subsidies, which have been used as anti-recession instruments, will not be discussed here.

In considering the role of subsidies, it is important to keep in mind which goal is being pursued and what the alternatives are. Thus, analysis of targeted employment subsidies to achieve equity objectives should consider: Is the group whose employment qualifies for the subsidy one that society wishes to redistribute toward? Are job and training opportunities the most appropriate means of redistribution or would simple income transfers be more cost-effective? Targeted employment subsidies to achieve expansion of total output could be compared with general, unrestricted government expenditures: the argument for subsidies is that they can improve the structure of the labour market such that more output can be produced or jobs provided for a given level of inflation.

To the extent that employment subsidies are being used to gain access to on-the-job training opportunities, the subsidies should also be compared with other ways of providing and financing human capital investment. An important issue here is the delineation of groups with low employment and earnings who could benefit from subsidies. One could picture a continuum or queue of hard-to-employ workers: for the most employable, small subsidies to potential employers might be all that is needed; for the next group it might be more cost-effective to first provide them with remedial education, counselling, institutional training or other assistance; and there might be another group for whom the choice is either very expensive employability assistance or straight income transfers.[5]

The Economics of Targeted Employment Subsidies: Summary

The broad outlines of the micro-economic theory underlying employment subsidies are quite simple: Employers will respond to an exogenous reduction in the cost of employing a class of workers by employing more of them. The responses by a firm will depend on the size of the reduction in costs and the elasticity of demand for this type of labour. If, for example, the subsidized labour is perfectly substitutable for other labour, and ignoring transaction costs, then the employer would attempt to replace all of the unsubsidized workers with subsidized ones; in this case, whether and to what extent total employment in the firm increased would depend on the responsiveness of the firm's total demand for labour to a reduction in labour costs.

The theory at the macro level is more complicated and varies according to one's view of how the overall economy works. But the potential of certain types of employment subsidies to expand total employment, for a given level of inflation, by more than could be achieved through the use of monetary and fiscal policies alone is generally acknowledged. The efficacy of employment subsidies depends on the state of the economy within which they are to operate, the reasons for difference between groups in their unemployment rates, the nature of the wage-setting mechanisms in the economy, behavioural relationships determining the demand for and supply of labour, and various institutional factors. Essentially, the trick is to subsidize the employment of members of a high-unemployment group whose wages are institutionally determined and maintained above the market-clearing rate. The existence of high youth unemployment and wages that are determined through awards would appear to make Australia a good candidate for employment subsidies targeted on youth.

The state of the art of the economics of subsidies is very well set forth in two Brookings Institution volumes (Palmer (1978) and Haveman and Palmer (1982)). The former includes a major article by Baily and Tobin, describing a model for analyzing the macro-economic potential of targeted employment subsidies. This section summarizes the major findings from these volumes and other recent studies that are applicable to the Australian subsidy issues.

First, under the right conditions, targeted employment subsidies can improve the terms of trade between inflation and unemployment available to an economy. It is generally acknowledged that the application of macro-economic stimulation, alone, to expand employment and reduce unemployment is constrained by inflationary pressures. The constraint is depicted in the Phillips curve literature by a non-linear trade-off between inflation and unemployment, at least in the short run. More recent literature depicts the constraint by a non-accelerating inflation rate of unemployment (NAIRU) or a natural rate of unemployment. All of these models tell a similar story: beyond some point, conventional macro-economic policies cannot lower unemployment any further (at least without generating politically unacceptable or accelerating rates of inflation); further reductions require changes in the underlying structure of the economy. Targeted employment subsidies are offered as one means of changing the structure.

Second, the mechanism through which targeted employment subsidies operate is by changing the relative costs of labour inputs to employers. This can increase relative employment in the subsidized market at the expense of relative employment in the unsubsidized market. This may be desired to achieve equity goals, even if the terms of trade between aggregate (un)employment and inflation are not improved.

Third, whether subsidies can succeed in improving the terms of trade depends, in part, on the characteristics of the labour market in which it is to operate. Within the Baily-Tobin framework, at least one of the following conditions should exist: minimum wages that generate involuntary unemployment in low-wage markets; rigidity of relative wages; or sectoral wage rate increases trend, in part, on relative wage rates.

Fourth, whether subsidies can succeed in improving the terms of trade also depends on their specific characteristics. In particular, the delineation of the eligible group is crucial. The group must be one whose labour market is characterized by one of the preceding conditions. Further, the group defined as eligible must closely match the group one wants to target on (whether for equity or efficiency reasons): if the eligible group is too narrow, the subsidy scheme could result in employers substituting members of the eligible target group for members of the ineligible target group, with no net gain in either non-inflationary employment or equity; if the eligible group is too broad, employers could hire from the eligible non-target group only, again with no net gain. Obviously, there will always be borderline problems (unless the size of the subsidy itself can vary).

Fifth, even under the most favourable circumstances, targeted employment subsidies are not likely to be able to shift the natural rate of unemployment or NAIRU very far. (This is not a criticism, only a recognition of their limitations; the decision about whether or not to have a subsidy scheme should be based on its cost-effectiveness compared with other means of achieving the intended goals.) For example, an empirical study of the US labour market by Nichols (1982), using the Baily-Tobin framework, concluded that a subsidy targeted on low-skill workers would reduce the national unemployment rate by between one-half and two-thirds of a percentage point without increasing inflation: the estimated government budget cost per net job created was between $10,000 and $25,000, a range below the amount required to create one by an across-the-board expenditure. His particular estimates are based on a narrow set of assumptions and should only be taken as illustrative; in any event, they are for the US economy and for a hypothetical subsidy in which eligibility was delineated by occupation.

III Targeted Employment Subsidies in Australia

Subsidization of employers to induce them to hire and train workers is a major instrument of Australian employment and training policy.[6] In financial year 1981–82 the two largest employment and training programs administered by the Department of Employment and Industrial Relations were subsidies: $78.7 million for the Commonwealth Rebate for Apprentice Full-time Training

(CRAFT) and $53.7 million for the Special Youth Employment Training Program (SYETP). Together, they accounted for almost two-thirds of the Department's employment and training expenditures.[7]

CRAFT is intended to increase the supply of skilled workers by subsidizing some of the costs employers incur in taking on apprentices. Since this is not a targeted scheme, it will not be considered here. SYETP, on the other hand, is specifically intended to expand opportunities for long-term unemployed youth. It is the type of scheme that the literature reviewed earlier suggests could be effective in redistributing the incidence of unemployment, and in reducing unemployment, for a given level of inflation, below what could be attained through conventional government expenditures.

This part of the chapter begins with a description of SYETP. Next, the available evidence concerning the impact of SYETP on the Australian labour market will be presented. This will be followed by an examination of employer responses to the existence of the scheme. In particular, we will consider whether, and to what extent, employers have responded to the particular incentives provided by the scheme in ways consistent with economic theory.

Although this chapter is only concerned with targeted employment subsidies, it is important to note that the Commonwealth provides a number of other programs that assist young people to prepare for and find employment and provide support for them while they are unemployed. These include education-based assistance, such as the Education Program for Unemployed Youth, and labour market information and job search assistance through the Commonwealth Employment Service. There are also special employment and training programs for Aboriginals, disabled persons, and other groups; the majority of participants in these programs are under age 25 (Hoy and Paterson (1983)). Unemployment benefits are another substantial component of Australia's assistance to unemployed youth; the majority of unemployment beneficiaries are young people.

The Special Youth Employment Training Program (SYETP)

SYETP was begun in November 1976 as a means of helping school leavers obtain work experience. Essentially, it is a hiring subsidy to induce employers to provide work experience and training to long-term unemployed youth. During the six-year life of SYETP, the major changes in the program elements have been in the duration of unemployment required to qualify for the subsidy, the weekly payment, and the duration of the payment.[8]

SYETP currently includes three schemes: (i) 'standard SYETP' for subsidizing firms to employ young people who have been unemployed at least four months; (ii) 'extended SYETP' for young people who have been unemployed at least eight months; and (iii) 'Commonwealth SYETP' for subsidizing Commonwealth departments and instrumentalities. The Com-

Table 1:   Major Provisions of Targeted Employment Subsidies in Australia and the US.

Program Element	Special Youth Employment Training Program (SYETP)	Targeted Jobs Tax Credit (TJTC)
Eligible Workers		
Standard	Ages 15–24, who have been unemployed and away from full-time education at least four of the last twelve months	Ages 18–24, with low family income during preceding six months, and certain other persons from low-income families
Extended	Ages 18–24, who have been unemployed and away from full-time education at least eight of the last twelve months	
Amount and maximum duration of subsidy		
Standard	$75 per week for up to seventeen weeks	50 per cent of first $6000 of wages paid during first year of employment and 25 per cent of first $6000 during second year
Extended	$100 per week for first seventeen weeks and $75 per week for second seventeen weeks	
Maximum potential subsidy		
Standard	$1275	$4500
Extended	$2975	
Method of payment	Employer claim	Tax credit
Special conditions	Training plan, award wages, some limits on number and type of jobs	Limited to for-profit employers
Administrative agency	Commonwealth Employment Service	US Employment Service, Internal Revenue Service
Expiry	Indefinite	December 1985

monwealth SYETP scheme is quite small, accounting for about 7 per cent of participants, and differs from the others in that it reimburses employers for 100 per cent of the participants' wages during the subsidy period. This chapter examines the schemes for private employers and will consider the Commonwealth employer scheme only tangentially.[9]

The main elements of the program, as it currently exists, are outlined in table 1, along with the corresponding elements of the American Targeted Jobs Tax Credit for comparison. The most important one is that the group for whom employers can obtain a subsidy is limited to young people who have been looking for work for at least four months. The terms of the subsidy are more generous to employers for hiring young people who have been unemployed for at least eight months.

The subsidy, itself, is a flat rate: $75 per week for up to seventeen weeks for the standard SYETP; $100 per week for up to seventeen weeks and then $75 per week for up to an additional seventeen weeks for the extended scheme.

Employers are required to pay award or prevailing wage rates. Preliminary estimates by Bureau of Labour Market Research (BLMR) staff indicate that, since 1979, the standard SYETP rate has been between 35 and 44 per cent of average junior wages.

The maximum subsidy that an employer can receive for each covered worker is $1275 under the standard scheme and $2975 under the extended scheme. There is no minimum duration required for an employer to receive the weekly subsidy. The employer receives the money by filing claims with the administrative agency.

Another important aspect of SYETP is that participation by employers is not automatic; that is, they cannot merely file a claim with the government after the fact. Instead, an agreement must be reached with the Commonwealth Employment Service (CES) in which the CES has certified that the young person meets the age and unemployment duration requirements and the employer has agreed to provide work experience and training to the new employee. The requirements for the employer include that the employer and/or the CES develop an individual training plan for the new employee. In practice, since 'training' can include normal orientation and the 'plan' can be quite simple, neither the preparation of the plan nor its implementation need be very costly to the employer. Likewise, the CES must approve the particular type of job for which the employer proposes to use the eligible worker. This, too, does not appear to be very restrictive.

A potentially more important condition is that the employer must agree to pay award wages or prevailing wages. For employers that do so anyway, this is not restrictive. But for those who would employ youth at lower wages, the scheme would only be useful if the subsidy were sufficient to compensate the employer for the higher wages.

Finally, although the scheme has undergone a number of changes since it was introduced in late-1976, it has no fixed date of expiry. This is important in that, if employers are convinced that the scheme is reasonably permanent, they would be more likely to arrange their staffing patterns in ways that take into account its existence. Likewise, if the program is successful, its usage by employers will increase over time, both because information about the scheme will spread and because of repeat business. A program to alter the structure of the labour market, as opposed to a counter-cyclical program, should be a long-term one.

What Impact Is SYETP Having on Australian Employment and Unemployment?

The short answer is that the scheme has been too small to have had much of an impact on the national statistics. SYETP appears to be reducing the proportion of unemployed teenagers who are long-term unemployed; it is not clear whether it is also reducing total teenage unemployment, or simply redistributing it.[10]

Each year the seasonal peak participation in SYETP-subsidized employment is in August. BLMR has extracted participation by age going back to 1978 (Hoy and Paterson (1983)). These data, along with ABS statistics on employment, unemployment and unemployment duration [ABS, (monthly)], are reported in Table 2. For reasons to be examined later, there was a policy-induced drastic reduction in the level of SYETP participation between August 1978 and August 1979, from 33.7 thousand to 10.4 thousand teenagers and from 6.4 thousand to 1.7 thousand older youth. Between 1979 and 1981 there was a building up in participation and then a substantial decline by 1982. Meanwhile, for the labour market as a whole, unemployment fell from August 1978 to 1979, remained fairly stable to 1981, and then rose sharply by August 1982.

The first question which can be answered from this table is: Under the most generous assumptions about windfall and substitution, how much impact could SYETP have had on Australian unemployment during this period? To answer this, I have recomputed the ABS employment and unemployment statistics by subtracting SYETP-subsidized employment from the former and adding it to the latter. The differences between these hypothetical statistics and the actual statistics provide estimates of the impact of SYETP *if* all subsidized employment had been net additions from the age group's stock of unemployed and there had been no secondary effects; these differences are shown in the bottom panel of table 2.

Under the stated assumptions, the existence of SYETP would have reduced the aggregate Australian unemployment rate in the peak month (August 1978) by 0.6 percentage points and in the other months by only 0.2 or 0.3 percentage points. The impacts on the unemployment rate of the age 20–24 group were of similar magnitudes. The major impacts, of course, were for teenagers. If all of the SYETP-subsidized employment translated into one-for-one reduced unemployment, the impact on the teenage unemployment rate in August 1978 would have been 4.5 percentage points and in the other months between 1.3 and 1.9 points.[11]

Employment subsidy schemes, regardless of how they are structured, must, to some extent, subsidize firms for employment that would have occurred anyway. (The same point holds for subsidies to stimulate other activities, such as investment and job creation in the public sector.) The only available estimates of the extent to which subsidized employment actually expanded total employment are from surveys of participating employers. These, at best, provide some indication of whether the employers, themselves, viewed the employees hired under the scheme as net additions or substitutes for workers who would have been hired in any event. Their responses indicate that only about one-third of the subsidized employees were net additions.[12]

The extent to which these were also net additions to total employment in Australia depends on the employment that could have been generated through

Table 2: SYETP Participation and Selected Employment Statistics, 1978–82

Group	August 1978	August 1979	August 1980	August 1981	August 1982
Age 15-19					
SYETP Participant	33,741	10,376	13,432	14,372	10,778
Employed	630,800	617,700	650,900	652,000	625,400
Unemployed	127,600	129,700	130,700	105,600	125,400
Under 13 weeks	61,400	56,200	55,100	48,200	57,600
13–25 weeks	24,100	22,700	21,300	18,200	19,300
26 weeks-plus	42,100	50,800	54,300	39,200	48,500
rate (%)	16.8	17.4	16.7	13.9	16.7
Age 20–24					
SYETP Participant	6,420	1,681	2,249	4,594	2,934
Employed	845,000	885,200	914,300	943,300	934,600
Unemployed	85,200	78,800	88,000	87,700	106,100
Under 13 weeks	42,700	36,700	42,000	46,200	54,000
13–25 weeks	16,300	14,100	16,200	11,100	15,100
26 weeks-plus	26,200	28,000	29,800	30,400	37,000
rate (%)	9.2	8.2	8.8	8.5	10.2
Age 15 and over					
Employed	5,969,600	6,041,500	6,246,700	6,356,000	6,347,600
Unemployed	395,700	373,800	392,300	377,100	458,500
rate (%)	6.2	5.8	5.9	5.6	6.7
Maximum impact of SYETP on unemploy-ment rates (%)					
Age 15–19	4–5	1–3	1–7	1–9	1–4
Age 20–24	0–6	0–2	0–2	0–5	0–3
Age 15 and over	0–6	0–2	0–2	0–3	0–2

alternative uses of the expenditures and on the impacts of the expansion of the subsidized firms' activities on other firms' activities. Moreover, the net impact on unemployment depends also on the labour supply response generated by the increased employment induced by the scheme. Since teenager participation rates are influenced by job availability (the 'hidden unemployment' phenomenon), the translation from employment impact to unemployment impact is certainly less than one-to-one.

Some indication of the extent to which the subsidized employment might have represented net additions to employment can also be seen by closer examination of the changes that occurred in the teenage statistics between August 1978 and 1979, when SYETP participation fell by 23,000 teenagers. The aggregate employment and unemployment statistics indicate that this was a period of improvement in the labour market: employment rose by about 70,000, unemployment fell by 20,000 and the unemployment rate fell by 0.4 percentage points. Yet this was not reflected in the ABS statistics for teenagers. Instead, employment fell by 13,000, unemployment rose by 2,000 and the unemployment rate rose by 0.6 percentage points. Since we do not know the impact of other factors at this time, the impact, if any, of the SYETP reduction cannot be estimated. But this does provide circumstantial evidence that at least some of the SYETP employment had been net additions to teenage employment.

The same 1978–1979 event also provides circumstantial evidence in support of the hypothesis that some of the impact of SYETP is simply to redistribute unemployment among teenagers, such that long-term unemployment is lower and short-term unemployment is higher. Recall that eligibility for the program included unemployment during four of the past twelve months (i.e. seventeen weeks). The unemployment duration statistics in table 2 refer to the duration of the current spell of unemployment, not the amount of unemployment over the preceding twelve months. Nonetheless, they indicate that the sharp reduction in SYETP employment was accompanied by an increase in long-term unemployment and a reduction in short-term unemployment. The same pattern occurred, but to a lesser extent, in the unemployment duration statistics for the age 20–24 group, which had a smaller reduction in the number of SYETP participants. And, to provide further circumstantial support, there was a decline in the number of long-term unemployed in the oldest group — the group not directly affected by SYETP. Again, in the absence of a model that is capable of accounting for fluctuations in age-duration unemployment levels, one should not push these numbers too far — they are suggestive only.

SYETP could also increase aggregate economic output and employment and redistribute income and employment opportunities to the extent that human capital is developed through the subsidized work experience. As with any training program, this macro-economic benefit would occur through the increased productive capacity of the work force. A necessary condition for this to occur is that the post-program earnings of the participants themselves exceed what they would have earned in the absence of the program. BLMR staff are attempting to estimate these direct impacts, although the absence of adequate comparison groups makes it impossible to estimate these impacts accurately (Stretton (1982)). Whether the gains to the individual participants translate into overall gains for the economy depends on whether the on-the-job training opportunities would have otherwise gone to persons who would have benefited to the same extent. No attempt will be made in this chapter to assess these human capital effects.

Are Australian Employers Responding to the SYETP Incentives?

The specific characteristics of SYETP — flat-rate subsidy, short duration, targeted, and requirement to pay award wages — provide specific incentives to employers to behave in certain ways. As per the goal of the scheme, they are encouraged to hire long-term unemployed youth. In addition, the incentive structure might influence more precisely whom they chose to hire from among the eligible unemployed and what they do with them. It is important to determine whether employers are, in fact, responding to the specific incentives for two reasons. First, this provides some indication of whether the subsidies taken by employers are anything other than pure windfall. Second, if employers are found to be responding to specific elements of SYETP, this provides some basis for expecting that changes in these elements could change their behaviour. Support for the proposition that Australian employers are behaving as economic theory and common sense suggest they should is found in: (i) the age distribution of the subsidized workers; and (ii) the reduction in participation following a large reduction in the size of the subsidy.

The clearest indication that employers are taking account of specific terms of the subsidy scheme comes from the age distribution of the workers whose wages were subsidized. In 1980–81, 59 per cent of the subsidized youth in the standard SYETP scheme were between the ages of 15 and 17; 28 per cent were ages 18 or 19; and the remaining 13 per cent were ages 20 through 24.[13] The oldest age group is distinctly underrepresented in the scheme, relative to the group's percentage of the eligible population and relative to its share of total youth employment. In this period, approximately 40 per cent of the long-term unemployed between the ages of 15 and 24 were in the ages 20–24 group.[14] Thus their representation in the standard SYETP scheme was approximately one-third their representation in the eligible pool of the unemployed.[15] This skewing of the age distribution toward the youngest workers may be explained by the nature of the subsidy, along with the customary positive age-earnings relationship: the flat-rate subsidy covers a smaller percentage of weekly earnings of the oldest eligible group.

In August 1978 there was a sharp reduction in the weekly subsidy rate and in the maximum number of weeks subsidized. Information on the subsequent reduction in employer participation *suggests* a rather large elasticity in demand for subsidized workers. In August 1978, there were 33,741 teenagers whose employment was being subsidized through a SYETP scheme.[16]

Under the agreements between employers and the CES when these youth would have been hired, the subsidy was $67 per week for six months, for a total potential subsidy of $1742. From the scheme's inception, the subsidy rate had been set at 45 per cent of the male adult average award wage for 6 months. In the August 1978 budget it was announced that henceforth new hires would be subsidized at $45 per week (30 per cent of the male award wage) for four months. Thus the total subsidy per worker that an employer could receive was reduced from $1742 to $765, only 44 per cent of the previous amount.

By the same month a year later, after hiring decisions would have adjusted to the new incentive structure, only 10,376 teenagers were in the scheme. As pointed out in a BLMR report (Hoy and Paterson (1983)), some of this reduction can be explained mechanically: if employer behaviour had not changed, a reduction in the potential duration of the subsidy to two-thirds of its former number would result in a reduction in the number of participants at any given time of the same magnitude.[17] This effect can be adjusted for by reducing the August 1978 subsidized employment level to two-thirds its actual size. Even with this adjustment, the reduction in employer participation is dramatic: from 22,494 subsidized teenagers to 10,376, only 46 per cent of the adjusted initial level.

The response by employers to the reduction in the SYETP terms provides a vivid illustration of the extent to which their participation in the scheme could be influenced by changes in its terms. However, lest the reader translate the similarity between the magnitudes of the employment reduction and the subsidy reduction into a unity elasticity estimate, it must be noted that it isn't that simple. For example, when the amount and duration of the subsidy were changed, the agency staff were given new instructions which emphasized the training objective of the scheme. To the extent that this was enforced, the potential benefit to employers was further reduced. Moreover, some of the reduction could have been due to less aggressive marketing by the CES. However, a survey of employer attitudes to the changes in terms found that over 40 per cent claimed they would reduce or terminate their participation.[18]

It is necessary to emphasize that these individual bits of evidence about employer responsiveness are, at best, suggestive. Adequate information simply does not exist at this time. In particular, the key issue of the extent to which the subsidy is changing the level and composition of national employment cannot be determined, given the absence of information about elasticities of demand for the eligible group and substitution between this group and other youth and adults. Nonetheless, as shown earlier, the scale of the program, thus far, has been so small that — under the most generous assumptions — it could not have reduced Australia's unemployment rate by very much.

A thorough economic analysis of SYETP would require estimates of the elasticity of demand for SYETP-eligible employees and elasticities of substitution between this group, other youth, and adults. A recent study by Lewis (1983) suggests that demand elasticities for young people in Australia might be quite large; that young males (age 21 and under) are most substitutable with females; and that young females are most substitutable with adult females. His specific estimates are for full-time employees only and are much larger than corresponding estimates in the US.[19] For example, he estimates that a 1 per cent increase in the weekly earnings of young females would be associated with a 4.6 per cent decrease in their employment; the estimate for young males is 1.8 per cent. His estimates imply that an across-the-board reduction in the wages of youth relative to adults of 1 per cent would increase the relative employment of young people by about 3 per cent. As is stated in that paper, such estimates should not be interpreted literally; they suggest that changes in the relative wages of young people could increase their employment, but not necessarily by these amounts.

SYETP, of course, is *not* a general youth wage subsidy. It differs in several critical respects: (i) it only covers a subgroup of young people; (ii) the subsidy per worker has a limited duration; (iii) and there are a number of conditions attached to it, making it more a hiring and training subsidy. Conceptually, it is difficult to even define the factor of production that is being subsidized through SYETP, since an individual's eligibility changes as his or her duration of unemployment changes. One would expect that, at least at around the 17-week cutoff point, subsidized and unsubsidized youth would be highly substitutable. If so, then the most obvious impact on the unemployment statistics would be a change in the composition of youth unemployment by duration. Whether the scheme also increased total youth employment (and reduced youth unemployment) and the extent to which this was associated with a reduction in adult employment would then depend on the relevant demand elasticities.

A further complication is that there is very little information available on the percentage of employment costs that is being subsidized — a critical element for estimating demand elasticities. We know the size of the subsidy, but do not know: (i) the wages paid to the subsidized employees; (ii) other costs incurred by employers during the subsidy period; and (iii) expected tenure of the subsidized employees.

The studies of SYETP that have been completed to date indicate that employers who use the subsidy are behaving in ways consistent with assumptions commonly used in economic models about rational, profit-maximizing economic agents.[20] The cost of employing certain types of labour has been reduced by the subsidy, but this does not suspend the rules of the market. Thus, some of the eligible pool are made more attractive than others and they are the ones most likely to be hired under the scheme. And some employers can benefit more from the scheme than others and they appear to be the ones most likely to participate in the scheme. Surveys of employers who have participated in the scheme also provide some information concerning the extent to which they have expanded total employment as a result of the scheme, although responses to this sort of survey are difficult to interpret.

IV Conclusion

Review of Australia's Special Youth Employment Training Program illustrates many of the issues involved in converting the theory of employment subsidies into practice and in measuring their effectiveness. The immediate purpose of SYETP is to induce employers to hire long-term unemployed young people and provide them with work experience that might help them to secure stable employment. Studies of the program participants indicate that this is being accomplished. The issues raised in this chapter have to do with the overall impacts of SYETP on the Australian labour market: Is it redistributing jobs? Is it permitting Australia to have more employment and less unemployment for a given level of inflation than could be achieved otherwise?

The program is too small to expect to be able to estimate its impact on the labour market from time series analyses of national statistics. Since it began in 1976, there were never more than 40,000 subsidized workers at any one time. During most of the period, less than half this number participated. Given reasonable assumptions about the extent to which participation represented net additional employment and about labour force responses, the program at its peak enrollment would not have reduced the teenage unemployment rate by more than 1.5 percentage points and the aggregate unemployment rate by more than 0.2 percentage points.

The available evidence suggests that employers are responding to the SYETP incentives as theory and common sense say they should. The size of the subsidy appears to influence their level of participation and the form of the subsidy appears to influence who among the eligible pool they hire. The number of long-term unemployed youth in Australia is probably lower than it would be in the absence of the program. It is a reasonable assumption that a reduction in the unemployment of this group has put less pressure on wages than would have resulted from an across-the-board unemployment reduction of similar magnitude; however, there is no direct evidence with which to test this assumption.

In sum, SYETP appears to be playing a useful, though not a large, role in the Australian economy. In considering what future role it or other employment subsidies might play, its relationship to other policies needs to be considered. More attention needs to be focussed on determining the most cost-effective methods of attracting employer interest while achieving the program's objectives. To the extent that targeted employment subsidies redistribute job opportunities, it is particularly important to examine the implications of the current and alternative eligibility rules. At this point, it is not clear whether the use of unemployment duration as a qualifying criterion is the best approach.

Notes

1   This chapter was written while the author was a Senior Research Fellow in the Department of Economics, Research School of Social Sciences, Australian National University. The views expressed are the author's own and do not necessarily reflect those of any organization with which he has been affiliated.

2   In Australia this approach has been suggested by CORDEN (1979), HARRIS (1982) and WITHERS (1982).

3   Targeted employment subsidies also provide on-the-job training. As such, they should be considered as one part of a government's strategy for investing in human capital. Issues involving the cost-effectiveness of subsidized private work experience and on-the-job training vs. education, off-the-job training, public work experience, and other methods of government support for human capital investment will not be directly addressed here.

4   HAMERMESH (1978) defines the various types of subsidies in a slightly different manner. He distinguishes between employment subsidies and hiring subsidies, with the former applying to the entire period of a worker's employment.

5   NATHAN (1982) uses a similar categorization, except that he further distinguishes between subsidization of private vs public employers, with the former assumed to be more selective.

6   Programs started after March 1983 are not included here. For further analysis of SYETP's impacts on unemployment, see SMITH (1984a and 1984b).

7   Programme expenditure statistics are from Minister for Employment and Industrial Relations (1982b). Some of the other programs, such as the Special Apprentice Training and the Skills in Demand programs, also include subsidies to employers to provide training.

8   These are described by HOY and PATERSON (1983).

9   The Commonwealth employer subsidy is examined in Department of the Employment and Youth Affairs (1980c).

10 These findings do not indicate whether SYETP has been cost-effective. They only indicate that it has operated on a small-scale. Moreover, its stated objectives have not included macro-economic ones as such. Also, only the impacts of SYETP are considered in this chapter. As of August 1982, approximately 6000 persons under age 25 were enrolled in education-based programs also intended to improve their job prospects and 3000 youth were receiving specialized assistance through other Commonwealth programs (HOY and PATERSON (1983)).

11 Among teenagers, persons under age 18 account for at least two-thirds of the SYETP-subsidized employees, though less than half of the teenage labour force. Therefore, the maximum potential impact on this group's unemployment rate is larger.

12 In late-1979 approximately 20 per cent of employers who had hired SYETP employees in April 1979 were asked how the vacancy arose (extra workers needed for business expansion, replacement of another SYETP worker, or replacement of a non-SYETP worker who left) and whether, in the absence of the scheme, they would have filled the position with a worker who was more experienced, older, or not have offered the position. Thirty-three per cent responded that they would only have hired a subsidized worker; about half of these were for expansion and the rest were for replacement or specially created for the scheme (DEYA (1980b)). A survey of 1981 SYETP placements provided similar estimates (HOY and PATERSON (1983)).

13 These are for first assistance under the non-Commonwealth scheme. The source of all 1980–81 program participant data in this section, unless otherwise cited, is HOY and PATERSON (1983).

14 During the year ending 1981, 120,000 of the 282,000 (43 per cent) persons under age 25 who were unemployed thirteen weeks or more were between the ages of 20 and 24; 74,000 of unemployment were in the older group (ABS (1982b) p. 17). During the same period, 1,064,700 of the 1,911,400 (56 per cent) persons under age 25 who were employed were between the ages of 20 and 24 (p. 13).

15 The comparison is not exactly the right one in that the time periods and eligibility rules are slightly different and the ABS unemployment statistics themselves would be affected by the program.

16 All program data reported in this section are from HOY and PATERSON (1983). August is the peak month in participation every year.

17 The relationship isn't exact because many employers do not stay with the employer for the maximum duration.

18 In early-1979 over 1000 employers who had participated in SYETP in 1978 or 1979 completed a questionnaire that included questions concerning their reactions to subsidy reductions announced in August 1978. Twenty-five per cent indicated that they would no longer participate; 17 per cent said they would reduce their level of

participation; 37 per cent indicated they would participate at the same level; and the remaining 21 per cent either didn't respond or didn't know (DEYA (1980a) p. 45).

19 See MILLER (1983) and HAMERMESH and GRANT (1979) for reviews of the US studies.

20 BLMR studies have also found, for example, that the industries in which disproportionate numbers of SYETP-subsidized workers are located tend to be ones with low wages and high turnover, such as manufacturing and retail industries; this is consistent with the incentives provided by a flat-rate, fixed-term subsidy (HOY (1983)).

References

AUSTRALIAN BUREAU OF STATISTICS (1982a) *Earnings and Hours of Employees, Australia, October 1981*, Catalogue no. 6304.0, Canberra.

AUSTRALIAN BUREAU OF STATISTICS (1982b) *Labour Force Experience During the Period February 1980 to February 1981, Australia*, Catalogue no. 6206.0, Canberra.

AUSTRALIAN BUREAU OF STATISTICS (monthly) *The Labour Force, Australia*, Catalogue no. 6203.0, Canberra.

BAILY, M. and TOBIN, J. (1978) 'Inflation-unemployment consequences of job creation policies' in PALMER, J. (Ed.) *Creating Jobs: Public Employment Programs and Wage Subsidies*, Washington, Brookings Institution, pp. 43–76.

BUREAU OF LABOUR MARKET RESEARCH (1983) *Employment and Training Programs for Young People: Analysis of Assistance in 1980–81*, BLMR Research Report no. 2, Canberra.

CORDEN, W.M. (1979) 'Wages and unemployment in Australia', *Economic Record*, 55, March, pp. 1–19.

DEPARTMENT OF EMPLOYMENT AND YOUTH AFFAIRS (1980a) *Special Youth Employment Training Programme Employer Survey*, Melbourne, processed.

DEPARTMENT OF EMPLOYMENT AND YOUTH AFFAIRS (1980b) *SYETP in the Private Sector: Follow-up Survey of April 1979 Placements*, Melbourne, processed.

DEPARTMENT OF EMPLOYMENT OF YOUTH AFFAIRS (1980c) *Training and Work Experience in Commonwealth Establishments — A Study of 1000 Trainees*, Melbourne, processed

HAMERMESH, D. (1978) 'Subsidies for jobs in the private sector' in PALMER, J. (Ed.) *Creating Jobs: Public Employment Programs and Wage Subsidies*, Washington, Brookings Intitution, pp. 87–115.

HAMERMESH, D. and GRANT, J. (1979) 'Econometric studies of labor-labor substitution and their implications for policy', *Journal of Human Resources*, 14, Fall, pp. 518–42.

HARRIS, G. (1982) 'The case for marginal employment subsidies', *Australian Quarterly*, 54, winter, pp. 161–72.

HAVEMAN, R. and PALMER J. (Eds) (1982) *Jobs for Disadvantaged Workers: The Economics of Employment Subsidies*, Washington, Brookings Institution.

HOY, M. (1983) *Review of Five Years Operation of the Special Youth Employment Training Program*, BLMR Conference Paper no. 18, Canberra.

HOY, M. and PATERSON, P. (1983) *Data on National Training and Employment Programs*, BLMR Technical Paper no. 6, Canberra.

HOY, M. and LAMPE, G. (1982) *Women in National Training and Employment Programs*, BLMR Conference Paper No. 13, Canberra.

KIRBY, P. (1981) 'An overview of Australian experience with manpower programmes' in BAIRD, C., GREGORY, R. and GRUEN, F.H. (Eds) *Youth Employment, Education and Training*, Canberra, Centre for Economic Policy Research, Australian National University, pp. 4.1–37.

LEWIS, P. (1983) *The Role of Relative Wages in the Substitution Between Young and Adult Workers in Australia*, BLMR Working Paper no. 19, Canberra.

MILLER, P. (1983) *The Role of Labour Costs in the Youth Labour Market: An Overview of the Evidence*, Australian National University, Centre for Economic Policy Research, Discussion Paper no. 65, Canberra.

MINISTER FOR EMPLOYMENT AND INDUSTRIAL RELATIONS (1982a) 'Commonwealth response to the labour market situation', *News Release 108/82*, 9 December.

MINISTER FOR EMPLOYMENT AND INDUSTRIAL RELATIONS (1982b) *Employment and Industrial Relations Programs*, 1982–83, Canberra, Commonwealth Government Printer.

NATHAN, R. *et. al.* (1981) *Public Service Employment: A Field Evaluation*, Washington, Brookings Institution.

NATIONAL COMMISSION FOR MANPOWER POLICY (1978) *CETA: An Analysis of the Issues*, Washington, US Government Printing Office.

NICHOLS, D. (1982) 'Effects on the non–inflationary unemployment rate' in HAVEMAN, R. and PALMER, J. (Eds) *Jobs for Disadvantaged Workers: The Economics of Employment Subsidies*, Washington, Brookings Institution, pp. 131–55.

PALMER, J. (Ed) (1978) *Creating Jobs: Public Employment Programs and Wage Subsidies*, Washington, Brookings Institution.

SMITH, R.E. (1984a) 'Estimating the impacts of job subsidies on the distribution of unemployment: Reshuffling the queue?', Discussion Paper no. 95, Canberra, Centre for Economic Policy Research, Australian National University.

SMITH, R.E. (1984b) 'How effective has the SYETP job subsidy really been?', Discussion Paper no. 104, Canberra, Centre for Economic Policy Research, Australian National University.

SOLOW, R. (1980) 'Employment policy in inflationary times' in GINZBERG, E. (Ed.) *Employing the Unemployed*, New York, Basic Books, pp. 129–41.

STRETTON, A. (1982) *The Short Term Impact on Participants of Selected Youth Employment and Training Programs*, BLMR Working Paper no. 15, Canberra.

WITHERS, G. (1982) 'The concerned politician's guide to countering inflation and unemployment', *Australian Bulletin of Labour*, 9 December, pp. 55–68.

ACOT

2 5 NOV 1986

LIBRARY

Urban Vocational Education and Managing the Transition from School to Work

Paul E. Peterson and Barry G. Rabe

All students are engaged in vocational education. From the beginning of their school years they learn abilities, skills and orientations that will benefit them in later life in their varied activities, including the work they perform in the jobs they hold. Of greatest vocational value to them will be their ability to read, write, calculate and communicate. Of far less value to most of them will be the specific information they acquire about a particular job or industry, for they may never be employed in such a position, or, if so employed, they may change occupations a short time later.

If the most important 'vocational' training often takes place in what is thought to be a conventional academic classroom, what then is the purpose of what is specifically designed to be 'vocational'? We shall suggest that the specific skills taught in vocational programs are valuable largely because they provide a mechanism for allowing students to develop direct contacts with a labor market. Managing the transition from school presents one of the greatest challenges to young Americans. At a time when youth attend school for an ever increasing number of years, or suffer high rates of unemployment if they do not, finding useful, interesting occupational careers is particularly difficult. The problems are most severe in economically distressed urban areas. It is, therefore, especially important for vocational education to assist in developing market contacts for urban youth.

The studies upon which this chapter depends found that vocational programs vary considerably in their capacity to provide relevant vocational training and valuable market contacts. In fact, a three-level system of vocational education programs seems to have developed in which: junior and community colleges and exceptional secondary level programs offer sophisticated training; vocationally-oriented and comprehensive high schools, which are circumscribed by resource limitations, tend to rely on older, more primitive technologies; and manpower training programs financed under the Comprehensive Employment and Training Act (CETA), now succeeded by programs of the Job Training Partnership Act (JTPA),[1] and the weakest of the secondary school programs, provide relatively unsophisticated training to individuals who have not successfully parlayed their prior educational experiences into employment. These three differing types of vocational programs are distinguishable in the kinds of students served, the quality of programs offered, the resources available, and the relationships established with both employers and trade unions.

The impact of federal policy on this differentiated system of service-delivery is two-fold. In the first place, federal funds, in conjunction with state and local resources help sustain vocational programs in high schools and junior colleges. The exact consequences of federal dollars are difficult to measure because of the commingling of federal, state and local funds, and the ease with which federal funds can act as substitutes for local resources. While this poses a difficulty for the analyst attempting to discern a federal impact, the commingling of resources may be very beneficial for the programs themselves. Quite clearly, they ease local school systems' administrative burdens and permit allocation of resources into areas where local administrators believe they can be of greatest benefit. The impact of federal funds on CETA (and now JTPA) programming is more substantial. Without federal dollars most of these programs could not survive. Whether or not the federal fiscal role in manpower training programs should be sharply separated from its role in other vocational programs is another question, which is discussed at some length later in the chapter.

If federal fiscal support has had definite local consequences, the second aspect of federal policy — attempts to shape the use of federal funds through program regulations and guidelines — has had much less of an impact. The Vocational Education Amendments of 1976 call for increased local planning, evaluation and participation by private sector groups. The legislation also calls upon local programs to reduce and eliminate sex bias and sex stereotyping. Most of these requirements, however, have had but the most minimal local impact. This can be attributed, in part, to their recent creation. If left intact over the course of a decade or more, more substantial consequences might become discernible. Yet, in one locality after another, administrators perceived many of the federal guidelines as largely irrelevant to their central mission. Planning and evaluation deadlines were met with a flurry of paperwork and a perfunctory yawn; sex stereotyping problems were gradually being addressed at the local level, but the impetus seemed to have little to do with federal recommendations; and private sector participation in local vocational education programming remained substantial in the most prestigious programs and barely recognizable in the least prominent, just as it was prior to the passage of the 1976 Amendments.

Most importantly, federal policy seems largely oblivious of the fact that vocational programs vary considerably in their capacity to provide appropriate vocational training and valuable market contacts. Instead of building on strength or seeking to unify a divided system that competes with itself, federal policy helps perpetuate a system that contains programs serving distinctive student constituencies with wide discrepancies in the quality of programs offered, the instructional and equipment resources available, and the capacities to manage the transition from school to work. The greatest infusions of federal funds have been directed toward creation and maintenance of the lowest tier of existing vocational programs, those funded through JTPA, which to use a popular political metaphor, served as a vocational 'safety net'. A significant repercussion of this noble effort, however, was the creation of a separate vocational training system that was largely divorced from its more prominent public school counterparts and possessed little political incentive to narrow these gaps if it was to remain an independent entity.

On the basis of these findings we recommend in conclusion that the federal government could best meet urban vocational education needs not only by continuing to provide supplemental funding to local districts but also by encouraging increased contacts between schools and the private sector and between the various levels of vocational programs. Instead of encouraging multiple levels through perpetuation of a bottom tier with relatively little exposure to more prestigious vocational programs and minimal private sector support, federal policy should attempt to bridge existing gaps. Federal funds were scattered thinly across the myriad of existing secondary and post-secondary programs and funnelled into CETA; they did little to broaden the access of minorities to more prestigious institutions, despite the fact that not all such schools were at peak enrollment levels. Instead of emphasizing an extensive series of requirements — such as planning and evaluation — which meet with largely perfunctory state and local responses, federal vocational policy might be redirected to build bridges between existing delivery systems, instead of imposing common obstacles upon each semi-autonomous level.

Our analysis and conclusions are based upon four case studies of urban vocational education in Atlanta, Chicago, Rochester and San Francisco, which were commissioned by the Vocational Education Study Group in the National Institute of Education.[2] In each of these case studies information was collected by reading state and local reports on vocational education and by interviewing a wide variety of school officials, including teachers, principals, directors of vocational education, administrators of programs under the Comprehensive Education and Training Act, and other informed observers. A wide variety of vocational programs were observed in all four cities. We supplement these case study findings with information gathered by the National Opinion Research Center (NORC) on the impact of vocational education programs as reported in a preliminary analysis of a 1980 survey of all high school sophomores and seniors in the United States.[3] This data set includes information on the background, abilities, educational programs, current work situation and future plans of the nation's high school sophomores and seniors.

Managing the Transition from School to Work

The main purpose of vocational education is to manage the transition from school to work. The ways in which this transition is managed will differ, depending on the skills that are taught to the students and those that the job market requires. For some students the period of transition will be prolonged; for others, a relatively brief period of specific occupational preparation will be sufficient. But for all of its variable components, the element which makes vocational education noticeably different from other forms of education is its specific interest in the processes of transition from the schoolhouse to the workplace.

Historically, vocational education was understood as involving training in certain kinds of subject matter and specific kinds of manual skills. The main divisions within vocational education were agriculture, domestic economics, industrial education, and business and commercial education. More recently, new areas of training such as the health and computer sciences have been incorporated as major components in vocational education. As functional specialization has increased, the number of specific occupations within these broad areas has multiplied, and as the technology has changed, the kinds of skills required and the specific areas where occupational opportunities exist have been dramatically altered. Clearly, there is no single body of knowledge that forms the curricular core for vocational education.

At the same time, it has become increasingly obvious to many educators that the most useful vocational skills include the very basic capacities to read quickly, comprehend easily, write clearly, and calculate accurately. Inasmuch as specific kinds of skill capacities quickly become dated, general verbal and numerical abilities, which can be translated into specific skill attributes with additional training, provide essential preparation for long-term career success. Thus, the two best predictors of earnings throughout a working career are one's overall verbal ability and the years one has remained in school.

In a sense then, all of one's educational experiences comprise preparation for an occupation. Yet, if all education is in part occupationally related, it is important to distinguish clearly those specific educational experiences which can be usefully identified as primarily and distinctively vocational. In our view, there is a growing sense among policy analysts and policy-makers that the distinctive contribution to be made by vocational education involves the successful management of the complex transition from school to work.

Skills and Contacts

In order for vocational education programs to manage successfully the transition from school to work, they must provide students with two separate but complementary attributes — skills and contacts. Until very recently, vocational education has focussed primarily on the provision of skills, leaving the development of market contacts either to the discretion and initiative of local administrators or to the individual job hunter. Recent economic analysis, however, has emphasized the independent importance of market contacts for finding suitable employment.[4]

We are now beginning to appreciate the complexity of the labor market, and recognize how awkward and cumbersome exchange relations in this market have become. As one economist observed recently, labor markets do not operate like grain markets, where the quality of the commodity is quite easily determined.[5] Instead, labor markets are more like marriage markets, where everything is uncertain and unpredictable. In the first place, when individuals search for jobs, and when firms search for employees, each side seeks a complex package of characteristics that best suits its interests. On the one side, individuals are interested not only in their prospective salary or wages, but, in addition, they are concerned about distance from home, work environment, hours of work, camaraderie of associates, and quality of benefits. On the other side, firms are interested in not only the potential employee's specific job related skills, but also in his or her dependability, collegiality, likelihood of remaining in the position, basic health, and overall mental abilities and learning capacities. Secondly, accurate information with respect to all the relevant characteristics of employees, on the one side, and jobs, on the other, is difficult to obtain in advance of employment. The most agreeable person in an interview situation may easily lose his or her composure under pressure. Work that seems fascinating from afar may become tedious and boring upon greater familiarity. Thirdly, once a job has been accepted and a person hired, disengagement is difficult and costly. For the employer, union rules and legal requirements may impede discharge. For the employee, the costs of searching for a new position and the danger of developing a reputation for transience and undependability discourage frequent job switching. Just as prudent people enter the marriage market cautiously and make commitments only after gathering a good deal of information, firms and potential employees similarly must consider many factors before a 'match' can be made.

Where exchanges are difficult and complex, both employers and employees use simplifying devices to gather the information they need. On the one side, individuals seek work with large, well-established, prestigious institutions whose reputation for permanence and continuity are well-known. They may even forgo more interesting, lucrative employment with smaller, newer firms, because the reliability of the employer is less well-established. On the other side, employers, too, use simple cues that tell easily and quickly who is likely to be an appropriate employee. Education has come to be one such cueing mechanism in the United States. Firms have discovered that those who do well and persevere in their school work will generally perform ably on the job. Conceivably, one of the reasons why length of schooling is such a good predictor of future occupation and earnings is the importance of education as a cueing device for employers.

Race, sex and age cues also seem to be used by many employers. Social stereotypes have in the past stigmatized racial minorities, women, and young adults. They can persist even in the face of significant changes in the characteristics of the stereotyped population, and are retained, in part, because the cueing characteristic is easily ascertained. Unfortunately, the ease with which the cueing characteristic is detected encourages its use even when the information being supplied may be erroneous in a large number of cases. Employers may know that a large number of women, blacks and young people may be quite satisfactory employees, but may still use this readily available cueing device to sort applicants for a position. Or, if selection of a person from a negatively stereotyped group is to be made, the employer will try to obtain additional information to ensure that the individual in question does not conform to the group stereotyped.

In making such a search, employers may rely on another type of cue, the recommendation of friends. Where reliable information is important but difficult to ascertain, formal channels of information are often supplemented by confidential suggestions made through informal networks of friends and acquaintances. According to Granovetter, many individuals rely on informal connections in their search for employment; if jobs are found this way, then employers must be using informal contacts as an important informational source.[6]

The Changing Labor Market For Young Adults

Such informal connections may be particularly important for persons who are members of negatively stereotyped groups. In this regard, young non-white males and females may be the most disadvantaged of the ascriptively defined social groups. Youth unemployment for non-white males and females aged 16 to 19 nearly doubled between 1957 and 1978, and was more than twice the rate for white youths of the same age and sex in 1978. Similar trends were evident among youths aged 20 to 24, suggesting that the youth unemployment problem is substantially more serious for ethnic minorities (see table 1). White and non-white labor force participation rates were equally distinctive. For example, 65 per cent of white males aged 16 to 19 were labor force participants in 1978, compared to only 45.4 per cent of the non-white males who were the same age (see table 2). If not confined to non-white youth, the difficulty of successfully managing the transition from school to work was nevertheless disproportionately severe for them.[7]

These trends are aggravated by the economic difficulties experienced by many urban areas, where youths who are members of minority groups are concentrated. Technological innovations in transportation and communication have reduced the need both for face-to-face contact and for the concentration of manufacturing facilities near central distribution points. As a result, many firms have moved from large central cities to suburbs, smaller cities and rural areas, where labor is less expensive and public amenities — open space, reduced pollution, and less crime — are more amply provided. Except for a few cities in the south and western parts of the United States, central cities are exporting capital, labor, and people. As central city economies decline, employment opportunities for young people are especially scarce.

Table 1: Youth unemployment rates in the civilian population by age, race, and sex: selected years* (in per cents)

	1957	1964	1978
All Youth			
16–24 years old	9.0	11.5	12.2
All Youth			
16–19 years old	11.6	16.2	16.3
20–24 years old	7.1	8.3	9.5
White Males			
16–19 years old	11.5	14.7	13.5
20–24 years old	7.1	7.4	7.6
Non-white Males			
16–19 years old	18.4	24.3	34.4
20–24 years old	12.7	12.6	20.0
White Females			
16–19 years old	9.5	14.9	14.4
20–24 years old	5.1	7.1	8.3
Non-white Females			
16–19 years old	20.2	31.6	38.4
20–24 years old	12.2	18.3	21.3

Sources: US Department of Labor, (1980) *Factbook on Youth*, Youth Knowledge Development Report 2.5, May, pp. 44 and 46; and *Employment and Training Report of the President, 1979*, p. 244. From US Congressional Budget Office, (1982) *Improving Youth Employment Prospects: Issues and Options* Washington, D.C., US Congressional Budget Office, p. 7.
* These years were selected because, in each, the unemployment rate for white males aged 35 to 44 was constant, at 2.5 per cent.

With large numbers of young minority adults unemployed, employer perceptions are likely to be stereotyped. These young people are likely to be perceived as unsteady, irregular workers without a sufficient sense of responsibility to the work situation. Given their probable need for at least some on-the-job training, the uncertainty of their long-term commitment to the firm makes investment in their recruitment all the more dubious. In sum, as unemployment rates among young minority adults persist at high levels, they suffer discrimination at the hands of potential employers, who are tempted to treat their age and race as negative cues.

Vocational Education and the Establishment of Market Contacts

The adverse stereotypical image of the young adult and limitation on employment opportunities complicate the transition from school to work. Successful vocational education programs cannot simply provide students with the necessary skills that lead to employment opportunities; in addition, they must provide students with market contacts as well. If a vocational education program is considered a trustworthy source of reliable employees, firms will treat the recommendations of the program staff with respect, giving

Paul E. Peterson and Barry G. Rabe

Table 2: Civilian labor force participation rates, by age, race, and sex: selected years* (in per cents)

	1957	1964	1978
All Youth			
16–24 years old	57.2	55.3	68.2
All Youth			
16–19 years old	49.6	44.4	58.8
20–24 years old	64.0	66.3	76.9
White Males			
16–19 years old	59.2	52.7	65.0
20–24 years old	86.7	85.7	87.2
Non-white Males			
16–19 years old	58.8	50.0	45.4
20–24 years old	89.6	89.4	78.0
White Females			
16–19 years old	42.1	37.8	56.8
20–24 years old	45.8	48.8	69.3
Non-white Females			
16–19 years old	33.2	31.7	38.2
20–24 years old	46.6	53.6	62.8

Source: *Employment and Training Report of the President, 1979*, pp. 240–44. From US Congressional Budget Office, (1982) *Improving Youth Employment Prospects: Issues and Options*, Washington, D.C., US Congressional Budget Office, p. 10.
* These years were selected because, in each, the unemployment rate for white males aged 35 to 44 was constant at 2.5 per cent.

program graduates a valuable credential that will assist them in securing a position. Even better, if the students find work related to their schooling while still in the vocational education program, the transition from school to work can be made smoothly without a period of disruptive unemployment. Such connections between vocational programs and the marketplace are the most easily achieved if the program itself is of high quality. At the same time, such market contacts help to maintain such quality. This dynamic is illustrated repeatedly in the most prominent vocational programs in the cities included in the case studies. Without the ability to place its graduates, vocational programs find it more difficult to attract good students, and teachers begin to lose enthusiasm for their work. The quality of the educational level of the program begins to slip. Quality vocational programs and market contacts are like the proverbial chicken and egg; which comes first is difficult to ascertain.

Data from the NORC study suggest that vocational education programs, on a nationwide basis, have helped to ease the transition from school to work for many young adults. The survey reveals that teenagers are interested in employment opportunities and pursue them well in advance of graduation. According to students' own reports, more than one half of the sophomores and seniors are employed in some capacity for at least one hour in the week preceding the interview. The percentage of students employed increases to well above 60 per cent for those 17–18 years of age. Of those working, the mean number of hours worked per week was 12.6 for sophomores and 19.4 for seniors. The mean hourly wage was $2.63 for sophomores and $3.28 for seniors. Among sophomores, 40 per cent of the employment was in odd jobs, babysitting, or farm work, and another 23 per cent of the workers did not classify their position in any of the categories available. But for seniors the percentages employed in these less structured occupations declined to 10 per cent, although another 20 per cent did not specify the exact nature of their work. A full 70 per cent of the seniors employed were engaged in trade, commerce or industry in apparently well-defined positions of employment.

Given the large number of high school students who are employed, the number of hours a week that they work, the substantial average compensation which they receive, and the significance of this work for future employment, it is of interest to examine the effect of vocational education programs on student employment. When students who reported being engaged in vocational programs were compared to those in academic or general education programs, in almost all comparisons students in vocational education were more likely to be employed. The greatest differences were between those in vocational and college preparatory tracks. For example, among senior males, the percentage employed among those in vocational programs was 73 per cent, while it was only 61 per cent for the college preps. Even more significantly, students in vocational education programs were also more likely to be employed than students in general education programs. Elsewhere in the survey, it was shown that the characteristics of vocational and general education students were generally similar; for example, while college preparatory students scored significantly higher on tests of verbal ability, there were almost no differences between vocational and general education students. Yet, the 'vocies' were more likely to be employed. Among seniors, for example, 68 per cent of the vocational education students were employed, as compared to only 62 per cent of the general education students. Moreover, differences between vocational and general education sophomores and seniors persisted even after controlling for the student's age, sex, family income, and the region of the country in which he or she lived. Finally, the percentage of students who sought jobs but who were unable to find them was lower for vocational education than for general education students.

These differences did not necessarily carry over into other aspects of the employment situation, however. For example, vocational education students earned less than the college prep students who were employed, and they earned no more than those in general education programs. Nonetheless, these findings did suggest recognizable distinctions between vocational and general education programs and students.

Varieties of Vocational Education Programs

These findings from survey research identify the role that vocational programs can and do play in managing the transition from school to work. However, they do not distinguish among the great variety of vocational education programs that are to be found in urban areas, or the varying ways in which differing programs manage the transition. The four-city case studies discovered that some vocational education programs are exemplary in quality, enjoy abundant resources, admit a limited number of students from a large number of applicants, receive materials and supplies from the private sector, and boast enviable placement records. Less well-endowed programs admit students without other educational options, have limited facilities and equipment, maintain routine course offerings, and have few contacts with the private sector.

Three types of vocational education programs have emerged, with each type serving a distinctive clientele. The premier tier of vocational education includes many post-secondary institutions, including community and junior colleges and some unusually prestigious secondary schools and programs; the middle tier includes the vocational schools and programs in many public school systems; and the bottom tier includes the many and varied manpower training programs funded under federal programs such as JTPA, as well as the weakest of the public school programs. The federal role has been limited in all but this third tier of programs.

Premier Vocational Programs

The post-secondary vocational programs have expanded rapidly over the past two decades, as increasing numbers of high school graduates are extending their education. These programs that were in our case studies were notable for their attractiveness to students, the amplitude of resources that were available to them, the ease with which they could modify course offerings in response to changing market demands, and the many connections they established with commerce and industry. They also circumvented the problems associated with enrollment decline, which limited vocational education programs at the secondary level.

The San Francisco case study examined the post-secondary institutions with special care, and its findings demonstrate the considerable potential for vocational education at this level. Post-secondary education in 'the city' was carried out by the City College of San Francisco and by community college centers. The City College offered an accredited two-year transfer program, while the centers, scattered about the city in eight locations and numerous satellite facilities, offered courses without credit in a continuing education program for adults.[8] Nearly half of the City College students were enrolled in vocational programs, and each of the centers had a primarily vocational emphasis. This two-pronged effort in vocational education allowed for considerable diversity. As one administrator observed, 'The different delivery systems provide much flexibility and freedom, both for our programs and our students'.[9]

Both the City College and centers conveyed a sense of confidence and optimism, especially when compared with vocational education in San Francisco's secondary schools. Administrators emphasized that their programs had facilities and instructional resources superior to the high schools. 'The high schools are compulsory', said one city college administrator, 'and that produces some problems; anyone in our program is there because they want to learn something'.[10] 'The city colleges are driving hard', observed one of his colleagues, 'and the high schools have given in quite a number of times'.[11] While the high schools are finding 'it difficult to maintain old programs, much less get new ones off the ground', the College and centers find it easy to hire new faculty and adapt and modify curricular offerings in response to changing market demands.[12] The flexibility in faculty recruitment that the College and centers enjoyed was especially important in this regard. A permanent faculty was maintained, but it was supplemented with a substantial number of part-time teachers. This allowed the programs the opportunity to review the quality of their instructional resources and to alter offerings as student interests and needs change. The desirability of teaching at the College level provided a substantial pool of talent which the College and centers drew upon. Private sector relationships, moreover, were generally quite good. Every College vocational program had an advisory council, which was composed of experts within each occupation who advised on curricular and personnel questions. The extent of council participation varied, but many were active and influential.

Two of the centers had particularly impressive programs. The John O'Connell Community College Center provided training in trade and industrial skills for 8000 students each year, including 1200 in apprentice programs that were closely coordinated with labor and industry. The Downtown Community College Center focussed on such subjects as accounting, banking, communications, computer studies, real estate and secretarial work. Its programs were diverse, its offerings popular among students, and its linkages with San Francisco's growing downtown business community close and mutually satisfactory.[13]

Some secondary vocational programs in urban areas approached the high performance levels that characterized programs in most post-secondary schools. These secondary level successes, however, were exceptional in several respects. First, they occurred in typically specialized vocational high schools that recruited students city-wide and developed reputations for excellence in certain vocational areas, whether it be industrial trades or business skills. Second, they were given a degree of autonomy from general secondary school policies, allowing them to recruit staff and build private sector relations not typically found in comprehensive high schools. The private sector, in turn, found them highly attractive sources of potential labor. Third, many of their students were college-bound. Although they operated as vocational schools, they were not directly responsible for the transition from school to work of many of their students. In fact, they rivaled college preparatory secondary schools in their reputation for overall academic excellence.

The Edison Technical and Occupational Education Center, which opened in 1979 on a thirty-acre site as part of an industrial park in north-west Rochester, was the most prestigious vocational program of that city. Serving 13 per cent of the secondary school population, it offered instruction in such areas as automobile and aeronautical power, business and marketing, construction, graphic arts and printing, human and health services, mechanical and electrical engineering, and the sciences. The racial composition of the school was roughly equivalent to that of the Rochester school system taken as a whole. The success of the programs at Edison was indicated by the ease with which graduates obtained positions; about 95 per cent of graduates entering the job market were able to find employment upon completion of the school's program, although a large number of them got jobs outside the field in which they were trained.[14] Ironically, Edison's full and part-time enrollments remained well below capacity, despite its preeminence among city secondary vocational programs.

Four high-quality, prestigious secondary schools were visited in Chicago. These included a trade school with an apprentice program, a business and commerce school located in downtown Chicago, and two high-quality, predominantly black vocational schools on Chicago's South Side. In these four schools were as attractive a set of program offerings as is likely to be found anywhere in public school education; one quickly forgets the school system's recent political and economic traumas upon visitation to such schools. The schools had excellent facilities and equipment, first-rate administrative leadership, a stable faculty, good relations with relevant industries and trade unions, and attentive, energetic student bodies. While the trade school remained predominantly white, the three other schools were overwhelmingly black in 1979: 99.8, 99.8 and 78.8 per cent, respectively. The minority with the most limited access to the best of Chicago's vocational education was the Hispanic community. Only in the commercially-oriented school were they found in percentages roughly equivalent to their presence in the city-wide school system.[15]

The flagship of the San Francisco secondary vocational enterprise was hardly auspicious on first inspection, located in a former elementary school, but the School of Business and Commerce offered comparatively sophisticated instruction to its students. Like Edison, the school did not approach maximum enrollment; the present facility could accept approximately 30 per cent more students, and it may eventually house evening school classes. Enrollment expansion was possible in part because of the part-time nature of participation in the school's programs. Students divided their time between the school and their neighborhood high school, and bus service was provided for students in both morning and afternoon sessions. As in Rochester, the local school district was unable to fill vocational classrooms in its premier vocational institutions due to a series of administrative complications.[16]

Enrollment was limited to juniors and seniors, and approximately 60 per cent of the students participated in placement and internship programs located throughout San Francisco. Many were also often involved in leadership roles within their neighborhood high school. As one administrator explained, 'Our students are quite prominent wherever they go'. The school's largest feeder high school, in fact, was Lowell High School, the most celebrated academically-oriented public high school in San Francisco.[17]

Close connections with leading institutions in the private sector served to supplement instructional effectiveness, both through extensive internship and placement positions with institutions and cooperative instructional ventures provided within the school. Private sector support undergirded many aspects of the school's curricular development, and approximately 100 local companies supported the school either with cooperative training programs or financial support. Diverse local groups, ranging from the Chamber of Commerce to the Teamsters Union played a role in the initial development of the school and remained enthusiastic supporters. 'Business seems to like what we're doing and has been very helpful', said one administrator. 'One of the advantages of focussing many of our more sophisticated vocational courses into one school has been the enhanced ability to obtain private sector support'.[18]

Specialized vocational high schools have not historically been a part of the Atlanta experience. The city has always emphasized academic, college preparatory programs, and even after major shifts in racial composition and racial direction of the schools, this orientation toward academic programs has continued. However, the Atlanta Area Technical School, operated by the Atlanta Public Schools in conjunction with Fulton County, provided a partial exception to the dominant tendency. Although the school was at one time known for the quality of its offerings, which included many post-secondary programs, competition from junior colleges intensified in the 1970s, and the reputation of the school has declined. About half of the students in the school took remedial courses in reading, and some observers characterized the school's curriculum as 'watered down'.[19]

Nonetheless, Atlanta resembled the other cities in that the highest quality vocational schooling was offered in the more specialized high schools. Although not all specialized high schools were of such stature, the case studies indicated a general tendency for their offerings to be of higher quality. The reasons for this pattern appeared to be multiple. Many students preferred specialized schools as a way of avoiding some of the disciplinary problems of the comprehensive high school. Administrators of specialized schools generally had greater flexibility in recruitment of staff and deployment of resources. Federal funds for vocational equipment were often directed more toward specialized schools, where the impact was more readily identified. Finally, such schools were able to build relations with the private sector more easily. As a San Francisco administrator observed, 'We wanted one quality school that could offer finished training, and (we) considered (the development of a specialized school) the best way to achieve that goal'.[20]

Paul E. Peterson and Barry G. Rabe

The Middle Tier of Vocational Programs

By comparison with offerings in specialized high schools and at the post-secondary level, vocational education within comprehensive high schools was of generally inferior quality. Instruction was limited in many high schools by inadequate facilities, outdated equipment, and the wide range of curricular responsibilities that had to be met. Purchase of materials and supplies was often difficult for comprehensive schools, both because of the expense of sophisticated equipment and the difficulty of distributing it equitably among city schools. The premier schools, in contrast, were seen as more legitimate recipients of such equipment and material, whether from public sources or private donation. Moreover, administrators of less well-endowed vocational schools had less staffing flexibility than their counterparts who managed premier schools and programs. In Atlanta, where vocational programs were broadly scattered and not concentrated in more prestigious institutions, support for vocational education was understandably unenthusiastic. 'Vocational programs get a fair share of Atlanta's education budget, but they do not get full support in terms of recognition and leadership, areas which are crucial if vocational training is to be seen by students and taxpayers as a complete, viable alternative to academics'.[21]

Advanced skill training was seldom provided in the majority of comprehensive high schools. Instead, general work-related skills were emphasized and introduced students to the basic language of specific vocational areas and to the expectations of employers in various industries. This was supplemented by some project-oriented training, although much of this training was not directly applicable for a student seeking immediate employment upon graduation.

Clerical and general business courses may be somewhat more thorough in their introductory courses, perhaps because of reliance on more static technologies. They can provide graduates, for example, with typing and machine transcription skills that might qualify them for certain kinds of employment. 'The wisest investment we could make, if the money was available, would be to update all our typewriter labs so that they were entirely electric', explained a Chicago administrator.[22] This might be followed by acquisition of new equipment for accounting and data processing courses. More sophisticated equipment and programs were reserved for premier institutions.

Vocational training in comprehensive high schools was handicapped by a number of diverse factors. First, except in unusual circumstances the administrative leadership of the school was likely to be more concerned about maintaining the quality of the academic programs; vocational education emerged as an afterthought by comparison. Secondly, equipment and supplies for comprehensive schools were likely to be distributed among all schools within the large city system according to a standard formula. Obtaining the special instructional and curricular resources necessary to mount exciting, innovative programs ran contrary to central office policies which required that neighborhood-based, comprehensive schools be treated equally. Third, in sóme cities personnel recruitment for comprehensive schools was highly centralized, leaving school-level administrators without the flexibility that the more specialized schools enjoyed. Fourth, relationships with the private sector were harder to develop and sustain. Fifth, many of the more studious and serious-minded students left the comprehensive school for a more specialized institution, less dominated by neighborhood youth culture.

The problems faced by the comprehensive school were noticed with such regularity in all four cities that one cannot begin but wonder whether this institution has begun to outlive its original purpose. Especially with regard to vocational education, instruction must now be so specialized and the necessary equipment must be so sophisticated that it is difficult to create complete vocational programs in all of the high schools of the city. At the same time the comprehensive high school, by attempting to respond to all tastes, orientations, and abilities, lacks a focus or purpose of its own. Instead, the school acquires its meaning from the culture of the neighborhood in which it is embedded. In many central city neighborhoods, teachers and students alike are searching for alternatives.

The Bottom Tier

The least prestigious vocational training was provided through the types of programs that were funded by CETA. Such rudimentary training was provided independently of public school systems, although comparably limited programs were also evident in the weaker comprehensive and vocational high schools. These types of programs were often intended to serve those who have performed poorly in (or left) the public schools and have been unable to secure employment. However laudable the intent of such programs, they illustrate the kind of training that emerges where unemployment and low educational attainment is the greatest. They have considerable difficulty in establishing working relationships with other, more solidly established government agencies. The number of student contact hours for instruction is high, instructor salaries are relatively low, relationships with industry are difficult to initiate or sustain, facilities and equipment are modest and often outdated, and successful placement of graduates in stable positions of employment is difficult.

CETA programs have had as much — and possibly more — difficulty in establishing sound relationships with private business firms as have the less prestigious vocational programs in the public schools. Many firms seemed to doubt that CETA trainees have learned the requisite work skills, and, as a result, most CETA on-the-job training placements were within the public sector. In the late 1970s and early 1980s, the federal government tried to rectify this arrangement by creating 'private industrial councils' to advise local programs and by giving tax credits to firms that hire individuals enrolled in

CETA or comparable training programs. Several CETA administrators were encouraged by these developments: 'Private institutions', one said, 'simply don't want to mess with the government; they say that once you let them in you never get them out, and they're right. They don't want paper work, and they don't want government inspectors snooping around their shop floor. But they will respond when an incentive is offered, and I think this might work very effectively. It means that businesses can save some bucks and our people can do more than move leaves around for a few months.'[23] Although the observation was expressed in optimistic terms, it pointed to difficulties with CETA programs. Businesses and industries demonstrated repeated willingness to embrace prestigious vocational education programs, but tended to shun less-established programs serving a low-income clientele, such as those of many CETA programs and certain high schools. Thus, many CETA placements were in low-level positions of transitory help to public service agencies, which offer little 'training' other than to encourage regular attendance. Tax incentives may change the pattern, but this still remains uncertain. As Richard Elmore has noted, the 'weakest link' among federal programs such as those included in CETA, as well as the overall youth employment delivery system:

> is the connection between youth employment services and private sector employment. Private employers seem generally to have adopted an arms-length posture toward youth employment programs — occasional token involvement in advisory groups, modest cooperation in work experience programs, and a generally critical view of the ability of schools to prepare young people with the skills needed for entry-level employment. *The few outstanding cases of private sector linkages seem to have come about as a result of school system actions rather than CETA-initiated activities* ... (our emphasis).[24]

Such programs themselves vary considerably in quality, and there are, no doubt, some programs in nearly every city that are of exceptional value. Foremost among these examplary programs was a tool and die training program developed in Rochester that was largely run by private industry and boasted an exceptional training and placement record.[25] Such impressive program performance, however, remained unusual in the cities surveyed. The Rochester report acknowledged, 'Apart from the tool and die program, the other Rochester CETA programs appeared much less selective and far less likely to lead to permanent unsubsidized employment.'[26] This was reflective of findings in the other cities. These programs labor under an especially severe constraint in that they are officially designated as a service delivery system specifically reserved for the low-income population. Moreover, they have to engage in basic institution building, finding facilities, equipment and staff, unlike experienced vocational education programs in well-established public schools.

The NORC survey data emphasized the extent to which CETA programs were in fact aimed at the low-income, minority population. Employed black students were five times as likely as whites to have a CETA or other government sponsored job: 22.7 per cent of black sophomores and 27.8 per cent of the seniors reported their job in these terms, while only 4 per cent of the white sophomores and 5.3 per cent of the white seniors so described their position. Hispanic students fell roughly in between blacks and whites. Moreover, a much larger proportion of students from low-income families had jobs sponsored by the government than did higher income students. The extent to which CETA served a distinctive social clientele was also evident when one compared student participation in the cooperative education programs operated through the public schools with participation in CETA programs. While the cooperative education programs had similar percentages of all racial groups participating within them (13 per cent of black seniors, 11 per cent of Hispanics, and 10 per cent of whites), CETA programs were marked by strong minority predominance (26 per cent of black seniors, 15 per cent of Hispanics, but only 5 per cent of whites). Similarly, income differentials among participants in the cooperative education program were large, while CETA programs were aimed largely at low income groups. Viewed positively, these data indicate the critical role that the government has played in recent years in providing employment opportunities for minority youth. Without the strong federal presence in youth employment, it is likely that the race and income differentials in youth employment would have been even greater than they had been. Viewed negatively, these data also suggest the extent to which CETA programs served a racially and class segregated clientele, leading to stereotyped assessments of the quality of their programs and the marketability of their graduates. As our case studies suggested, these programs were not likely to produce candidates capable of competing for employment with graduates of prestigious programs.

Federal Support of Vocational Education

At the same time that the federal government has played a major role in funding many of the least prestigious programs, it has also played a modest, supplemental role in the other two tiers of vocational education. Since the enactment of the Smith-Hughes Act in 1917, the federal government has provided limited amounts of funding for vocational education. These funds have historically been broadly allocated, with a minimum of federal requirements shaping their use. Over the decades, the program became somewhat more restrictive, and the 1976 amendments to the 1963 Vocational Education Act imposed a range of new requirements on funding recipients. As we shall see, however, the impact of these changes on local vocational education was slight. Although the federal government would be the driving force behind CETA-type programs, it was far less influential in other areas of vocational education.

Paul E. Peterson and Barry G. Rabe

Fiscal Impact of Vocational Education Amendments

The impact of Vocational Education Act funds on urban education was both fiscal and regulative. Fiscal impacts, though probably significant, were difficult to discern accurately. VEA funds paid for less then 10 per cent of all vocational education, down from 36 per cent in 1917 and 22 per cent in 1962.[27] These funds were commingled with state and local vocational dollars, making it difficult, in many instances, to specify exactly how federal monies were used. In many places equipment, materials, and supplies were paid for with federal funds, presumably because local authorities could easily account for such expenditures and because such purchases could be varied as the flow of federal dollars went up or down. But many of these purchases would have to be made from state and local resources if federal dollars were not forthcoming, which would constrict other aspects of the vocational program.

It can be said that in many parts of the country urban school systems have serious financial needs, and federal dollars alleviate the fiscal strain somewhat. In all four cities investigated, federal vocational dollars were used by secondary schools largely to maintain existing programs and equipment. Only in the case of the San Francisco community colleges were federal resources perceived to be an 'extra' that supplied other than basic resources. In that single case, an administrator observed that 'most of the aid goes into non-essentials, things we would like to have but could conceivably do without . . . If federal funds were suddenly withdrawn, there would probably be no need for us to remove or severely alter any present programs we consider really important.'[28] In contrast, at the secondary level federal vocational dollars were distributed broadly to programs throughout each city. They were channelled generally toward basic system maintenance. Of course, this did not allow for many flashy programs that readily impressed outside observers. Nevertheless, the fiscal impact of federal policy on urban areas could very well be substantial. The amount of money allocated for vocational education, and its distribution among school districts, provided urban school systems with valuable re-sources that seemed to be essential for maintaining basic services but which were insufficient for mounting innovative, prestige-garnering training pro-grams. The precise effects of marginal changes — upward or downward — in the size of the vocational dollar were difficult to specify, yet it would be idle to suggest that such changes would not be noticed by hard-pressed urban school systems.

Regulative Impact

Although the exact fiscal effects of federal policy were hard to specify, the impact of federal regulations which were coupled with the grants-in-aid could be assessed more directly. In this case one could examine Congressional legislation and federal regulations, and then compare these requirements to local practice. If practice seemed highly responsive to federal rules, then the regulative impact could be regarded as substantial. The case studies found little evidence that local practice was significantly influenced by federal policy. Congress' increased effort to direct vocational education programming was perhaps best illustrated by the dramatic increase in the actual length of the legislation authorizing the program. In 1963 the Vocational Education Act was but thirteen pages in length, but in 1968 it expanded to thirty-three pages, and by 1976 was forty-seven pages long. While it was impossible to examine in these studies the way in which all features of this complex piece of legislation were being implemented, the case studies did examine four areas that Congress in 1976 deemed particularly important. These parts of the legislation required that states and localities (i) develop a planning capacity that would allow for adaptation of vocational programs to changing market needs; (ii) evaluate programs to establish their effectiveness in training students for employment; (iii) reduce sex bias and sex stereotyping; and (iv) increase private sector involvement through the creation of a variety of advisory committees at state and local levels.

In general, the case studies found that Congressional regulatory efforts in each of these four areas had but little effect. Even where Congressional mandates were stated clearly, it was difficult to ascertain significantly altered behavior at the school building level. The federal effort, of course, was conducted through each state; nonetheless, local administrators, the individuals who were to oversee the implementation of federal regulations, were largely uninformed about the Vocational Education Amendments, suggesting that the business of vocational education was continuing largely unaltered. To be sure, this judgment may be premature. The full effects of Congressional legislation cannot be expected to be fully apparent four short years after the legislation was passed. As one administrator in Atlanta observed, 'The laws were passed in 1976; it took most of 1977 to reach our level; 1978 was spent figuring out what to do; and only in 1979 and 1980 has anything been done.'[29] In Chicago, too, it was noticed that minimum compliance with even state information requirements did not occur until 1979. In all probability the legislation, if left unchanged in the next reauthorization, would have an increasingly substantial effect on local practice. Concluding that legislation has no immediate effects does not necessarily mean that it will not shape local thinking and practice in the longer run;[30] about that our case studies can only be agnostic. The findings that follow must therefore be understood as only providing information about the short-term consequences of Congressional policy.

Planning

Any state that received federal vocational education funding was required to produce a five-year plan that, among other things, must 'set out explicitly the planned uses of federal, state, and local vocational education funds for each fiscal year of the state plan and show how these uses will enable the state to achieve these goals'.[31] States were also required to submit an annual program plan and an accountability report for each of the fiscal years included in the five-year plan. They relied on local educational agencies for provision of information necessary for completion of the report.

The state plans were often lengthy booklets, adorned with numerous tables and charts, many of which proclaimed vigorous vocational education activity that successfully prepared students for entry into the labor market. Their utility in shaping policy, however, was highly suspect. Many local administrators conceded that they were little more than documents that formally complied with the planning requirements and did little to shape actual policy choice. One administrator acknowledged that statistics were 'massaged' to assure federal examiners that progress was being achieved, while making the process of data accumulation and translation into planning documents as painless as possible for states and localities.

States did not appear overly aggressive in securing local compliance with federal objectives. In Chicago, for example, the state interpreted federal guidelines in ways that were as lenient for local administrators as possible; when it prepared its own accountability report for 1978 to the federal government, it made no mention of specific instances of local malfeasance or non-compliance but instead justified any and all programs throughout the state as operating according to federal expectations.[32] In San Francisco, the planning process was also concerned mainly with securing a smooth flow of funds to localities with a minimum of federal scrutiny. As a 1977 analysis of state vocational education planning described it, required plans 'have been largely oriented toward compliance with federal regulations rather than toward comprehensive planning.'[33] In Atlanta, relations between state and local officials were less collaborative, but the difficulties seemed to have little to do with local non-compliance with federal guidelines.[34] Overall, procedural compliance with federal planning provisions did take place in the cities studied, but it seemed more geared toward satisfying federal guidelines than providing an opportunity for introducing purposive changes in local service delivery.

Evaluation

Federal legislation required that

> ... each state shall evaluate, by using data collected, wherever possible, by statistically valid sampling techniques, each such program within the state which purports to impart entry level job skills according to the extent to which program completers and leavers: (i) find employment in occupations related to their training; and (ii) are considered by their employers to be well-trained and prepared for employment.[35]

As was the case with the planning requirements, the evaluation activities were hardly in accord with the spirit of the law.

The demands and sophistication of the legal requirements notwithstanding, evaluation of vocational education programs in urban areas relied on traditional approaches and techniques that in the end left school officials largely in control of the process and product of their own evaluation. It is true that local schools generally filed an accountability report which recorded for each program the number of students by race, sex, handicap, and whether or not they were disadvantaged. External monitoring of local programs was also conducted. In Chicago, for example, a state-sponsored evaluation team visited each school once every five years to assess the strengths and weaknesses of the school's vocational offerings.

If the evaluation team found that a particular course or program was deficient, they could suggest changes or even recommend that the program be denied federal funding. If changes were recommended, local officials were to respond to these suggestions in their next five-year plan. While in theory these arrangements implied a good deal of central direction, in practice local administrators felt that it was up to them to determine whether or not they wished to modify practices in light of their evaluations.[36]

Local administrators were not only unlikely to dramatically alter programs based on external evaluations, but they also frequently scoffed at the data included in many evaluation projects. Numerous vocational program administrators noted that one of the major information-gathering methods was the post-graduation interview, which was intended to determine the effectiveness of vocational curriculum in preparing students for direct entry into the work force. They argued that this method was highly unreliable because of the extreme difficulty in locating and obtaining the cooperation of former students. Reliable data was reported to be most difficult to obtain from student constituencies in the least prestigious vocational schools. In Chicago, for example, the school that pioneered post-graduation evaluation ranked among the outstanding secondary institutions in the city; by contrast, schools of lesser quality had far less experience with evaluation, and understandably less motivation to produce detailed reports.[37] The Atlanta study revealed a similar difficulty in the accumulation of reliable data. In fact, Georgia vocational education officials were unable in 1980 to supply basic statistics for the 1978–9 school year.[38] While states such as California and Illinois proved more adroit at compiling evaluation data, the utilization of this material for programmatic purposes was virtually non-existent.

Sex Stereotyping

The 1976 Amendments expected local institutions 'to develop and carry out such programs of vocational education within each state so as to overcome sex discrimination and sex stereotyping'. They contained a number of specific provisions designed to achieve this objective.[39] Local response to these provisions was also quite limited. While local vocational administrators were not opposed to altering the sex composition of their programs, there was little evidence that they were doing much to facilitate the change.

The most common local response to the requirements appeared to have been the creation of open enrollment for virtually all vocational programs to members of both sexes. It proved impossible to determine whether these new developments were a direct consequence of federal guidelines or whether they represented more general societal changes. It was also difficult to find much evidence that opening course access significantly altered the sex composition of vocational programs historically skewed on the basis of sex, although each of the cities could demonstrate certain examples of breakthroughs.

Administrators consistently emphasized their support for addressing sex imbalances, and many were able to cite some enrollment changes in recent years. Some principals recruited outside speakers and designed programs to attempt to heighten awareness of curricular and vocational alternatives. In San Francisco, federal funds were channelled toward specific projects designed to introduce women into vocational areas traditionally dominated by men; these experiments occurred in the Community College District, which enjoyed greater latitude in program experimentation.[40] Nonetheless, local officials reported little progress and contended that change took place very gradually. Interviewers heard comments such as the following in explanation of the slow pace of change: 'girls dislike loud, dirty work'; 'boys realize that the income in traditional female occupations is relatively poor'; 'boys do not have the fine motor skills that girls do'; schools 'cannot counteract the influence of the home'. Given these perceptions, many program directors and principals foresaw little likelihood of dramatic breakthroughs in sex stereotyping.

Private Sector Involvement

Somewhat more tangible results of the Amendments could be discerned in private sector involvement in local vocational education service delivery. The most recent federal vocational education legislation required that each funding recipient 'establish a local advisory council to provide ... advice on the current job needs and on the relevancy of courses being offered'.[41] The Amendments called for broad participation on these councils, including members of the general public and experts in specific vocational areas germane to local programs. Such councils were, to a large extent, created, but their mere existence did not insure valuable contacts between training programs and the private sector.

The premier vocational institutions have long relied upon advisory councils and enjoyed extensive private sector support. In Rochester, this support was largely directed toward the new Edison Technical High in Rochester. Other schools in the city offered vocational instruction, but Edison emerged as the leading recipient of private sector attention and support. A local industrial management organization was 'a staunch supporter of the movement to create a new, more up-to-date and sophisticated' school and it concentrated its energies on Edison.[42] In Chicago and San Francisco, the premier vocational institutions had close ties to the private sector, but had cultivated these relations well in advance of federal council requirements. This supportive base provided curricular advisement and equipment donations to schools, as well as internships and job placements for students.

But such councils were less active in less prestigious institutions. Predictably, advisory councils at the least able and equipped schools were largely perfunctory. Parents were sometimes amassed to lobby the school board or the central office, but meager substantive returns were gained from these efforts. In particular, few reliable contacts with potential employers of program graduates were established. Federal requirements may have provided a general framework for such participation, but their effect depended greatly upon local school conditions and showed few signs of bolstering institutions that most readily needed private sector support.

Limited Impact of Federal Regulations: Some Explanations

The reasons for the limited impact of federal directives on local vocational education policy are multiple. In the first place, federal allocations for vocational education in urban areas were a small percentage of total state and local expenditures. If federal vocational education policy was significantly affecting local practice, it would have to be the proverbial tail wagging the dog.

The way in which vocational education funds were distributed made such wagging highly unlikely. Under the 1976 Amendments, most funds were distributed among the states according to a pre-established formula that was based largely on the population size of each state in certain age categories. The states were responsible for allocating the funds among school districts, community colleges, and other vocational institutions. State guidelines were interpretations of federal regulations, and state enforcement depended on the eagerness of state officials to pursue national policy objectives. In practice, state officials seemed to identify more with the interests and concerns of local school officials than with national policy objectives. These practices maximized the autonomy of local administrators. At both state and federal levels, resource allocation did not vary according to the extent to which local officials were vigorously pursuing federal objectives. As a result, vigorous enforcement of the regulatory provisions of the federal program became more difficult.

Furthermore, vocational education funds are allocated among the states on a matching basis. For every federal dollar spent under the basic grants program, states and localities were to allocate a similar amount. Though this was designed to ensure that local governments were genuinely committed to a federally funded program and reduce the fiscal burdens of the federal government, it also meant that federal objectives must roughly coincide with state and local objectives. Where the two conflicted, federal objectives could not be pursued too assiduously without jeopardizing state and local willingness to participate. If policies with respect to evaluation and sex stereotyping in vocational education were too stringent, many localities might forego federal funds under the Act rather than allocate matching local resources for programs found burdensome or distasteful.

Slippage in federal policy objectives occurred not only as the state reformulated federal concerns, but at various local steps as well. By focussing much of the research attention on vocational education at the school-building level, the case studies were able to identify perceptions and activities at the level where services were being delivered. For federal policy to affect activities at this level, they had to be transmitted from Washington to the state capital, from there to the school system's department of vocational education, from the vocational assistant superintendent to many other administrators, and, finally, to principals and teachers in individual schools. The slippage in this process was substantial. Shared perceptions were rare among various levels of the so-called chain of command. At the school level there was scarcely any awareness of a Vocational Education Act or Amendments at all. Many school-building personnel were simply unaware of the federal presence in vocational education. The impact of federal directives on local vocational programs, in turn, remained largely insubstantial, once filtered through these numerous levels.

Conclusions and Policy Recommendations

Perhaps federal policy needs to further encourage the search for alternatives. Vocational dollars used to support rudimentary vocational programs, whether in public secondary schools or CETA-type programs, may only sustain an institutional framework that is increasingly out of date, especially in contrast with other local programs that boast more relevant curriculum and more substantial contacts. Federal dollars have been scattered widely among the various institutions that offer vocational training and have done little to reconcile the considerable discrepancies in service quality. In fact, the good programs only become better with supplemental federal funds; they are able to make innovative investments while their less prominent counterparts merely try to maintain present services.

Instead, federal assistance to management of the transition from school to work could include placing more students in the best possible programs available rather than leaving many in static vocational programs such as those offered by the weakest public secondary schools and those funded through CETA. 'Substantial gains in employability are possible for disadvantaged youths when they are offered a combination of services including remedial education, well-structured work experience, and training', observed a 1982 study by the Congressional Budget Office.[43] Such commingling of services might best be provided in the schools with the strongest vocational programs. Nonetheless, some of the leading vocational institutions — those that get ahead and stay there — operate with less than full enrollments. Rochester's Edison and San Francisco's School of Business and Commerce and some of its community college centers are reflective of 'underenrolled' programs which could assist more students without facility expansion. Rather than scattered thinly across the lot of all vocational education programs, federal funds could be directed toward providing maximum educational opportunity at the best possible local institutions, thus providing a bridge for students into programs more likely to manage effectively the transition from school to work. Funds for remedial education, where necessary, might be provided through a compensatory education-type program targeted at the secondary level and on vocational programs.[44] The CBO study suggested that VEA funds might be better used in such a manner.[45]

An example of the potential bridging of the polar extremes of vocational programs are provided by the Chicago case study. The city's premier trade school, long known for its extraordinarily successful ability to provide its students with excellent contacts, has long been intransigent to federal participation of any kind in its affairs. Anticipated 'federal interference' was seen by school administrators as outweighing revenue benefits. However, many of the program's students were potentially eligible for support funding from CETA because of their low socio-economic status. Combined with the recent traumas of the Chicago school system, trade school officials and CETA representatives began to seriously consider working in tandem. Bridges were also being constructed between introductory skill programs and the trade school, and the latter may absorb entire programs. Similarly in San Francisco, community colleges have gradually assumed responsibility for many programs that have become too expensive to be maintained by secondary schools. Both secondary and community college vocational education instruction were frequently offered in identical sites, but program coordination was rare, as static secondary institutions were unable to tap the relatively rich instructional and equipment resources of neighboring community colleges.

Federal policy could be designed to encourage such cooperation and make the most of existing local resources, instead of perpetuating the clear lines of demarcation among existing programs and waiting for local crises to encourage cooperation. Such a strategy would seem particularly promising given declining enrollment in each of the four cities studied, thereby emphasizing the healthy coordination — potentially consolidation — of programs in order to maximize local strengths. Instead of proliferating dated programs at the secondary level and a segregated CETA system at the bottom, limited federal funds could underwrite placements of students in respected, proven institutions whose enrollments and services could be expanded.

The lack of coordination between the Vocational Education Act and

CETA funds was illustrative of the federal contribution to creation and perpetuation of distinct levels of vocational education service delivery. When the programs were viewed at the local level, cooperation was largely non-existent. VEA and CETA programs served overlapping constituencies, but neither found much occasion to collaborate or seek ways in which mutual resources might best be focussed to provide services. Instead, they coexisted autonomously, often entirely unaware of vocational services offered by the other, even when located nearby and offering programs of conceivable benefit to one another. Although they sought similar ends — managing the transition from school to work for their participants — they pursued this matter independently of each other.

In Chicago, for example, most lower-ranking vocational school officials knew little and cared less about CETA programs. Many contended that the law did not allow them to inform any enrolled student about the availability of these training programs, regardless of the potential applicability of training. They generally complained about the quality of any CETA workers assigned to work in the public schools — unless the school administrator was able to select one of his or her own students for a CETA-paid position. They regarded CETA dollars as wasted money, paying exorbitant funds for programs that included stipends to trainees. We found no school-building level administrators who showed any awareness of vocational programs being provided by CETA outside the public schools. For the Brahmins in the school system, CETA programs seemed 'untouchable'. Given these attitudes toward CETA, it was difficult to translate formal cooperation into substantive programs. School administrators, of course, were not the sole sources of intransigence. CETA administrators were equally uncharitable with regard to the public schools. They claimed that they were educating those that the schools had 'failed', and that CETA-type training programs would never have been necessary had the schools functioned effectively. Even two decades after the passage in 1962 of the Manpower Development and Training Act, there was little evidence of coordination among various vocational training programs.

Forging Contacts with the Marketplace

Although Congressional capacity to direct vocational training is limited to the extent to which it directs local resource allocation, it should encourage further emphasis on building relations between vocational programs and the private sector. If vocational education is to continue to have an important role in a society where basic skills that can be applied to a wide variety of circumstances remain highly valuable, it needs to see its major role as assisting students in managing the transition from school to work. Because youth, as a group, seem to be facing significant problems of discrimination and negative stereo-typing, it is all the more important for young people, as individuals, to have their own specific market contacts. Training programs that place students directly in touch with employers, giving them an opportunity both to explore alternative work situations and to demonstrate their seriousness and competence, are likely to yield the greatest individual and societal benefits.

Numerous creative initiatives have already been made in this area; federal efforts should take note of these and build upon them. For example, recent research on the Youth Incentive Entitlement Pilot Projects (YIEPP) has indicated long-term benefits for 16- to 19-year-old youths who participated in this program. YIEPP guaranteed employment, part-time during the school year and full-time during the summer, to participants who remained in or returned to school and met special school attendance and performance standards. According to the Manpower Demonstration Research Corporation, which studied the program in exhaustive detail, YIEPP reduced short-term youth unemployment, particularly for black youths. It also 'led to substantial earning gains' among participating youths upon leaving the program, 'as compared to eligible youths in comparison sites' who were not invited to participate. The MDRC report explained that 'the increased earnings were primarily due to the improved employment rates of the young black youths . . . although more hours of work and slightly higher wage rates also contributed to the effect'.[46] Such a guarantee of employment in exchange for continued schooling helps ease the transition from school to work, as do the more successful vocational programs.

Eliminating Systems of Institutional Stratification

In a society and economy as open and changing as that of the United States, clearly definable levels of vocational education services are counterproductive both for the individuals participating within them and for the country as a whole. American schools have long been known for their comprehensive, integrative quality. Because they serve all the children in the community, they have traditionally represented American ideals of liberty and equality. Current efforts to desegregate the nation's schools are merely the latest chapter in a long history of attempts to bring educational practice into harmony with the country's finest ideals.

It is therefore unfortunate that Congress, as a matter of national policy, has in the area of vocational education encouraged the development and extension of a set of service delivery systems that institutionalize race and class differences. The distinctions between junior colleges, secondary schools, and CETA training programs developed without conscious planning on the part of federal or local officials, yet they provided distinct populations with varying quality services. The most elaborate, well-supported, and occupationally useful programs seemed to be increasingly concentrated within junior and community colleges. The secondary institutions provided some high-quality programs through a limited number of specialized schools, but, for the most part, their offerings were much more poorly staffed and equipped and much less well connected with the private sector. Finally, most of the manpower training programs funded under CETA and some secondary school programs had the fewest resources and the least prestige. Not surprisingly, it was the CETA programs that served disproportionately high numbers of low-income minorities.

The problems produced by the coexistence of these three types of vocational offerings are exaggerated by the particular problems of youth in the labor market. Since youth generally have little proven job experience, the particular place that they received their training is especially significant for the kind of job they obtain and even whether they are offered any position at all. The best credential a new employee can have is the backing of a prestigious vocational training program. The weakest credential — perhaps a credential of only negative value — is to have a diploma or certificate from a training program of little or no repute. Such degrees or programs may only compound the problems facing minority youth who ultimately seek employment. It is questionable whether federal policies that maintain institutions of different status and rank can reduce the employment problems of low-income minority youth or increase the overall productivity of the American economy.

Bridging the Existing Gaps

Attempts by Congress to redirect local vocational education programs through its 1976 amendments generally have had little effect — at least in the first years of the program. The processes of policy implementation are so complex that in the short run it is very difficult for Congress to achieve specific, detailed objectives. These difficulties have been compounded by the small federal share of total vocational education expenditures and the historically limited role of federal oversight of its vocational education funding. Instead of attempting to apply identical and complicated policies in each program, Congress should confine itself to stating realizable objectives and arranging an institutional framework for achieving them. Congress cannot escape its obligations to uphold and enforce fundamental Constitutional requirements, but its present approach seems unlikely to achieve the desired objectives. The present types of regulations are likely to generate high administrative costs and cause local officials to substitute procedural compliance for commitment to policy goals. The case study findings suggest that this is occurring at present.

Alternative federal efforts might seek to bridge gaps between the various kinds of vocational programs. There are institutions that successfully manage the transition from school to work, even in cities fraught with problems of high youth unemployment. Ironically, not all of these programs function with capacity enrollments, and all could conceivably be expanded to absorb more students and programs beneath their sound institutional umbrellas. Federal dollars could be directed toward expanding the access of low-income and minority students to these programs, building bridges between the premier, middle-tier and weak programs and institutions instead of continuing to drive wedges between them.

Increasing Variety

At the same time, we do not advocate a full uniformity to all vocational education programs in the United States. On the contrary, secondary schools are perhaps the single weakest link in the American educational system, marked by 'broad decline in academic performance among black and white students alike — in reading and mathematics, in science and social studies'.[47] Many of the problems of American secondary schools stem from their attempts to provide an enormous range of educational services to all students living within the community. The greatest advance in secondary education in urban areas might well come from introducing greater curricular specialization among schools. It is significant that many of the most successful high schools in the large central cities that we have studied are those that have narrowed their scope and purpose — the magnet schools, performing arts schools, and premier vocational schools. If schools are defined by the particular approaches and programs they offer, not by the neighborhood in which they are located, the identity and mission of the school is determined by its curriculum rather than by its efforts to satisfy all tastes and interests. Moreover, students can be given a sense of autonomy and freedom that goes with the capacity to choose among a variety of high school alternatives. If the exemplary secondary schools and community colleges can be taken as a model for what is possible at the secondary level, perhaps some of the uncertainty and malaise that pervades the comprehensive high school can be reduced, if not eliminated altogether.

If vocational education is understood to be managing the transition from school to work, it becomes relevant for all students and it can play a key role in giving distinctive identities to the variety of schools located within a central city. Vocational education then need not be the inferior component of a comprehensive high school, but a key element in a curriculum which emphasizes both the need for developing basic, transferable skills and the desirability of obtaining meaningful contacts with the marketplace.

These suggestions are more than can be accomplished by any minor modification of federal vocational education policy. They can only be achieved through prolonged discussions of the changing role of secondary education in the United States. Yet, the difficulties faced by American youth, by secondary schools, and by government-sponsored work programs are too great to require anything less.

Notes

1 The Job Training Partnership Act of 1982 differed from the Comprehensive Employment and Training Act in a number of ways. JTPA eliminated public

service jobs in favor of an exclusive emphasis on training, provided a larger advisory role for businesses and industries, and shifted considerable responsibility for program administration from the local to the state level. Nonetheless, JTPA resembles CETA in many respects, particularly in its emphasis on training for the disadvantaged. See (1982) 'Job Training Program Replaces CETA', *1982 Congressional Quarterly Almanac* Washington, D.C., Congressional Quarterly, pp. 39–42.

2   The four case studies include: WAYNE J. URBAN and CHARLES A. STARRATT, (1981) 'Vocational Education in the Atlanta Schools', Georgia State University, National Institute of Education; PAUL E. PETERSON and BARRY G. RABE, (1981) 'Career Training or Education for Life: Dilemmas in the Development of Chicago Vocational Education', University of Chicago, National Institute of Education; MICHAEL W. KIRST and BARRY G. RABE, (1981) 'Vocational Education and Federal Policy in San Francisco', Stanford University, National Institute of Education; WILLIAM LOWE BOYD and HAROLD CLINE, (1981) 'Vocational Education in a Technical Labor Market: Rhetoric and Reality in Rochester, New York', Pennsylvania State University, National Institute of Education.

Portions of this chapter depend heavily and explicitly on these four case studies. Although we have generally not burdened the text with quotation marks when drawing upon these studies, notes indicate the particular case study which is being directly or indirectly quoted. We thank the authors of the case studies for their permission to use their material in this way. The views expressed herein are those of the authors, not necessarily those of the case-study writers or of the National Institute of Education. We also wish to thank James McKee and Gary Mucciaroni for their comments on the manuscript and Eve Dimon and Robert Londis for typing the various versions.

3   LEWIN-EPSTEIN, N (1981) 'Youth Employment in High School', Report to the National Center for Education Statistics, Chicago, National Opinion Research Center.

4   NATIONAL OPINION RESEARCH CENTER, (1981) 'A Proposal for a Center for Research on Poverty', submitted to the US Department of Health and Human Services.

5   We are indebted to Robert Michael, National Opinion Research Center, for his perceptive comments on these issues.

6   GRANOVETTER M.S., (1973) 'The strength of weak ties', *American Journal of Sociology*, 78, pp. 1260–380.

7   DAVID T. ELLWOOD and DAVID A. WISE have observed that from 1970 to 1980 employment rates for both black men and women aged 16 to 24 declined approximately 14 per cent relative to those of similarly aged whites. See ELLWOOD and WISE, (1983) 'Youth Employment in the Seventies: The Changing Circumstances of Young Adults', working paper, Cambridge, National Bureau of Economic Research.

8   KIRST, M.W. and RABE, B.G. (1981) *Vocational Education and Federal Policy in San Francisco*, Stanford University, National Institute of Education, pp. 51–2.

9   *Ibid.*, p. 52.

10   *Ibid.*, p. 53.

11   *Ibid.*

12   *Ibid.*, p. 54.

13   *Ibid.*, pp. 59–65.

14   BOYD, W.L. and CLINE, M. (1981) *Vocational Education in a Technical Labor Market:*

Rhetoric and Reality in Rochester, New York, Pennsylvania State University, National Institute of Education.

15 PETERSON, P.E. and RABE, B.G. (1981) *Career Training or Education for Life's Dilemmas in the Development of Chicago Vocational Education*, University of Chicago, National Institute of Education, pp. 38–9.

16 KIRST, M.W. and RABE, B.G. (1981) *op cit*, p. 36.

17 *Ibid.*, p. 37.

18 *Ibid.*, p. 39.

19 URBAN, W.J. and STARRATT, C.A. (1981) *Vocational Education in the Atlanta Schools*, Georgia State University, National Institute of Education.

20 KIRST, M.W. and RABE, B.G. (1981) *op cit*, p. 36.

21 URBAN, W.J. and STARRATT, C.A. (1981) *op cit*, p. 76.

22 PETERSON, P.E. and RABE, B.G. (1981) *op cit*, p. 51.

23 *Ibid.*, pp. 82–3.

24 ELMORE, R.F. (1980) 'The Youth Employment Delivery System', Policy paper for the Vice President's Task force on Youth Unemployment, Brandeis University, Center for Public Service, pp. 13–14.

25 BOYD, W.L. and CLINE, H. (1981) *op cit*, p. 35.

26 *Ibid.*, p. 37.

27 WOLFE, M. (1979) 'The Vocational Education Act of 1963 As Amended: A Background Paper', Washington, D.C., Congressional Research Service, p. 4; and GALLADAY M.A. and WULFSBERG, R.M. (1981) *The Condition of Vocational Education*, Washington, D.C.: National Center for Education Statistics, p. 129. From US Congressional Budget Office, (1982) *Improving Employment Prospects: Issues and Options*, Washington, D.C., US Congressional Budget Office, pp. 60–1.

28 KIRST M.W. and RABE, B.G. (1981) *op cit*, p. 76.

29 URBAN, W.S. and STARRATT, C.A. (1981) *op cit*, p. 63.

30 A more longitudinal approach to policy analysis can differ markedly from short-term assessments, and may reveal increasing intergovernmental collaboration and effective management of federal programs. See PETERSON P., RABE, B.G. and WONG, K. (1984) *When Federalism Works*, Washington, D.C., National Institute of Education.

31 Vocation Education Amendments of 1976, Public Law 94–482, 12 October 1976, 90 Stat. 2180.

32 PETERSON, P.E. and RABE, B.G. (1981) *op cit*, p. 73.

33 KIRST, M.W. and RABE, B.G. (1981) *op cit*, p. 70.

34 URBAN, W.J. and STARRATT, C.A. (1981) *op cit*.

35 Vocational Education Amendments of 1976, 90 Stat. 2187.

36 PETERSON, P.E. and RABE, B.G. (1981) *op cit*, pp. 60–1.

37 *Ibid.*, p. 34.

38 URBAN, W.J. and STARRATT, C.A. (1981) *op cit*, p. 70.

39 Vocational Education Amendments of 1976, 90 Stat. 2169.

40 KIRST, M.W. and RABE, B.G. (1981) *op cit*, pp. 81–2.

41 Vocational Education Amendments of 1976, 90 Stat. 2176.

42 BOYD, W.L. and CLINE, H. (1981) *op cit*, p. 5.

43 US Congressional Budget Office, p. 48.

44 More than 90 per cent of all federal compensatory education funds are used at the elementary school level.

45 US Congressional Budget Office, pp. 65–66.

46 FARKAS G., OLSEN R., STROMSDORFER E.A.W., SHARPE, L.C., SKIDMORE F., SMITH D., and MERRILL S., (1984) 'Post-Program Impacts of the Youth Incentive Entitlement Pilot Projects', Washington, D.C., Manpower Demonstration Research Corporation, pp. v-viii.
47 PETERSON P.E., (1983) 'Did the Education Commissions Say Anything?' *The Brookings Review*, winter, p. 5.

ACOT

2 5 NOV 1986

LIBRARY

Youth Employment: National Policy and Local Delivery in Three US Settings

Richard F. Elmore

This chapter summarizes research on the local implementation of national policies affecting youth employment in the United States. The research was conducted in three sites — two medium-sized cities, Seattle and San Francisco, and one small metropolitan/rural area, Clark County, Washington — during the 1981–82 school year.[1] It was designed to examine how national policy works at the delivery level. The study focussed exclusively on 'high-risk' youth, defined as those who, by virtue of family income, race, or language, have a higher-than-average likelihood of being out of school, unemployed, or both. Because of this focus, our interviews were conducted mainly in local programs that were funded under the Comprehensive Employment and Training Act (CETA), the federal government's major employment program for disadvantaged adults and youth, which has recently been superceded by the Joint Partnership Training Act (JTPA).[2] For reasons that will become clear in the body of the chapter, the analysis goes beyond a simple description of how CETA youth programs were implemented to the question of how service delivery organizations and the adults who work in them affect young people's access to the labor market.

The mode of analysis is 'backward mapping'.[3] The logic of backward mapping begins by specifying the behavior that is the target of policy; it then examines the ways that various instruments of policy affect that behavior, either through organizations or by working directly on individuals; and finally, it examines how policy affects the structure of relations and the allocation of resources among key actors in the delivery system. Backward mapping focuses attention on how policies affect the choices of the individuals to whom they are addressed, rather than on how policies are elaborated into formal regulatory and organizational structures. In this sense, backward mapping reverses the usual view of how policy is implemented. Instead of asking whether specific provisions of policies are being carried out consistent with the intent of policy-makers, it asks whether we can expect policy to have its intended effect, given what we know about the individual and organizational behavior that policy is trying to influence.

The data and conclusions reported in this chapter describe modal responses to structured interviews with young people, front-line workers, and local administrators in the three settings we analyzed. The analysis is meant to be suggestive of how one might analyze the implementation of public policy 'from the ground up', taking into account problems of individual choice and street-level operations as well as broader strategic and political questions. Our sample does not permit generalization to the overall effects of national policy on local delivery.

The chapter is divided into three main sections, each following the logic of backward mapping, and concludes by addressing the policy consequences of the analysis. The first section deals with the perceptions, experiences, and behavior of high-risk youth toward school and work. The second deals with the perceptions, experiences, and behavior of front-line workers who deal on a daily basis with high-risk youth. And the third deals with the effects of policy on youth, front-line workers, and the organizations that implement policy.

School and Work Choices for High-Risk Youth

In aggregate terms, young people's behavior toward school and work in the United States can be characterized as follows:

(i) *A large proportion of teenagers and young adults are labor force participants*; that is, they are either employed or looking for work. Labor force participation among 16–17-year-olds rose from 46 per cent in 1960 to over 51 per cent in 1979; for 18–19-year olds, it rose from 69 per cent to 72 per cent; and for 20–24-year-olds, it remained in the neighborhood of 86 per cent. Labor force participation has risen for teenage males and females in all population groups, except black males, where it has declined by roughly 25 per cent between 1960 and 1979.[4]

(ii) *Young people's labor force participation is relatively unresponsive to aggregate demand for labor, and unemployment among young people increases disproportionately with increases in adult unemployment.*[5] Labor force participation among young people has not declined proportionately as overall unemployment rises. In fact, it has continued to increase steadily as unemployment has fluctuated over the past twenty years. This relationship suggests that young people are entering the labor force not just in response to excess demand for labor, but as an expression of their preference for work over other activities. The ratio of youth to adult unemployment over this period has fluctuated directly with increases and decreases in unemployment, between about 2.5 and 4.5.

(iii) *A large proportion of teenagers and young adults pursue school and work at the same time.* About 50 per cent of young people aged 16–19 who were enrolled in school in 1979 were also labor market participants. This proportion has grown from about 35 per cent in 1960.[6]

(iv) *Labor force participation among teenagers and young adults is characterized by a high rate of movement among jobs.* The rate of job turnover, the number of periods of unemployment, and the duration of unemployment are high for teenagers, but gradually decline and stabilize as young people reach their mid-twenties.[7]

(v) *Though high school completion is positively related to both earnings and employment, the proportion of high school drop-outs remains relatively high (in the neighborhood of 10 per cent overall, as high as 40 per cent in some urban areas) and low-income, minority youth are significantly more likely to drop out of high school.*[8] In other words, higher risk youth, defined in terms of income, ethnic group, and linguistic status, are more weakly attached to school.

We constructed a sample of ninety-five young people by choosing them at random from participants in local employment programs. They were all classified as low-income according to federal eligibility criteria, most were members of minority groups, and about one-quarter either did not speak English at all or used English as their second language. In the two cities we studied, Seattle and San Francisco, about one-quarter of our sample was composed of youth who were participants in 'out-of-school' programs; that is, they had dropped out of high school at some point and were now attempting to finish a high-school-equivalency program as well as to enter the labor market. In our sample of in-school youth, a small proportion (less than 10 per cent) had been out of school for more than one month at some point in their high school education. Those enrolled in in-school programs tended to be younger (most in the 17–18 year interval) than those enrolled in out-of-school programs (most in the 19–20 year interval). All were either employed at the time we interviewed them, as a result of their participation in an employment program, or were preparing to enter the labor market. Our sample was constrained by the selection processes of the programs we studied, so it can't be characterized as representative of the youth population as a whole or of high-risk youth in particular. It does provide a fair representation of the kind of young people who are likely to find their way into local programs designed to help high risk youth enter the labor market.

The attitudes and behavior of young people in our sample toward school and work were similar to those of the youth population at large. They were active participants in the labor market; they did not see school and work as mutually exclusive choices; and they saw themselves as continuing to work, regardless of their future educational plans.

Beyond these broad patterns of similarity between our sample and the youth population at large, a number of more specific patterns emerged. First, while they attached a high value to education, they did not perceive adults in school as playing a large role in their entry to the labor force. Asked to respond to the statements 'how well you do in school makes a big difference in how well you do in later life' and 'how well you do in school depends on how hard you try', all but a handful agreed. Likewise, about two-thirds said they planned to pursue some form of post-secondary education, vocational or academic, after completing high school. This response should be viewed with caution, however. It sometimes appeared that young people assumed it was the appropriate answer to give, and at other times that they had not gauged their present skills or past performance against their aspirations. When they were asked to respond to the statement 'most adults I have known in school care whether I succeed or fail' about half agreed and half disagreed, and when they were asked to identify adults who had been helpful to them, most cited family members or adults they had met through employment programs, rather than teachers, counselors, coaches, or administrators they had met in school.

Second, school did not seem to have played a strong role in shaping their preferences for work, except in a negative sense. More than half said that they had taken vocational or career education courses in school. These were predominantly clerical (typing, business machines) or shop (metal or wood) courses, and in only a few isolated cases did the courses correspond to what young people said they were currently doing in the labor market or what they said they would like to do. A common theme in our interviews was that young people found work satisfying because 'I'm taken seriously and made to feel important', 'it keeps you busy', 'you learn how to be independent', or 'you learn how to get along with people'. These comments reflected a relatively strong preference for work over school and they also showed that, for many young people, the social aspects of work took precedence over more tangible benefits such as making money or gaining experience and status.

Third, the young people in our sample were positive, if somewhat episodic participants, in the labor market. The majority had been employed two-to-three times, most jobs lasting six months or less. Most had plans to continue working as long they could find jobs. Virtually all agreed with the statement' 'my work will be an important part of my life'. Likewise, more than two-thirds said that their two closest friends were working and liked to work. When asked to respond to the statement 'most people I know like to work', however, they were about evenly divided between agreement and disagreement, which suggests that they did not perceive other people to be as positively disposed to work as they and their friends. Many young people drew a distinction between adults and other young people in their responses, saying that while most of their friends like to work, their parents and other adults they knew did not.

Fourth, most of the young people in our sample identified certain key adults as being the critical factor in guiding their entry to the labor market, rather than institutions or organized processes. In the majority of cases, the adults young people identified as being helpful worked in CETA-funded employment programs, which was not surprising given that this was where we did our interviewing, but in a significant number of cases they were relatives (brothers, sisters, uncles, parents). In only a handful of cases did young people say that they got their jobs by themselves without any help. This finding does not mean that institutions and organized processes were unimportant in guiding young people's entry to the labor market. Rather, it means that young people, when asked to describe how they got their jobs, identified certain key adults, rather than the organizations or processes of which these adults were a part. This pattern did not hold, however, when we asked young people to identify what they would do if they had to find a job tomorrow. Their responses to this question tended predominantly to take the form of standard processes and institutions — classified ads, personnel offices, employment services, etc. In a small number of cases they cited individual adults who had already been helpful. The tentative picture that emerges from these responses, then, is that young people see specific adults as having been crucial in helping them get where they are, but they haven't yet projected that view into the future.

The picture of young people's entry to the labor market that emerges from this profile is one characterized, first, by a relatively high degree of movement betwen school and work; second, by a relatively low degree of reliance on school as a means of entry to the labor market; and third, by a relatively heavy reliance on significant individuals rather than institutions or organizations. Movement from school to work appears not to be an orderly, step-wise progression; it appears instead to be a process of short-term engagement and disengagement, of search through familiar adults, and of decisions made on the basis of immediate opportunities, rather than long-term objectives. Individuals — especially key adults — play a significant role in this world, by helping young people negotiate entry to adult institutions. But organizations, especially schools, don't seem to play a decisive role, at least in the eyes of young people.

Both the aggregate evidence and our limited sample of interviews suggest that the term 'school-to-work transition', which is so often used to characterize the youth employment problem,[9] does not give a very accurate picture of how young people make school and work decisions. To be sure, there is a 'transition' from school to work, if only in an aggregate statistical sense; as people get older, they spend less time in school and more time in the labor force. But as a characterization of how young people make decisions, there are at least three potential problems with the notion of a school-to-work transition. First, it probably overstates the importance of schools, as organizations, in positively shaping the decisions of young people, especially those we have characterized as high risk. Second, it implies a gradual, step-wise movement from school to work, when the actual pattern appears to be more episodic and disconnected. And third, it suggests that school, as an institution, is the major force-creating movement in the labor force, when in fact this movement seems to be influenced much more by specific attachments that young people form with adults, more often outside school than inside. Both the aggregate data and our interviews suggests that the school-and-work behavior is better described as a process of idiosyncratic, trial-and-error search that is anchored by adult contacts young people have made through work and various intermediary institutions — employment programs, family, etc. It is probably not a sequential, organized, developmental process. This conclusion tracks closely with the views of adults who work with young people, as we shall see.

If true, this view helps to explain some of the peculiarities of demand for organized services designed to help young people enter the labor market that we discovered in the process of our study. Our interviews were conducted during a period of growing unemployment and declining federal funding for youth employment programs. We found several instances of dramatic instability in demand for youth employment services. In Seattle, for example, the program for in-school youth changed, between June and September of 1981, from a predominantly black program into one predominantly populated by Asian refugees. Front-line workers were unable to explain this dramatic shift at the time it was occurring; they simply accepted it, and enrolled large numbers of Asian refugees, despite the fact that many did not yet speak English well enough to take jobs with English-speaking employers. Only well after the fact did we discover that the shift in demand was probably attributable to the fact that newly arrived refugees had formed strong networks of peers and adult 'sponsors' — American families, church groups, neighborhood associations — who played a significant role in negotiating their entry to Seattle. The black youth, who had previously accounted for the majority of participants in the program had essentially 'disappeared'. Front-line workers speculated that 'they probably found jobs on their own' or that 'they might be involved in after-school athletics', but were unable to offer more specific explanations. What probably happened is that they had been bumped from the program because of the eagerness and initiative of the Asian refugee youth, who had moved from the summer program and filled the available positions in the program. Black youth had, over time, come to expect that there would be subsidized jobs waiting for them at the beginning of school. The Asian students, on the other hand, had received encouragement from their peers and from adults to seek the benefits of the work programs.

Another example of erratic demand comes from two out-of-school programs in San Francisco, one serving a predominantly black population, the other a predominantly Hispanic population. In both instances, despite increasing unemployment, demand for positions in the program had fallen below the number of participants the programs were authorized to serve. In one program demand had fallen by about 50 per cent; in the other, it had fallen by about 25 per cent. Front-line workers were unable to give specific explanations for the shift in demand. One possibility they suggested was that publicity surrounding federally-funded employment programs had given potential clients the impression that the programs were being disbanded. Another explanation was 'word is out on the streets that there aren't any jobs, period, regardless of whether you're enrolled in a program'. Both explanations suggest that young people arrive at their decisions to enter programs based on networks of advice, rather than by utilizing formal points of access.

Whatever the explanation for instability of demand, access to employment programs for high-risk youth is clearly not a simple matter of setting eligibility criteria and admitting students. Demand is heavily influenced by factors outside the control of those who deliver the services — the level of employment in local labor markets, informal networks among young people, and knowledge of programs among adults who take an interest in high-risk youth. The one potentially influential factor that lies within that control of service deliverers is individual contacts with youth. Local employment and training organizations do not use standardized mechanisms for finding and enrolling clients. They do not, for example, use the records of schools or social service agencies to identify potential clients and solicit their participation, as is done in European countries.[10] Nor is it likely, as we shall see later, that such mechanisms would work if they existed. Those mechanisms that have the highest likelihood of working are ones based on interactions between individual adults and individual young people.

Patterns of Interaction Between Young People and Adults

The actual work that adults do to influence the labor market participation of high risk youth is a product of two main factors : *policies* communicated from outside the organizations in which adults work and *practices* agreed upon within the organization. This section deals primarily with practice. We attempted to understand the work of delivery-level personnel, first, in terms of their own descriptions of practice, and second, in terms of the influences that organization and policy exercise on practice. In doing so, we asked adults working directly with high-risk youth to describe what they did, what the purposes of their work were, what differences and similarities they observed among the young people they worked with, and what the most significant problems were that their clients faced. We also asked a number of questions designed to elicit how their work was influenced by the organizations they worked in — for example, how their caseloads were determined, how much discretion they had in making decisions about their clients, what proportion of their time they spent working with young people individually and in groups, how often and in what context they met with other adults doing the same kind of work as they, and how their work was supervized and evaluated.

There are a limited number of services one can offer to influence the labor market participation of young people. One is to provide direct employment, which can involve either subsidizing employers for hiring young people or recruiting employers without the aid of a subsidy. Another is to provide information on alternative career possibilities, assistance in searching for jobs, and assistance in making choices. Another is to provide training designed to prepare clients for specific jobs. Still another is to provide remedial education for students who lack some specific skill or credential — English-language instruction or a high school completion certificate, for example — that could influence their employability. In the language of those who work on youth employment these activities are called, respectively, work experience, counseling and career development, job training, and remedial education. They take place separately or in various combinations in a variety of different types of organizations financed in whole or in part by grants from the federal government.

There are no standard roles or job descriptions for youth employment specialists, unlike school systems, for example, where the terms 'teacher' and 'counselor' have relatively uniform meanings from one setting to another, or social service systems, where 'case worker' or 'eligibility worker' have come to mean similar things. Still, the work of youth employment specialists involves a cluster of relatively well-defined tasks that recur consistently from one setting to another. One task might be called counseling or advising. It involves one-on-one advice about job-related matters, such as career choice and on-the-job behavior, and personal matters. A second task might be called job development. It involves recruiting and maintaining relations with employers of young people involved in work experience. A final task might be called simply teaching. It involves actual group instruction in such areas as basic skills (reading, math, grammar), English language, occupational skills, and knowledge of the job market. Often these tasks are all performed by the same person. The in-school program in Seattle, for example, was designed around employment counselors who were paid from federal employment funds and were part of a separate organization within the school system, but were physically located in the city's high schools. These workers did counseling and job development primarily, with a small amount of teaching on career-related subjects. In other organizations, however, the tasks were differentiated. One community-based organization in a Hispanic neighborhood of San Francisco, for example, had separate roles for job development and teaching; counseling was assumed by all staff members.

The sixty front-line workers in our sample reported that they spent the largest share of their time (between 40 per cent and 60 per cent) working directly with young people; of that portion, they spent the majority working with individuals, and the smallest share working with groups. They viewed their work, in other words, as predominantly composed of one-on-one relationships with clients. Beneath this basic pattern of adult-youth interaction, however, lay large variations in caseloads. In our three sites, we found caseloads as low as five youth to one adult and as high as 140 youths to one adult (the caseload in the latter program had been over 400:1 in the previous year). The school-based programs, with the exception of the rural schools in Clark County, had much higher caseloads than the programs based in other governmental agencies or community based organizations. At the high end of the distribution there was less one-to-one interaction and more time spent on routine paperwork, group instruction, and dispensing paychecks for subsidized work. The modal caseload in our sample, though, was fifteen to twenty-five youths, but the school-based programs were sixty and 140 in Seattle and San Francisco. The typical pattern of work for an individual consisted of (i) a large number of one-on-one contacts with young people, on a daily or weekly basis, depending on whether the program involved short cycles of three-to-four weeks or whether it extended over the whole school year; (ii) a limited number of group contacts, which usually involved teaching or group discussions; (iii) a regular schedule of visits to employers and young people at worksites; and (iv) periodic recruitment of employers to take students for work experience. In some instances, as noted above, these tasks were done separately by different people, but even in those cases there was a high degree of interaction among workers, so the organizations did not appear to be highly differentiated. Two features of this combination of tasks are especially noteworthy. One is the heavy emphasis on one-to-one contacts between adults and youth, which contrasts dramatically with what most young people experience in high school, where contacts tend to be between one adult and relatively large groups of students. The other important feature is the role that delivery-level workers play in negotiating entry to the workplace and in negotiating the boundary between school and work. Having adults develop initial job contacts and periodically visit employers at the work site gives the young people a kind of legitimacy with the employer that they would not otherwise have.

The duration of programs varied considerably. Most programs for in-school youth ran over the entire school year, although there was significant turnover in the course of a year as young people left the program for other jobs or simply lost interest. The in-school programs typically involved four hours of work experience per day, sometimes coupled with academic credit, plus individual counseling and periodic group workshops in career development. Before 1981–82, the year in which our interviewing took place, the typical in-school program involved full payment of students' wages from federal funds. Because these payments constituted a subsidy to employers, federal regulations restricted them to non-profit and governmental organizations, precluding placement of students with private firms. During the year of our interviews, a number of programs we studied were in the process of converting some or all of their work experience programs to unsubsidized, private sector jobs. This change was in response to reductions in federal funding. Programs for out-of-school youth were usually shorter in duration than those for in-school and more highly focussed. Some were individualized, in the sense that students entered the program to pass the high school equivalency exam and find a job, and left the program when these tasks were completed. Other programs had finite time periods attached to them, often as little as three-to-four weeks or as much as a full school year.

Two major themes emerged when we asked front-line workers to describe their work and its purposes. One might be called the 'developmental' view. This view emphasized the role that adults played in helping young people to develop the positive self-image, personal attributes, and cognitive skills that precede entry into the labor force. Another view might be called 'instrumental'. This view emphasized the role that adults played in helping youth to get jobs and deemphasized changing the attributes or skills of young people. A typical statement of the developmental view was , 'I work with kids who don't have the advantage of a strong home background and try to help them develop a good image of themselves and the confidence to sell themselves to an employer'. A typical statement of the instrumental view was, 'I help kids find jobs; beyond that, they're responsible for themselves'. The dominant view among the front-line workers we interviewed was the developmental view. Most workers saw themselves as being closely involved in the personal lives of the young people they worked with, whether they wanted to be or not, and as helping young people to develop certain skills and attributes. The more closely they became involved in the lives of their clients, the more front-line workers perceived their clients' problems to extend beyond work. Many front-line workers saw themselves as compensating for the failure of other adults — in families, communities, and schools — to form strong attachments with their clients. While the developmental and in-strumental views seem logically contradictory — the one stressing close interpersonal relations, the other detachment — they were often held by the same person. Often, front-line workers would begin by describing their work and its purposes in terms of helping young people to develop and end by describing how difficult it was to have an effect and how the pressures of their work led them to view placing young people in jobs as their primary activity.

This ambivalence between the developmental and instrumental views reflects a basic tension in the work of youth employment specialists. On the one hand, they see the young people they work with as demanding strong adult attachments and as needing help with a broad range of problems, from immediate income to personal relationships to education deficits to interpersonal skills. On the other hand, they see themselves as having limited access to young people for a relatively short duration and as having, in the final analysis, only one material benefit to confer on their clients — a job. A common resolution of this tension is to try to form strong attachments with young people in the early stages, in order to get the basic developmental tasks done, and then to attenuate those attachments as young people reach the end of their time in the program. A common refrain among front-line workers was typified by one out-of-school program counselor who said, 'it's important to love these kids ruthlessly, to get behind their defenses and to stay with them until they take charge of their own lives; then it's important to gradually pull away'. This view was corroborated as well by a number of young people, who would typically say, 'the important difference between this program and high school is that here they stay after you until you get the stuff. You get the idea that they really care. They want to you make it in the outside world.'.

The front-line workers in our sample were typically young (in their middle-to-late twenties), relatively mobile (two or three previous jobs), committed to work with youth (at least one prior job involving work with young people), and college-educated (about equally divided between general liberal arts degrees and specific degrees in teaching or counseling). The exceptions to these general attributes were a significant number of people in their forties and fifties who had left conventional teaching jobs and a few younger people who were products of programs like the ones they were working in. At the time of our interviews, federal youth employment programs were undergoing large funding reductions, and a significant proportion of the people we interviewed (one-quarter to one-third) were contemplating or actively involved in changing careers. They saw themselves as being involved in high-stress, low-paid jobs, for which society at large had little appreciation.

Most front-line workers viewed their immediate work environment as informal and unbureaucratic, and saw themselves as having a relatively wide range of discretion in the use of their skills. Virtually all front-line workers met frequently and regularly, individually and in groups, with their counterparts and supervisors within the organization. In only a few instances did we find formal, bureaucratic relations between front-line workers and their supervisors; these tended to occur where employment programs had been attached to school systems and were administered by career school people. In most instances, front-line workers said they had daily, or at least weekly, contact with their immediate supervisors, and these contacts were informal. Only about half said that their work was formally evaluated by a supervisor, but most reported receiving some kind of feedback about how well they were doing their jobs. When they were asked to whom they would take a major complaint about some administrative matter within the organization, virtually all answered that they thought such complaints could be resolved by their immediate supervisor. In one program — King County, surrounding Seattle — workers organized themselves into a cooperative structure, in which most decisions were made collectively in formal meetings among front-line workers and administrators that often occurred more than once a week. Most participants in this form of collective decision-making found it suited their expectations of how their work should be organized; a few found the constant meetings to be burdensome and an interference in their work with young people. Another program — within the Seattle school system — was more hierarchically structured and differentiated, but still maintained a high degree of collective decision-making; all important decisions affecting staff members were discussed in staff meetings. The typical pattern of work, in all but one or two programs, was informal, collegial, and highly decentralized.

While front-line workers had a high level of interaction with others in their own organizations, they had virtually no contact with people at the same level of other organizations doing related work. This pattern manifested itself in several ways. First, front-line workers in community organizations did not consult, even infrequently, with other workers in similar organizations. Second, front-line workers in programs administered within school systems had some contact with regular high school counselors, teachers of either academic or vocational subjects, or high school administrators, but they saw themselves as largely isolated from the regular school program and from each other when they worked in different schools. The isolation was often a matter of choice. Contacts between youth employment specialists and school people, when they occurred, were often formal and included resolving problems with individual students, such as class schedules, permission to leave school for part of the day, access to special courses, disputes over academic credit, etc. And third, front-line workers, whether they worked within schools or outside schools, in community organizations, were often critical of schools and school people for the way they treated their clients. The major criticisms levelled at the school system by youth employment specialists were (i) that young people were not kept busy and productive in school, hence they tended to see school as a waste of time; (ii) that teachers and counselors did not take individual students and their problems seriously, hence forcing students to look outside school for adult attachments; (iii) schools were not teaching basic skills to the hard-to-teach, hence leaving large numbers of students unprepared for either vocational training or employment; and (iv) schools were not interested or actively engaged in understanding the labor market in which they were located. Whether these criticisms were accurate or not, they expressed a strong division between the federally-funded youth employment system and local school systems at the delivery level.

These delivery-level divisions grew partly out of policy, partly out of the preferences of front-line workers, and partly out of administrative structure. Policy provided strong incentives to define one's interests in terms of employment for high-risk young people, vocational education, or counseling, rather than in terms of the whole population of young people who might benefit from all services. The administrative structure aggravated these distinctions by assigning separate tasks to separate central administrators. And the preferences of front-line workers reinforced policy and administrative structure by focussing attention inward rather than across organizational boundaries.

Front-line workers did not see themselves as controlling access to their programs or as exercising the determining influence on their clients' careers. With few exceptions, decisions about who would participate were made by centralized 'intake units' that were structurally separate from the service delivery part of the organization. In only one small organization did we find that final selection decisions were made collegially by the entire staff. Caseloads were likewise determined by dividing the number of positions authorized for the program under its funding agreement by the number of front-line workers and assigning clients on a more or less random basis. In addition, front-line workers saw themselves as having a very limited amount of time with their clients, relative to the time these young people spent on the street, at work, or in school, hence, exercising relatively little leverage on their aspirations and behavior.

One result of this limited control was a highly focussed view of what they wanted to achieve with clients. Most delivery-level workers saw themselves as imparting a limited number of specific skills and attributes that would serve their clients well in the labor market. If the objective was to prepare the client to pass the high school equivalency examination (the Test of General Education Development, or GED), as was the case in all the out-of-school programs we studied, the subject matter areas of the test would be broken into discrete pieces and short-term prep courses would be offered in each area. If the objective was to supplement work experience with general knowledge of career options, as was the case in nearly all the in-school programs we studied, then a single workshop or a short series would be organized around a specific topic of career choice. If the objective was to prepare young people to search for jobs on their own, an element of many programs, then delivery-level workers would lead young people through a structured exercise in preparing a resumé, getting an interview, going to the interview, and following up on initial contacts. What seemed to distinguish these activities, in the minds of both clients and front-line worker, was their specificity and their immediate pay-off. It was these attributes that were most often mentioned favorably as the things that distinguished what employment programs did differently from the school system.

Another consequence of limited control was the ability of front-line workers to focus on one or two attributes or skills of a given individual client at a time and, temporarily at least, to disregard others that might appear striking to other adults. Workers in out-of-school programs, for example, did not routinely hassle their clients about their dress, language, or behavior around their peers while they were teaching basic skills. Work on dress and behavior would come at the point where clients were ready to begin approaching employers, when it was clear what its utility would be. Workers in in-school programs, for example, would often stress maintaining acceptable performance in school and punctuality at work, and leave questions of dress and demeanor to the client and the employer. This focussing behavior seemed to result in working relationships between young people and adults that both viewed as favorable and helpful. Young people frequently observed that they were treated more as adults by the people they came in contact with through employment programs than by the people they came in contact with in the regular school program.

A final consequence of limited control was that front-line workers saw the outcomes of their work differently from higher-level administrators. As we will see in the following section, all the organizations we studied were under considerable pressure to produce measurable results. The most obvious measure of success for an employment program is, of course, placing a client in a full-time, unsubsidized job, although for the youth population progression to higher-level skill training or even to post-secondary education is often viewed as a favorable outcome. The view of what constituted a satisfactory result was considerably more complex and less determinant for front-line workers. In some instances, they argued that the more serious the problems presented by their clients the less likely they were to have a clear impact. One worker in an out-of-school program, for instance, said, 'when a 17-year-old kid comes in here with a second grade reading score, what's a satisfactory result? I would settle for sending him out of here, after three months, with an eighth grade reading score and entry to a solid vocational skills program, but I don't think that necessarily counts as a good result outside the organization.' Another worker in an in-school program said, 'a lot of these kids need money to buy things that other kids take for granted. If we make it possible for them to have some things that other kids have and to make contacts that might pay off later in the job market, can you ask for much more?'. Front-line workers, in other words, were much more likely to focus on proximate results — things they saw as feasible to achieve, taking into account their clients' backgrounds and the workers' limited leverage — rather than longer-term, more abstract results.

A final consequence of limited control was that front-line workers placed a considerable emphasis on motivation, in addition to cognitive skills and family background, when they were asked to describe the attributes that distinguished clients. Given their limited ability to influence young people, they saw young people's willingness to push themselves as a key factor in their own success as well as their clients'. Many said they would rather work with a highly motivated, unskilled client than with a weakly motivated, but relatively skilled client. 'If you show an extreme interest in working and going to school', said one worker of her pitch to clients, 'then we can help you. If you don't, nobody can.' Some front-line workers thought it was possible to build motivation through strong contacts between youth and adults, but as funding for employment programs declined and as emphasis on performance standards increased, most front-line workers said that programs were increasingly having to select on their perception of motivation. In terms of the earlier distinction between views of practice, many front-line workers saw themselves as being pushed by external circumstances from a developmental view of their work to an instrumental one — an occurrence that many viewed with alarm.

The world of front-line workers in youth employment organizations, then, is characterized by the following attributes: (i) adults working directly with young people are relatively young and have a demonstrable commitment to their clientele, judged in terms of their prior experience; (ii) they manifest an underlying tension between developmental and instrumental views of their jobs; (iii) their work involves a high level of individual interaction with young people and co-workers in their own organizations; (iv) they have virtually no contact with people performing similar jobs in other organizations; (v) they have a relatively informal work environment in which supervision and evaluation typically take place collectively or collegially; (vi) they perceive themselves as having limited control over both who comes into the program and what happens to clients after they leave; and (vii) they tend to focus on a limited number of skills and attributes that they think they can influence in a short period of time.

The Multiple Meanings of Policy and Organization

When we asked front-line workers what rules, procedures, or policies made their jobs easier, or more difficult, they generally found the questions hard to answer. When they did reply, they tended to focus on paperwork requirements (weekly reports on clients, payroll forms, reports on the disposition of clients leaving the program, etc.) or on eligibility requirements (income criteria). Policy, in other words, had a very specific meaning for front-line workers. It set limits on their work. It was not perceived as a grant of authority to engage in official action. It was instead seen as a set of constraints on practice. Most front-line workers readily expressed their judgments about what the young people they worked with needed. They did not see policy as playing a particularly important role in making it possible for them to do what was necessary. They saw policy instead as a necessary, if often annoying, set of limits that one had to accept in order to do what was necessary.

Nor did front-line workers see their work as being part of a national effort made possible by the existence of national policy. They did not see themselves as 'implementing' national policy objectives; they often did see themselves as protecting their interests and their clients' interests against an increasingly hostile public and an increasingly unsympathetic agency bureaucracy.

Yet beneath this largely negative view of policy lay a surprising willingness to adapt to changes in objectives that were communicated from above. During the time of our interviews, a number of significant shifts in policy were occurring at the national and local levels. Prime sponsors, the local administrative agencies for federal employment policy, were under pressure from the US Department of Labor to produce clearer evidence of program effects and provide better records of their grants to delivery organizations. This pressure resulted in nearly universal adoption of 'management information systems' that provided a central record of individual clients' progress, proportions of funding for different types of activities, and the performance of program operators. At roughly the same time, declining federal funding resulted in difficult expenditure decisions at the local level; expenditure reductions were based in part on performance criteria. These shifts had a significant impact on the nature of work in youth employment organizations and on the way front-line workers perceived their work. A number of organizations responded by reducing or eliminating stipends for participation in educational programs, by moving substantial numbers of young people from subsidized to unsubsidized jobs, by shortening the duration of educational and career orientation programs, and by focussing more resources on job development and placement. A large proportion of front-line workers we interviewed said, usually with qualified approval, that youth employment programs had shifted substantially in emphasis, from 'income support' to 'job placement' objectives. Many said that youth employment programs had gone too far in the direction of paying low-income youth for activities that had little to do with work and holding them in educational programs for long periods of time without encouraging them to seek unsubsidized employment. They saw the shift in emphasis as having given youth employment programs a new sense of direction, to which they gave their overall approval, even though they doubted that the new emphasis would work for the most difficult cases.

Perceptions of policy changed significantly as one moved from front-line workers to administrators in delivery organizations and to local government administrators of federal employment programs. At this level, people clearly distinguished between policies initiated at the federal level and those initiated at the local level, they clearly placed themselves in both the historical development of policy and the current delivery system, and they were acutely aware of (if often frustrated by) the movement of policy at the federal and local level. Furthermore, the administrators we interviewed at the local level were acutely aware of being part of a local political system in which important decisions were made about the allocation of resources among competing organizations and activities.

Like policy, organization meant different things at different levels of the delivery system. For both front-line workers and delivery-level administrators, organization meant *their* immediate organization, not the organization of the local delivery system. Their relations with their counterparts in other organizations were either non-existent or highly politicized. As noted earlier, there was little or no interaction among delivery-level workers in different organizations working on similar problems or populations. There was a higher level of interaction among administrators of delivery-level organizations, but this interaction took the form largely of representing the organization in local decisions. For example, in San Francisco, the local government administrative unit responsible for employment, the Mayor's Office of Employment and Training (MOET), gave considerable weight to the funding recommendations of its Employment and Training Committee, which was composed partly of representatives of the various delivery organizations. This was the main setting in which administrators of the various delivery organizations met face-to-face, and it was seen as an important political arena. In Clark County, there was a high level of consultation on administrative questions between county-level officials and representatives of delivery-level organizations, but since funding decisions were not included in these discussions, participants did not perceive them as political. In Seattle, decisions cutting across delivery organizations were made largely by the staff of the local government administrative agencies, so there was little interaction among administrators even on a political level.

Taken together, these views of policy and organization among front-line workers and local administrators reinforced a highly balkanized delivery system for youth employment at the local level. Front-line workers saw themselves working with *their* clients, in *their* organizations; higher-level policy decisions were constraints on their actions, not grants of authority to do things that would otherwise be impossible. Delivery-level administrators likewise saw the interests of their programs and their organizations as paramount; for them, higher-level policy decisions were important mainly for the effect they had on the allocation of resources among competing organizations, among competing programs within organizations, and sometimes among competing neighborhoods or ethnic groups. Local administrators of federal employment programs saw themselves as orchestrating the competing demands of delivery organizations, within constraints imposed by federal law and regulations. The result, in all three of our settings, was a structure in which separate organizations were doing separate things for separate populations, all within a given geographical area, but no one was especially concerned about the overall effects.

This delivery structure, or lack of structure, is partly a result of the incentives built into federal policy, partly a result of the peculiarities of local government organization in the US, and partly a result of adaptations to the school-and-work behavior of young people. Federal policy promotes a balkanized delivery structure by encouraging localities to create separate organizations for the administration of federally-funded employment and training activities rather than relying on existing structures. Funding formulas at all levels of government promote balkanization because they allocate money based on 'body counts' of students served by specific organizations, rather than on the basis of how well the total array of institutions is serving the total population. Local government organization promotes balkanization because school systems, community colleges, and general government at the local level are organized independently of one another, each with its own separate base of authority. The high rate of movement of young people between school and work promotes a balkanized delivery system because there is no single set of local institutions one can rely on to keep track of where young people are at any given time.

Even though this balkanized system represents a relatively successful adaptation to the basic forces shaping the implementation of federal youth employment policy, it creates its own special set of problems. The most obvious one is equity of access. The absence of any strong incentives for lateral coordination at the local level means that no one can assure that high-risk young people who need assistance negotiating entry to the labor market are actually getting it. Indeed, no one can say reliably how large the population of high-risk youth is in a given setting, or what proportion of that population is actually being served. Another serious problem is that the system promotes narrowly-focussed recruitment and job placement, often at the expense of attention to larger structural issues. The most difficult problems of high-risk youth have to do with their relative lack of preparation, by basic education, training, or experience, for mainstream jobs. The incentives embedded in federal policy encourage delivery organizations to recruit and place high-risk youth in jobs that are immediately available and for which they are either immediately qualified and can be trained to do in a relatively short period of time, without much regard for the changing structure of local labor markets. Delivery-level organizations adapt to these incentives by developing networks of contacts with youth and employers which they rely on over time to produce the outcomes that federal and local administrators expect. However, the economic base on which these jobs rest is frequently eroding. In Seattle and San Francisco, for example, the economies were becoming increasingly professionalized and service-oriented, and less hospitable to youth with basic high school or vocational training. In Clark County, the economy was shifting from one heavily reliant on forest product manufacturing to service and technical industry. This combination of policy incentives and economic shifts can produce increasing competition among delivery-level organizations for a declining pool of jobs.

Two findings in our research on local delivery systems were somewhat surprising. The first was the age of the delivery organizations in our sample. Most could trace their histories continuously back fifteen-twenty years. The in-school program in Seattle, for example, had been in continuous operation under various names and auspices since the Neighborhood Youth Corps was established by the US Congress in 1964. The community organizations in our San Francisco sample could trace their roots back thirteen, eighteen, twenty-one and twenty-five years, through various locally- and federally-financed programs. Despite this history, the typical front-line worker was relatively young and had relatively little experience with the organization. So the picture that emerges from our sample is one of very stable organizations, with highly mobile populations of workers and clients. The continuity of the organizations is expressed in their identification with the communites in which they work and in a few key leaders who stay with the organization for long periods of time. Within this continuity, there is a high level of turn-over at the staff level. These organizations are effectively the 'capital stock' of federal youth employ-ment policy. They continue to exist over time by responding to shifts in federal objectives and by turning over large numbers of staff and clients. Yet there is no explicit acknowledgement in federal policy of the role these organizations perform. Federal law and regulation speaks to the relationship between the federal government and designated agencies of state and local government, not to the role that delivery-level organizations play within state and local jurisdictions. There is a major risk in failing to understand that delivery-level organizations play a key, continuous role in implementing federal policy. The risk is that federal policy will be changed in ways that threaten the existence of the capital stock of delivery organizations, without understanding that it is they who actually deliver the most of the services, not units of local government.

The second surprising finding in our analysis of local delivery systems was that structure seemed to have little effect on delivery-level work. We deliberately chose our three sites to reflect the major structural variations in local administration of federal employment policy. Seattle is a system based largely on programs nested within other local government agencies; the school system, the city's Department of Human Resources, and the county's human services agency run the major youth employment programs. Clark County is a system in which the county government exercises the dominant influence in service delivery over a partly-rural, partly-metropolitan area, much like the 'county unit' system in the South. San Francisco is a system based primarily on ethnic community organizations, like many large US cities. What we found was that, while these structural variations were very well adapted to their local settings, they didn't produce any significant variation in either program content or delivery-level practice from setting to setting. Our interviews with delivery-level personnel and administrators produced basically the same descriptions of work in all three settings.

Two explanations come to mind. First, there are only a limited number of things one can do to help high-risk youth negotiate entry to the labor force. After twenty years, or more, of local experience, it is highly unlikely that dramatic new variations will arise. So what we were observing was a probably stable set of delivery-level patterns that had emerged after a long period of trial-and-error. Second, much of this trial-and-error learning has been institutionalized and codified in federal policy and local administration. Program guidelines, funding priorities and criteria, performance standards, and the like, all reflect the basic patterns of practice: counseling, teaching, and employer relations.

Conclusions

Our basic findings on the relationship between national policy and local delivery in youth employment can be summarized in three conclusions:

(i) Patterns of young people's movement between work and school suggest that the delivery structure most compatible with the actual behavior of youth is one that (a) relies on a number of different points of entry; (b) does not rely exclusively on schools as its main source of contact with young people; (c) promotes a high level of one-on-one contact between youth and adults; and (d) permits a high degree of flexibility in matching services to young people.

(ii) Both delivery-level practice and organizational structure have adapted well to these patterns. The practice of front-line workers, as we have described it, consists of a high level of one-on-one contact, a highly-focussed view of what adults can do to help young people negotiate entry to the labor force, and a relatively informal and flexible set of working relations with colleagues and supervisors. The local delivery structure is highly balkanized, which has the effect of creating multiple points of entry, but at the same time, it appears to involve a remarkably stable set of organizations which adapt readily to changes in policy.

(iii) The major deficiencies of the delivery structure are (a) its relative insensitivity to problems of equitable access to services; (b) its inability to account for anything like the total population of high-risk youth; and (c) its lack of incentives to adjust to major structural shifts in local labor markets.

The mode of analysis we've used in this study has been designed to address the question of how policy is implemented by reversing the usual process of looking first at policy objectives and then at law, regulations, and organization to see if they are consistent with those objectives. We have instead turned the process around and asked how one can get from an understanding of young people's school and work behavior, to an understanding of an appropriate delivery structure, and then to an understanding of how policy works on those things. In fact, the two modes of analysis go hand-in-hand, revealing complementary aspects of the process of implementation. Our major purpose here is to demonstrate that one can map backward from behavior to delivery-level practice and structure to policy, as well as forward from policy to practice to outcomes.

Acknowledgements

This chapter was prepared as part of a research project funded by the National Institute of Education, US Department of Education, under Grant # NIR-8-00-0138. Betty Jane Narver, Research Consultant at the Institute for Public Policy and Management, University of Washington, assisted in editing the chapter and in checking the consistency of its findings with the case study research on which it is based. Janet Campbell assisted in the research.

Notes

1   The research on which this chapter is based is summarized in ELMORE R.F. and NARVER B.J. *Youth Employment Delivery Structures: Case Studies of Three Settings,* Washington, DC Institute for Public Policy and Management, University of Washington.

2   Under the Comprehensive Employment and Training Act (CETA), responsibility for local administration of federal employment programs was delegated to units of local government — cities, counties, or consortia of local governments. These units were called 'prime sponsors'. In this chapter, we will call them local government administrative agencies. These agencies actually engaged in very little direct delivery of services. They contracted for most employment services with other public or private agencies — schools, community organizations, local government human service agencies, community colleges, etc. The exact mix cies and services varied considerably from setting-to-setting. This varia- what we attempted to represent by doing our research in three different

Under the Joint Training Partnership Act, passed by the US Congress in 1982 and scheduled to be implemented in the fall of 1983, the prime sponsor system, based on units of local government, has been replaced by a system based on joint business-government agencies at the local level and a stronger role for state government in designating and overseeing the operations of these local agencies. The Act also institutes stronger performance standards for employment programs and restricts uses of federal funds mainly to training.

3   See ELMORE R.F. (1979–1980) 'Backward mapping: implementation research and policy decisions', *Political Science Quarterly*, 94, 4, winter, pp. 601–16. Also, ELMORE R. F. *Forward and Backward Mapping: Reversible Logic in the Analysis of Public Policy*, Graduate School of Public Affairs, Washington, University of Washington; and LIPSKY M., (1978) 'Standing the study of public policy on its head', in BURNHAM W. and WEINBERG M. (Eds) *American Politics and Public Policy*, Cambridge, MA, MIT Press.

4   (1980) *Handbook of Labor Statistics*, US Department of Labor, table 4.

5   SENINGER S., (1980) 'Postwar trends in youth employment,' in ADAMS A. and MANGUM G., (Eds), *The Lingering Crisis of Youth Unemployment*, Kalamazoo, MI, Upjohn Institute for Employment Research.

6   (1980) *Handbook of Labor Statistics*, US. Department of Labor, Table 66.

7   *Ibid.*, table 67; and FREEMAN R. and WISE D. (1982) 'The youth labor market problem: Its nature, causes, and consequences,' in FREEMAN, R. and WISE, D. (Eds) *The Youth Labor Market Problem*, Chicago: University of Chicago Press.

8   RUMBERGER R., 'Why Kids Drop Out of High School', Program Report #81-B4, Institute for Research on Educational Finance and Governance, School of Education, Stanford University.

9   See, for example, (1976) *From School to Work: Improving the Transition*, Washington, DC National Commission for Manpower Policy; and STEVENSON, W. (1980) 'The transition from school to work', in ADAMS, A. and MANGUM, G. (Eds). *The Lingering Crisis of Youth Unemployment*, Kalamazoo, MI, Upjohn Institute for Employment Research.

10 In Norway, Sweden, and Denmark, the national government has experimented with programs designed to track young people after they leave secondary school and guarantee private or public sector jobs to those who are unemployed. The tracking is nearly universal and is done either by school personnel or local employment offices. It is made easier by the fact that Scandinavian countries use a single personal identification number for all transactions with the government — something that would be highly unlikely in the US, especially for high-risk populations. See, MAGNUSSON, H. (1982) 'Youth Unemployment Policy in

Sweden: Policy Change and Implementation Problems', paper presented to the International Working Group on Policy Implementation, June; and WINTER, SØREN (1982) 'Studying the Implementation of Top-Down Policy from the Bottom-Up: Implementation of Danish Youth Employment Policy', paper presented to the International Working Group on Policy Implementation, June and in this volume.

Studying Implementation of Top-Down Policy From the Bottom Up: Implementation of Danish Youth Employment Policy[1]

Søren Winter

The Bottom-Up Implementation Perspective

Since the early seventies, when Wildavsky and Pressman wrote their already classic work on 'implementation', many American implementation studies have shown that the capacity of government to implement its own policies is very limited. Most American and other implementation studies have used a top-down perspective, following the implementation process from the intent of the original political decision in parliament or government, step-by-step through the central governmental administration via different regional administrative levels, to the implementation and performance at local level, where the policy is delivered to the citizens.

When using this top-down perspective, we look upon implementation from the perspective of the top, i.e. parliament or government and the essential questions to be answered by research are: To what extent are the intentions and expectations, or rules, guidelines and plans realized and followed in central administration, and at the regional and local levels? Where and why do deviations occur? It is undoubtedly relevant to study implementation problems from the perspective of the top, focussing particularly on control and accountability questions. The top-down perspective has a tendency, however, to treat only a narrow range of possible explanations for implementation failures.[2] When using this perspective, there is a tendency to focus on single goals and programs as well as on single actors at the top and functionalized organizational actors on the lower levels, the organization thus reflecting a clear end-means chain.[3] Deviations from this pattern are often treated as dysfunctional behavior which should be remedied by approaching the rational, hierarchical model.

Very often implementation takes place in an arena characterized by a multi-organizational network where official goals are vague, where each actor is responsible for a number of different programs that might be conflicting, and where the different actors involved in each program are pursuing different goals. Furthermore, even if this picture runs contrary to the ideal rational hierarchical model, recommendations to make fewer and clearer goals and to reduce organizational complexity would often be the same as denying and renouncing the very existence of politics.

It is also often an underlying presumption of the top-down perspective that implementation is, or at least can be and should be, directed and controlled from the top,[4] just as there might be a tendency to concentrate research upon the upper levels of administration, which are supposed to be the most crucial to implementation. The belief in the rational, hierarchical administration dominates our minds to such an extent that we are confident that implementation can be controlled from the top. It is only a question of finding the effective steering and control instruments.

A growing body of research shows, however, that the ability of government to control implementation can be questioned[5] and that implementation at the bottom, at the delivery level, is often more important to the success of implementation than the upper organizational levels. Lipsky, Weatherley, Prottas, Elmore, and Hjern have shown how crucial the behavior of 'field-workers' or 'street-level bureaucrats' is to implementation.[6]

Another weakness of the top-down perspective in looking at the capacity of government to regulate and deliver services at the grass-roots is a tendency to focus the analysis, on the one hand, upon the government's will and capacity or resources to control the implementing organization, and on the other hand upon the will of the implementing actors to accent the guidelines of the government. However, several implementation studies, and particularly the studies on street-level bureaucrats, have shown that implementation failures can often be explained by limited capacity of the delivery personnel to implement the governmental programs. Perhaps implementation gaps are caused by lack of implementing capacity in the delivery system at least as often as by lack of will.

Because of the weaknesses of the top-down implementation perspective mentioned above and the importance of the delivery level in implementation, we have chosen a bottom-up perspective for the following study of the implementation of Danish youth employment policy. This bottom-up perspective is inspired partly by the studies of 'street-level bureaucracy' by Lipsky, Weatherley and Prottas[7] and partly by more systematic attempts by Elmore, Hjern and Hull, to look not only at the behavior of the delivery-personnel, but also to study the whole implementation process from the bottom up.[8] In this way, the upper organizational and governmental actors will also be studied, but only to the extent in which their behavior influences the street-level bureaucrats' work conditions.

The question of goals is very crucial in implementation research, since most implementation studies deal with processes involved in the attempt to implement goals. Most top-down studies have focussed on the manifest official goals of the government in laws and regulations, but some have also discussed the role of latent, unofficial goals that may be the real incentive behind political decisions.[9] Whether manifest or latent, the normal standard of top-down implementation studies has been the goals of the top decision-makers.

Some of the new bottom-up implementation researchers have been reluctant to let their analysis be guided by the goals of the top. Hjern, Porter, and Hull, whose main focus in implementation is on the role of interorganizational networks, find it irrelevant to evaluate the implementation only against the standards of the governmental goals. They see that implementation is characterized by multiple programs and multiple actors pursuing quite different ends. Accordingly, Hjern and Hull seem to maintain that there must be as many criteria for judging implementation success or failure as there are interests being pursued or otherwise affected by implementation.[10]

One of Elmore's key interests in implementation research is the problem-solving capacity of the government and the observation that not all political goals are able to solve social problems, even if completely implemented. Accordingly, Elmore's bottom-up implementation or 'backward mapping' analysis starts by defining the problem and identifying organizational operations which might change the problematic social behavior. Stepping further backward, Elmore wants to end his analysis by formulating those goals which can solve social problems. In this way goals will be the end-product of the analysis, not the point of departure.[11]

In this section we will study the implementation of top-down policy from the bottom up.[12] There are some advantages to using this perspective. Firstly, the resulting analysis will be of more direct relevance to decision-makers in answering the questions, What are the street-level bureaucrats' chances of implementing the political goals at the delivery level? And, what factors impede implementation at the local level? The following study, which has been financed by the Danish government, aims at evaluating the administration of a new experimental youth employment program. The government is naturally more interested in knowing if and how its goals are implemented than in being told what goals it should follow. Besides, seen in the light of value relativism, it is logically impossible to deduce political goals from problem definitions without applying political values. Neither, for that matter, can problems be defined without the application of some form of values. With this in mind, if the values of the political decision-makers are not applied as standard there is a risk that the implementation process may be analyzed and evaluated in terms of the values and goals of either the researcher himself or the street-level bureaucrats or the participants.

Nevertheless, the perspective applied here allows us to find out if there are any deficiencies in the goals–means chain of the government. The analysis might show that it is impossible to reach the goals of the government by using the means or instruments of the program in question. Thus, compliance in delivery-level behavior might dash the goal of the program and vice versa. And a deficient goal–means chain may help explain a possible implementation

Søren Winter

Figure 1: Top-perspective ('top-down')

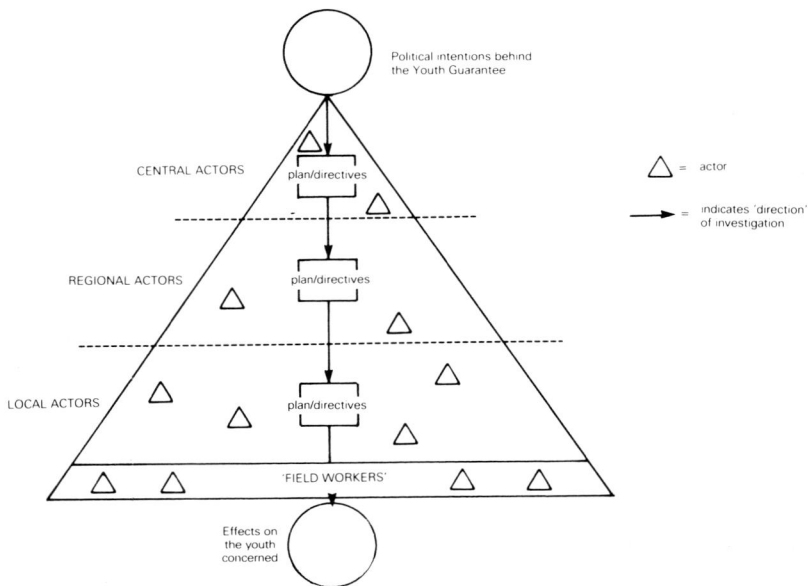

Figure 2: 'Field-worker' perspective ('bottom-up')

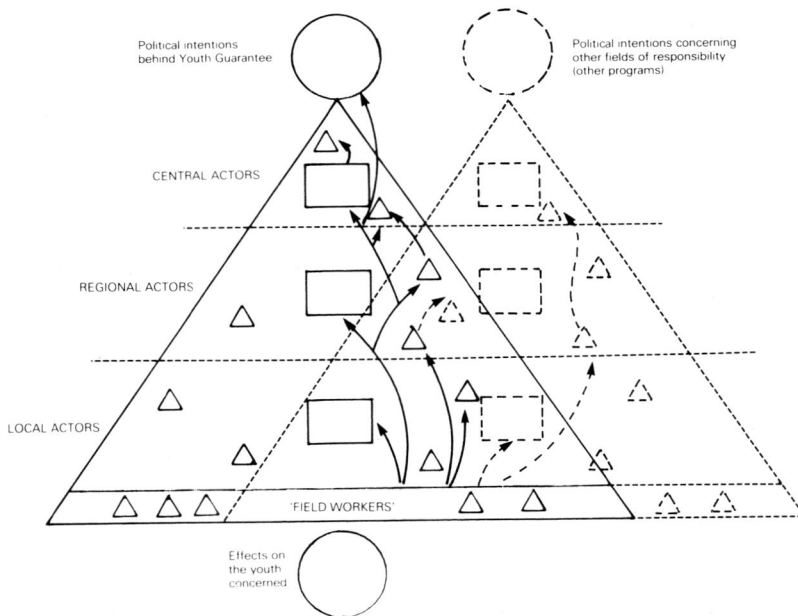

gap. At the same time it is possible to take the goals of different implementing actors into consideration, even if the main focus is upon government goals. Again, such goals conflicts can help explain the degree to which the policy is or is not implemented.

Figures 1 and 2 represent an attempt to illustrate the two different perspectives for implementation research: the top–down and the bottom–up perspectives. The following analysis of the implementation of the Danish youth employment policy will use a bottom–up perspective — our point of departure is the street-level bureaucrat and our central question to be answered is, What are his conditions of work in trying to solve the problems according to the goals of the governmental program? Or, What factors influence his possibilities of solving the problems according to the goals of the program?

Lipsky and Weatherley have shown how important the capacity and coping mechanisms of street-level bureaucrats are to implementation.[13] Hjern, Porter, and Hull have pointed out how crucial interorganizational networks and program conflicts are to implementation,[14] while one of Elmore's important contributions is the observation that the problem-solving capacity of the government is limited[15] and that it is important to analyze the interaction between the delivery-personnel and social environment and its implications to implementation and problem-solving. Finally, many implementation studies have focussed on the role of planning and control in the implementation process.

On the assumption that all these factors are very important in explaining the delivery level behavior and implementation, our model tries to integrate them all in a common framework for studying the implementation conditions of street-level bureaucrats.

Figure 3 illustrates the bottom–up perspective of this chapter and shows a model with some factors which influence the front-line workers' possibilities for solving the problems according to the goals of the governmental program.[16]

Danish Youth Employment Policies and the Experimental Youth Guarantee Program

This section focuses on one special program: the Youth Guarantee Program (YGP), which has been running as an experiment or pilot project in two counties, the county of Aarhus and the county of Storstrøm, from October 1980 to March 1983. I have been asked by the Danish government to evaluate the administrative implementation of this experimental program which, according to the original intents, was to be extended to the whole country if it proved successful.

Since the mid-seventies, youth unemployment has been growing rapidly in Denmark and, consequently, so have the number of countermeasures. The

Figure 3:   Model of the implementing conditions of the delivery-personnel

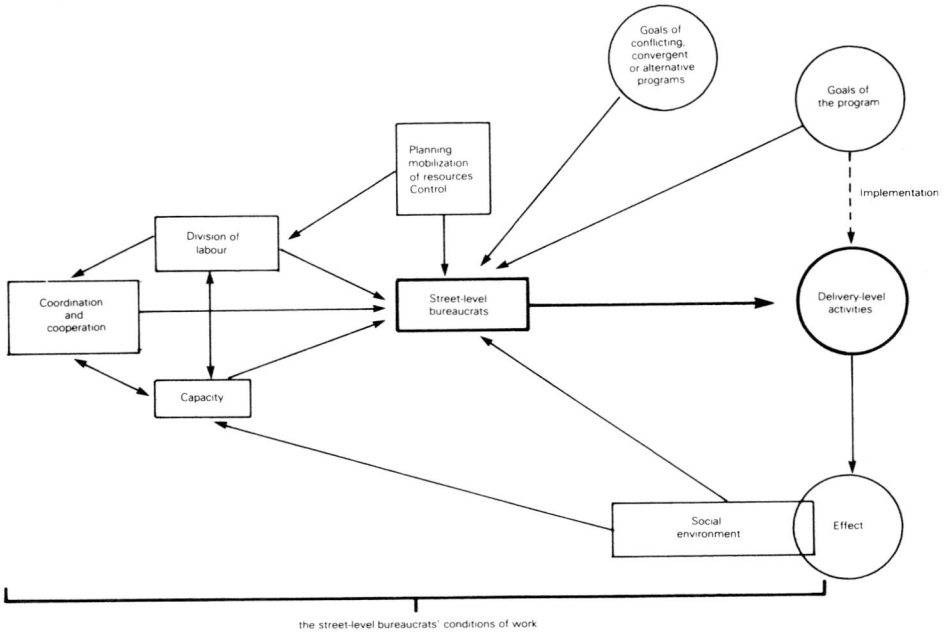

ordinary educational and vocational training system and the labor exchange functions have been supplemented by extraordinary measures such as workshop-type work experience projects, special and temporary public jobs, special traineeships and apprenticeships in public offices and institutions, subsidies for private firms to establish special traineeships and apprenticeships and extra jobs. In 1978, well over 30,000 young people were given an employment opportunity or an offer of education or training. However, a substantial number of young people, including even the long-term unem-ployed young persons, did not receive any such offer. Many returned to unemployment after participating in one of the above activities provided by the government's employment plan.[17] The target group for the employment activities differed from district to district and the offers seemed to be distributed among the young people somewhat accidentally. Besides, the program against unemployment was criticized for not giving the young people sufficient qualifications. Too few young persons entered education providing qualifications and training courses, many were not able to finish their vocational training because of lack of traineeships, while at the same time too many employment projects failed to improve the participants' qualifica-

114

tions substantially. In December 1979, 43,630 young persons were registered as unemployed, and only one year later this number had risen by 60 per cent to 69,728. In 1980, 11.9 per cent of all young people were unemployed with women hit harder than men.

The Youth Guarantee Program (YGP)[18] was an attempt to concentrate and intensify the existing efforts. Because of the unsystematic way in which the participants were chosen in previous effort, it was intended that the YGP should attach the greatest importance to the weakest group of unemployed young people. Accordingly, the main target-group was defined as young people who had been unemployed for a long time (nine out of the last twelve months was the original criterion specified in the program). The YGP also includes, however, some measures of a more preventive nature. Therefore, additional target-groups are youngsters just graduated from school ('school leavers') and all basic-year trainees of the vocational schools. With regard to the trainees, the goal was to secure a relevant trainee service place for all trainees who had completed the basis year of the basic vocational training whereas all 16–17-year-old school-leavers were to be offered careers and vocational guidance both before and after completing school. Furthermore, they should be offered an education or a job if they had been unemployed for not less than three months out of the six months immediately following school departure.

The core group of the YGP, however, is made up of young long-term unemployed people, who, according to the program, should be *identified*, *registered*, *singled out*, and offered intensive career and vocational *guidance* and a subsequent *'guarantee measure'* ('G-measure') consisting of further education, training or a job lasting for nine months. In order to increase the YGP-participants' chances of obtaining employment by making them competitive with other young people, it was the goal of the program not only to employ them for nine months, but also to ensure they were qualified. Therefore a remarkably clear order of priority was established for the G-measures:

(i) longer training or education with qualifications, mainly basic vocational training,

(ii) short, qualification-providing labor market courses *combined with* (a) jobs in the private sector; (b) jobs in the public sector; (c) participation in a training workshop (KUP) or a project-based work experience arrangement; (d) a job for nine months in the private sector if possible, otherwise in the public sector in an office or institution. Through guidance the clients should be motivated to participate in high priority measures, but the choice was to be their own.

While placed in their G-measure, the initial guidance and counseling should be continued by *follow-up* actions in order to pass the young people on to subsequent education, training or employment.

To What Extent Are the Goals Reached at Delivery Level?

This study is based on many different data sources. The most important data are (i) nearly 100 very long, loosely structured interviews with delivery-personnel in six selected settings in the two pilot counties and with 'higher-level administrators' on the local, regional, and central levels; (ii) survey of all municipal employment officers and work creation projects; (iii) data on the background and wishes of the clients and on the program measures adopted; (iv) a survey of the clients' situation after finishing program participation; (v) a survey of all young people of a particular year in one large district; (vi) plans and reports.

As the data-collection for this implementation study had to be carried out in the winter of 1981–82, when the program had only been running one to one-and-a-half years, it is difficult to give a completely fair estimate of the delivery level effects because new programs usually require some time to be implemented. This fact should be taken into consideration when reading the following.

The following analysis will concentrate on the key target group of long-term unemployed young people, who account for 95 per cent of all program participants. The YGP has had reasonable success in identifying and catching this target group. A survey in the municipality of Aarhus (a site encompassing one-third of all inhabitants in the pilot counties) shows that about 80 per cent of the target group have been registered and contacted by the program authorities, whereas only 20 per cent of this group had been caught by the previous programs. However, 20 per cent of the target group remain unidentified, and many of the YGP participants were contacted several months too late. The missing cases as well as those which were included at a late stage belong to an especially weak group, most of them being women with children.

Originally, clients were supposed to receive a G-offer when they had been unemployed for nine months out of the last fifteen months, but most of them have experienced even longer periods of unemployment by the time they are contacted and provided with a G-offer. By then, the average period of unemployment is about seventeen months. This means that measures to assist the participants are substantially delayed. Neither has the program been successful in terms of placing the clients where they gain the intended qualifications. In fact, the list of priorities has been turned almost upside down, as can be seen from Figure 4.

Only a few per cent of the G-persons have started vocational training. Fourteen per cent have participated in short training courses, normally combined with a job. This is fewer than anticipated, but more than in previous programs. About 18 per cent of the clients had jobs with private employers with or without employment subsidies — again, fewer than expected. But this figure has shown a rising tendency in 1982 after the main data collection was completed. The majority of the participants have, however, been placed in

Figure 4:   Priority of YGP-offers and Actual Distribution

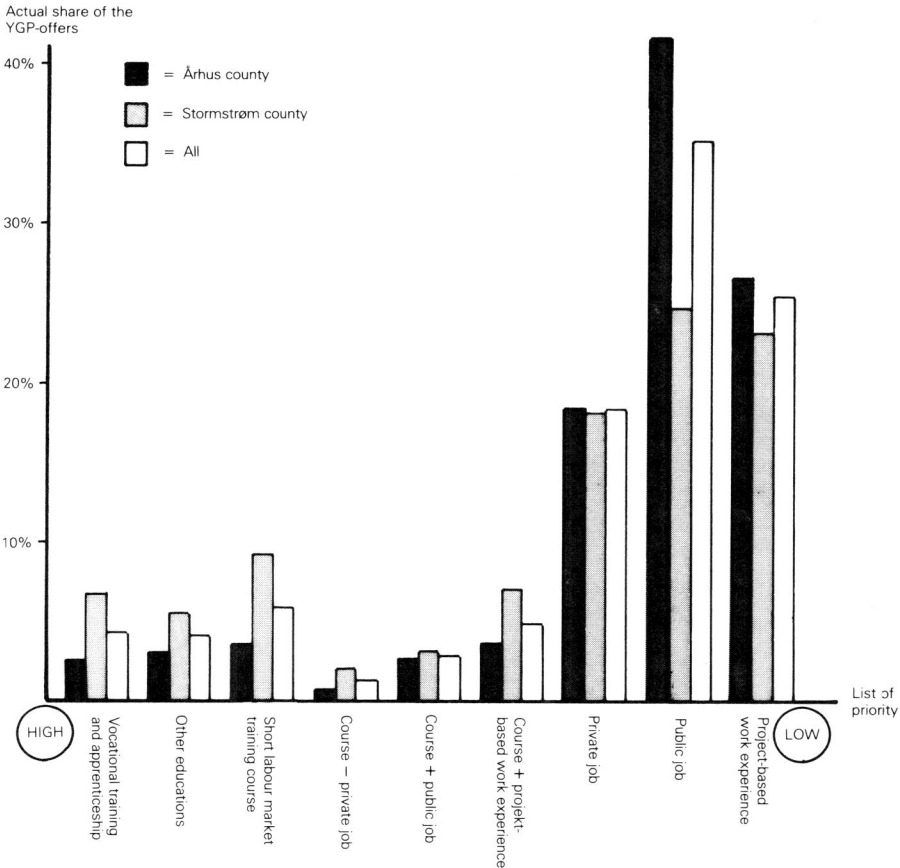

specially created public jobs or under work experience projects, although, according to the original plan, these projects were only to be accepted if combined with training courses. Moreover, most work experience projects were not of the expected quality.

Finally, it can be noticed that the last phase of the program — the follow-up and passing-on actions — has been neglected, with 62 per cent of the clients returning to unemployment after finishing their nine-months G-offer. A few months after leaving the program, only 11 per cent are recorded as participating in education/training, and only 21 per cent as having a job.

So, the objects of the program are far from having been achieved. Still it must be noted that the youth employment measures have been more focussed and more goal-directed than before and that the measures adopted have led to more participants than previously acquiring some form of qualification.

We will now try to explain these implementation effects by analyzing the implementation and working conditions of the delivery-personnel. The main emphasis will be on factors that hamper the implementation process — though space will allow only some of these factors to be discussed in this article.[19]

The Delivery-Level Personnel and Their Implementation Conditions

The Social Environment and Its Impact on Implementation

Most policy programs try to solve problems by changing the behavior of the citizens, who in this context may be conceived as the 'social environment' of the public sector. But the citizens' behavior is not only determined by politics, but also by many other factors more or less beyond immediate control of the government.

While the welfare state expands its activities to cover an increasing number of private activities, there is a growing body of evidence in implementation literature showing that in many cases policies can change citizens' behavior only marginally.[20] Therefore, the character of the 'social environment' may have a very crucial effect on the implementation conditions of the delivery-personnel. Delivery is not an automatic act or a one-way relationship between the street-level bureaucrat and his/her clients.

The basic problem in this context lies in the financial difficulties of private business and the rapid growth in unemployment. The number of vacant jobs has declined, while labor supply has increased because of a rise in the net influx of women onto the labor market. It is difficult for young people with little or no work experience to compete for jobs with more experienced adults. The growing rate of unemployment has increased the target group of the YGP and decreased the potential number of jobs in the private sector. At the same time, the crisis has meant a rise in the number of qualified applicants for the existing vacancies, thus making it all the more difficult for long-term unemployed young, who have normally had no vocational training, to compete for jobs. In a YGP framework, this fact makes it difficult to find more permanent jobs for the target group and even more difficult to pass the participants on into subsequent employment.

It is easier than under normal circumstances to get private jobs under the G-offer system because these are subsidized with more than 80 per cent of the normal salary. In spite of this large subsidy and extensive searching-out activities it was possible in 1981 to get jobs in the private sector for only 20 per cent of the clients. However, the number of private jobs has grown since the subsidy was increased in the summer of 1981. In 1982 about 30 per cent were placed in private jobs. But taking the subsidy and information into consideration, it is remarkable, first, that the number of jobs created was not even greater, and second, that there appears to be a considerable time-lag between the subsidy-increase and the employers' reaction to it.

Jobs for clients who have completed their program participation are not subsidized and that may help explain why so few get a job afterwards. Besides, the work creation experiences have a more doubtful reputation with the employers than can be justified when one takes into consideration the fact that these youngsters have, after all, reached a degree of qualification. In fact, program participation may have reduced employment opportunities for some of the youngsters.

Also the *attitudes of the target group* are very important to street-level bureaucrats. The main idea of the program was that most unemployed young people could be persuaded, by counseling, to enter further education or training to improve their employment situation, conditional on the capacity of the educational institutions.

It is, however, a clear experience of the field workers that counseling, persuasion, and capacity are not sufficient because of important social barriers to education and training. One demotivating factor is economy, since students in most education/training receive far less financial support than they could expect from a salary, unemployment insurance, or benefits. This problem is amplified by the fact that many clients have children or other responsibilities of maintenance. Besides, there are others who fear that they will not be able to complete vocational training because of lack of apprenticeships.

Problems of maintenance, problems of getting traineeships or apprenticeships, and traditional sex roles explain why the most popular education or training wish among female YGP-participants is to become an assistant nurse. In this program the students are salaried during the trainir_ period and field work placement is guaranteed.

One of the aims of the YGP is to fight the relatively high unemployment among women by motivating them to choose training or jobs which are typically male fields. This sub-goal has not been implemented and our study questions if the employment chances are likely to improve for women entering untraditional vocational training. Though normally only a few per cent of freshmen in vocational training for building construction and metal work in the pilot counties since 1974 have been women, only 25 per cent of those pioneer women, much fewer than the men, have completed their education. There is no reason why the weaker group of YGP-persons should be more successful. This is one example of social programs where implementation of one sub-goal or means may dash the ultimate goal. Also some of the other experiences of the street-level bureaucrats question the logic of the ends-means chain of the program.

The program has changed the behavior of most clients in the short run by moving them from unemployment to temporary employment, but it has not been able to motivate more than a tiny group to take up an education or training place, nor has it in the long run been able to cause more than a marginal change in the behavior of the participants, most of whom return to unemployment.

The Pool of Organizations in the Delivery-System: Division of Labor and Interorganizational Networks

The organizational structure of the implementation of youth employment policy in Denmark is very complex. The implementation process utilizes a large pool of different organizations, so that different sectors, different geographical layers of government, organizations with different types of authority (i.e., state agencies, local governments, and interest organizations) are all involved in implementing the policy.

In this section we shall focus on the organizational structure at the delivery level. We will concentrate on the delivery functions of guidance and exchange, which can be classified as follows:

(i)   identification, registration of clients
(ii)   reaching-out casework/contact with clients
(iii)   guidance
(iv)   reaching-out activities in relation to private and public undertakings
(v)   placement/exchange
(vi)   follow-up/passing clients on

This means, however, that some important delivery-functions shall not be analyzed, for example, the teaching and training activities related to the actual G-offers.[21]

The above guidance and exchange functions have been divided among a number of different local authorities, in particular among the state employment service and the municipal extended school counseling scheme, employment secretariat, and social welfare administration.

Compared with other countries, regional and local public administration in Denmark is highly consolidated as most delivery-functions are run by local governments. These consist of 275 municipalities and fourteen county councils. At regional and local levels, the national government is only in charge of, in the main, the following delivery-functions: employment service, vocational training, short training courses and higher education, post, railways, motorways, police and defense. But of course the state is involved in most public sector functions through the mechanism of mandatory rules and by controlling and/or giving financial support to, for example, the trade unions' unemployment funds and to the counties and municipalities to supplement their own income from taxes.

Originally, the national employment service was the main responsible authority for measures against unemployment at the individual level of application. These were supplemented by the unions' unemployment funds and the unemployment benefits distributed by municipal social welfare administration. The main functions of the employment service have been exchange, for example, individually matching demand for and supply of labor, educational and vocational guidance, approving apprenticeships and traineeships, reaching-out activities aimed at private firms and placement of the marginal labor force.

With the growth of unemployment, the number of organizations implementing youth unemployment policies has also increased. Because such a large part of the public sector delivery function is run by the municipalities and counties, it was natural to give them some responsibilities in fighting the increasing unemployment both by creating more jobs and by raising revenues for employment measures. In 1981, for example, the counties and the municipalities were required to spend at least 25 Danish kroner (Dkr.) and Dkr. 50[22] respectively per inhabitant for measures against youth unemployment. Any unspent money had to be paid to the state! However, many municipalities spent even more than demanded.

Most municipalities have an employment committee, often including politicians and representatives from the labor market and a type of employment secretariat (varying from several persons to one part-time officer) responsible for the employment budget of the local government, for creating extraordinary jobs in offices and institutions, for setting up work experience projects for young persons and subsidizing wages for unemployed persons in private firms.

Another new, so far voluntary, task of the municipalities is to give extended educational and vocational guidance to the pupils before and after leaving school. This function is often performed by teachers as a part-time job. In addition, each municipal school administration is required to offer youth school courses. Finally, the municipalities are involved in youth unemployment policy through their social assistance payments to persons who have had no stable connection with the labor market and who have no access to the unemployment funds. Beside paying benefits, the municipal welfare administration is among other responsibilities in charge of social counseling and rehabilitation.

The counties have also been ordered to participate in the measures against unemployment by raising funds, by creating public jobs as do the municipalities and by subsidizing extraordinary traineeships and apprenticeships. As in the municipalities, these efforts are normally run by a special committee and an employment secretariat. To this structure may be added the ordinary state run short training courses for unskilled workers and vocational training, the latter including training, guidance and reaching-out activities aimed at employers for the purpose of providing traineeships.

Thus, the employment implementation structure has experienced the kind of proliferation that is so very characteristic of western administrative systems. With the growth of the public sector, new programs are often followed by new administrative agencies. The resulting proliferation characterizes not only the external but also the internal division of labor in the organizations.

This run-down shows that several authorities are involved in delivering employment policies, even though it is important to stress that the Danish delivery system is much less diversified and complex than, for example, the American one, where so many private and semi-public service-providers are involved at the delivery level.[23] However, the Danish system has been sufficiently complex to create a number of coordination problems, especially between the state employment service and the different municipal agencies.

The YGP has used the existing structure, *cf.* Figure 5, but has also attempted to bring about a more distinct division of labor and better coordination. The state employment service is responsible for identifying, registering, and guiding G-persons, for reaching-out activities aimed at private enterprises, for placement of participants in private jobs and education/ training programs, as well as for follow-up and subsequent channelling efforts.

The municipal welfare administration is responsible for referring welfare cases to the employment service, while it is the task of the employment secretariats of the municipalities and counties to create extraordinary jobs in offices and institutions and especially to create work experience projects.[24] The placement of YGP-participants in public jobs is supposed to be a matter of teamwork between the employment service and the employment secretariats.

It may be added that the employment service identifies cases in receipt of unemployment insurance by consulting a central data encoding system for labor market statistics based on reports from the trade unions' unemployment funds.

Figure 5: Organizational network in identifying, guidance and placement activities in the YGP

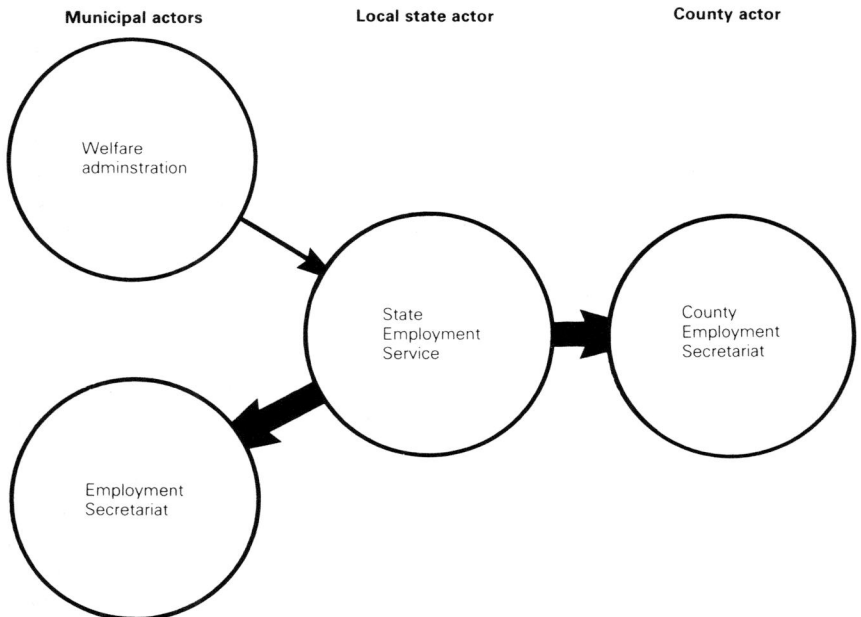

The simpler administrative structure and the new administrative procedures are responsible for the success in reaching the majority of the target group, a result which is remarkable even by international standards. However, there still are shortcomings in the cooperation between some social welfare administrations and the employment service (and also internally in the latter agency) implying that some individuals in the target group are not identified at all and many are identified too late.

In most local districts the cooperation between the employment service division and the municipality is reasonably good, but in certain sites there are conflicts which are often based on clashing organizational interests. Some welfare workers may be interested in moving some of their clients from welfare programs to the YGP to save money, and perhaps their own work, while the Employment Service division may be interested in keeping rather weak clients away from the YGP program, which is a labor market program.

The municipal employment secretariat may want the employment service division to finish most cases itself by guiding young people to education/ training activities administered (and financed) by the state, or by finding jobs in the private sector which are less costly and more convenient to the municipalities than public jobs and work-creation projects. Therefore most municipalities want the employment service divisions to increase their reaching-out activities to secure jobs and traineeships in the private sector, or allow the municipalities to participate in these activities if the employment service divisions lack sufficient capacity.

On the other hand, it is regarded as a core interest by most local employment service divisions to keep their monopoly in contacting private enterprises. As mentioned above, the municipalities and county councils are becoming increasingly involved in labor market policy, and this trend is regarded as a threat to the organizational interests of the employment service. Even though the employment service has been growing considerably under the economic crisis, the employment activities of the municipalities have grown even faster. The general experience within different public sectors has been that it is easier to raise funds in local governments with their own taxing capacity than in state agencies. The employment service wants both to keep its monopoly on contacting private enterprises and to receive a large supply of different quality jobs from the municipalities in order to make placement easier to handle. In fact, there are a few sites where the employment service divisions just submit a list of names of persons to be placed in the public sector to the employment secretariats, without any consideration of their individual clients or cooperation in the placement of them. This occurs even when the employment service personnel know their clients from guidance interviews.

However, the general impression given is that the cooperation between the two different sets of agencies is characterized by teamwork based on a common commitment and consensus of opinion with respect to the goals of the program. This teamwork can in part be attributed to the methods used by the municipalities and the employment service divisions when internally dividing the labor. In most districts the YGP tasks have been specialized and are the responsibility of certain persons who identify themselves with the program. Thus, despite an almost traditional conflict of interests between their parent institutions, the special YGP sub-units may to some extent feel more loyal to the common YGP enterprise than to their parent institution.[25]

In a way, a new organizational YGP structure with its own interests has been created, cutting across the normal organizational structure and borders. This teamwork is formalized in most districts by so-called 'team-groups' headed by the local employment service division and the employment secretariat, and usually including representatives from the municipal welfare and school administration (the latter representing extended school guidance service).

Even though the general level of conflict is low, this does not amount to saying that all authorities are managing to perform all their various duties. As we shall see later, lack of capacity prevents some street-level bureaucrats from performing all the delivery-activities expected of them.

Program Interaction and Implementation Consequences

When policy programs are made, the policy is often treated as if nothing but that program existed and as if all efforts of the implementing organizations would be directed towards implementing this particular policy. In reality, most programs interact to some extent with other programs in a manner which may be either *conflicting* (i.e. different goals, different means), *convergent* (i.e. different goals, but identical means) or even *alternative* (i.e. identical goals, but different means).

The employment service experiences a program conflict between the YGP and other programs concerning (a) job-offers for long-term unemployed who are eligible for unemployment insurance schemes (Law No. 277); (b) young unemployed people who are not YGP-persons (shorter periods of unemployment); (c) ordinary exchange; and (d) rehabilitation. In a period of economic crisis with only few jobs available, these programs are to some extent competing for the same jobs. One program can probably succeed only at the expense of others, even if it is a task of all programs to create new jobs. In this situation it is difficult to measure the effectiveness of the implementation of a single program.

As is normally the case, no clear governmental order of priority helps in solving this conflict, even though a de facto priority can be estimated from the relative resources of each program, if these programs are divided and resources earmarked for sub-units in the organization. This is indeed the case in most employment service divisions. Another de facto priority is set by the regulatory demands. For example, the 277-job-offer program for insured workers is written into a law which demands that the target group *must* have a job-offer *before* a certain time, whereas YGP-persons, due to an arrangement between the central and local authorities, are only to be offered education, training or jobs 'to the extent to which it is practically and economically possible'. As a consequence, the 277-program has been more successful in placing participants in extraordinary private and public jobs with the result that many of the YGP youngsters must content themselves with the generally unpopular low priority work experience placements.

Programs can also be *convergent*, so that one program can help in implementing another. Even though the 277-program is in some respects competing with and hampering the implementation of the YGP, it has in other ways also helped in the implementation of the YGP by taking over some members of the YGP target group, namely the young people who are in receipt of unemployment insurance. Because the 277 program receives re-latively more state support, and therefore is in a position to service clients originally included in the YGP target group, YGP is left with more money for fewer clients. Therefore the net result for the YGP of the expansion of the 277-program appears to be more YGP job-offers. These are, however, of a lower quality and priority.

Programs may also be *alternative*, so that the street-level bureaucrat can choose freely among alternative programs. For instance, a substantial propor-tion of the long-term unemployed youth consists of unmarried mothers receiving social benefits. For some of those clients the delivery-personnel can choose among a YGP-offer, rehabilitation under the Law of Social Welfare, a normal job through the exchange section of the employment service, and continued social benefits to enable the mothers to take care of their children (while at the same time sparing day-care center places). Even if the last alternative hardly can be found in any governmental program, it nevertheless is the policy of some welfare administrations to 'protect' such mothers. Thus the latter practice — or 'coping mechanism' (*cf.* below) — leads to a type of informal program. In this way delivery-personnel can often choose among programs as if they were drawing them from a vending machine.

However, this situation of interrelated programs may influence the implementation of one particular program at the delivery-level. This fact indeed complicates implementation analysis and calls for implementation studies that focus on packages of programs rather than on single programs.[26]

Delivery-Level Capacity

The capacity at the delivery-level is one of the most decisive variables affecting implementation. Detailed laws, regulations and orders do not make much difference, if the resources to implement are insufficient. Implementation research has paid increasing attention to the important of the local capacity.[27] It is a very common perception that implementation gaps are normally caused by lack of *will* in the implementing organization. In fact such gaps can be just as often explained by too little *capacity* at the delivery level. From a bottom-up perspective it is, however, important to distinguish between two different concepts of capacity, namely the capacity or *work-load/quality of the street-level bureaucrats* themselves and the *capacity concerning the measures* that can be offered by the street-level bureaucrats. Both variables have quantitative as well as qualitative dimensions.

Capacity of measures

It is evident that a social policy cannot be implemented if there are not enough measures to offer the target group, and in the Danish political and administrative debate the failing success of the YGP-program has very often been explained by too little educational capacity. In particular this has been the 'excuse' used by the local and regional authorities which are responsible for implementing the program.

Our study has shown, however, that though there has been a lack of capacity in some areas of education and training, there has been sufficient capacity in several others. The demotivating factors as described above are much more important than educational capacity in explaining the failure of the important goal of getting the target group into further education or training. During the program there has been a considerable expansion in the capacity of the vocational schools and the short labor market courses. Especially in the latter, capacity has exceeded demand. This can in the main be put down to bad planning and matching of the jobs (which are predominantly public) and the courses (which are predominantly targeted towards the private sector). The capacity-problems have fallen especially within typical female trades, for example, hairdresser, food service, and assistant nurse (which is the most popular education). This has implications for implementation since two-thirds of the target group are women. Within some professions, particularly the one first mentioned, it is, however, nearly impossible to get a job after training is completed, while the latter profession has very good employment prospects. Nevertheless the training program for assistant nurses has not been expanded. During the program the problems of getting enough traineeships and apprenticeships have become more serious because of increasing demand while the number of practice-places remains constant. This means that though it has become easier to start vocational training, it has become more difficult to complete it.

As to job-capacity, we have already discussed the reluctance of the private employers, and the competition for both private and public jobs from the 277-program. Here it might be added that though the program preferred private jobs over public ones because of their supposed higher quality, many private jobs have in fact very little to offer in the way of qualifications, since they represent functions no one else likes to perform, for example, cleaning or working in a burger bar. The capacity of work-creation projects has been more than sufficient in most of the pilot areas, but insufficient in several small municipalities in the county of Aarhus (see below). The average quality of the projects has improved compared to earlier projects but is still far below the program standards.

The capacity of street-level bureaucrats and coping mechanisms

Weatherley and Lipsky maintain that it is a fairly universal fact that the street-level bureaucrats' own resources are chronically and seriously limited in relation to their delivery tasks.[28] Even if that might not always be the case, no doubt it is a well-known situation and besides, it seems to be a general trend and part of the administrative culture that street-level bureaucrats *feel* their workload is too heavy. These feelings may be more important in affecting implementation than the actual workload.

Feelings of being hampered by an excessively heavy workload have also been widespread among the field-workers of the YGP. Especially the employment service has experienced a very heavy case load, even though it has varied from district to district. The case load can be illustrated by the fact that in 1981, eighteen street-level bureaucrats at the employment service had about 3700 clients for guidance and nearly 3000 to place in jobs or education and to follow up. This was in addition to continuing with reaching-out activities, administrative coordination, etc. That amounts to an average case load of about 200 clients per field-worker per year although the case load does vary geographically both in quantitative terms and qualitatively in terms of the character of the social problems of the involved youngsters.

Most of these bureaucrats feel they suffer under a very heavy workload as well as feeling that they have too few measures to offer their clients in the guarantee period and almost nothing afterwards. They experience a gulf between the demands from the ambitious program and from the clients on the one side and their limited resources on the other. Facing this dilemma it is only natural for the street-level bureaucrats to make use of some coping mechanisms in order to solve the problems and to survive organizationally. These coping mechanisms in the YGP are very similar to those that have been described in other studies on the behavior of street-level bureaucrats.[29]

One of these mechanisms is to prolong the decision-making time, but it is important to note that the relation between case load and decision-making time is very complex. The data of this study do not permit exact correlation analysis, but another study on disablement pension administration has shown no correlation at all between the two variables, giving support to a hypothesis or 'law of the constant pile of papers on the bureaucrat's desk'.[30]

Other coping mechanisms include *setting priorities* on different types of tasks, on different groups of clients, and on different types of solutions. These priorities may be controlled by the administrative or political leaders, but often this is not the case. In the case of the YGP, the regional management of the employment service has decided an order of priority that assigns the highest priority to registration, initial conversation with clients (containing interviewing and guidance), and exchange, whereas a low priority has been given particularly to follow-up and transfer activities. In the beginning of the program reaching-out activities on the labor market also had a low priority. Apparently this order of priority is in part established because registration, initial conversation, and placement were the first tasks when the program started and therefore also the first activities to become programmed. These were also visible and controllable activities registered and reported to a central register, thus providing a 'pin' in the statistics, whereas the other activities were not subject to registration.

These priorities were, however, reinforced by the street-level bureaucrats' own coping-mechanisms. According to Gresham's Law, programmed activities tend to dominate looser unprogrammed activities.[31] This tendency must be expected to increase with a growing case load. Interviewing youngsters and placing them in extraordinary public jobs are more tightly programmed and easier to carry out than reaching out, providing thorough guidance and counseling, and attending to follow-up and transfer activities. There has been a tendency to limit the guidance of clients to a short conversation for about half to three quarters of an hour, focusing the interviewing on filling in a mandatory questionnaire (for evaluation purposes!) about the clients' background and discussing concrete available possibilities of placement. In most cases very little time is used for discussing social problems and giving counseling and guidance about further education and training. In the same way there has been a tendency to make the placement of clients easier to handle. Particularly in the first period of the program reaching-out activities for jobs on the labor market had a rather low priority compared to other program activities. It was easier to ask the municipalities and counties for jobs.

The lowest priority has been assigned to follow-up and transfer activities. These are somewhat unprogrammed activities that are difficult to perform as the street-level bureaucrats feel that they have very little to offer. It is easier to put clients into the program than to pass them on to employment. Cooperation is also reduced because of this order of priority. There is a tendency to self-sufficiency when street-level bureaucrats feel they have a heavy workload. There is very little coordination between the employment service and the employment secretariat with regard to guidance and follow-up questions and as described above, in some districts the employment service is merely passing on the task of placing participants into public jobs to the municipal employment secretariat, which has very little information about the youngsters to be placed.

Maybe this behavior is also expressing another coping mechanism: *passing clients on to other authorities*. It is easier for the employment service officer to pass the clients on to the municipalities than to search for a private job. Similarly, some employment service officers believe that the social welfare administrations are trying to get rid of the weakest clients by shoving them on to the employment services.

Another coping mechanism is to *ration services* for the benefit of youngsters who may not be those who require the most assistance. For instance private jobs (which are most likely to be permanent than public ones) are often reserved for the most motivated and qualified young persons, who might be better able to get a job themselves. It is encouraging to succeed once in a while and such a placement may improve the attitudes of the employer and urge him to give more jobs to the program in the future. This means, however, that the most qualified and active people in the target group have the biggest chance to get a good job that may lead to subsequent employment, whereas the weakest persons are placed in work-experience projects with a more than 80 per cent chance of returning to unemployment.

The above mechanisms of fixing priorities, rationing and getting rid of clients are sometimes combined with certain mechanisms such as *categorization of participants and routinization of procedures*. Routines may sometimes be adequate, but are problematic for implementation if very rough standard classifications of participants are used and combined with rules-of-thumb regarding the further placement of each group of youngsters. For example, some employment service field-workers in the normal exchange section may have the idea that participation in work-experience projects generally disqualifies young people if they later ask for a job in the private sector. This kind of classification and establishment of rules-of-thumb may rest on generalizations taken from a few personal experiences.

A last coping mechanism is to justify the above actions by overstating the real problems by convincing oneself that it is impossible to motivate the clients for education, that there is no educational capacity at all, and that it is useless to perform follow-up activities because nothing at all can be offered. Some street-level bureaucrats also try to free themselves from the feeling of guilt because of the lack of success by creating a cynical, almost suspicious, attitude towards the clients. It is, for example, not unusual to use derogatory nicknames when talking with colleagues about clients.

It is very difficult to estimate how widespread the above coping-mechanisms have been in the YGP. All of them are in evidence, but it would be unfair to say that they totally dominate the program-performance. It is, however, interesting to note that very similar street-level behavior can be found both in different sectors as described in the works of Lipsky and Weatherley and in different political systems with very different programs and administrative systems.

The capacity of the street-level bureaucrats does not depend only on the number of staffers but also on their quality. The problem solving capacity of each field-worker is heavily dependent on his or her educational and vocational training, earlier job and experience of working with clients. Besides, the feeling of workload and stress described above may often be brought about by a sense of powerlessness and lack of problem-solving ability. The background of the YGP delivery-personnel varies considerably and implementation problems might in some cases be attributed to inexperienced and unskilled field-workers. In particular, the municipal employment secretariats are staffed by very different kinds of people and in some places long-term unemployed people with no earlier experience in guidance, pedagogical or administrative knowledge have been taken on as employment advisers. In addition the wage is comparatively low, and the personnel turnover is high. Half of the municipalities in the county of Aarhus changed employment adviser around new year 1982.

Planning, Mobilization of Resources and Control

Up to this point, we have focussed on the delivery-system and the actors performing these delivery-functions. We can also identify another pool of planning organizations, having its own mechanism and pattern of interests.[32] When we use a bottom-up perspective, the behavior of these planning actors on the central, regional, and local levels is relevant as far as it affects the implementing conditions of the delivery personnel.

The organizational system of planning, mobilization of resources and control is very complex involving different sectors, including local, regional, and central actors, and state agencies, local governments, and interest organizations. Space allows only a brief sketch of some of the important actors and interactions of this system.

Starting from the local level, the municipalities and their employment secretariats have important functions in planning services and mobilizing resources. The quality and quantity of jobs and work experience projects are very dependent on the planning process and on economic resources, a substantial part of which are financed by municipal taxes. The municipalities of the county of Storstrøm have formed inter-municipal employment committees and secretariats that encompass four-six municipalities, while each municipality of the county of Aarhus has its own committee and secretariat. For the YGP the government suggested a structure for the employment service and the employment secretariats similar to the one in the county of Storstrøm. From a top-down perspective one could say that the other kinds of structures represent deviations from the program, or an implementation gap. But the organizational structure being a means rather than an end in itself, we think it ought to be empirically tested to determine which of the structure should best be able to further implementation.

Our analysis shows that inter-municipal cooperation has both positive and negative consequences for implementation. It furthers implementation by making it possible to create a larger, more diversified supply of work-experience projects offering more qualifications than is possible for a single small municipality of about 7000 inhabitants. Each of those small municipalities has so few clients in the target group that it is almost impossible to create an effective work experience workshop — with diversified production — and at the same time create and implement programs of further education and training. The inter-municipal cooperation is very important in explaining why the work-experience projects in the county of Storstrøm are larger, cover a broader geographical area, and are more differentiated and lead to better qualifications than the projects in the county of Aarhus.

It seems, however, to be more difficult for the inter-municipal employment secretariats to create extraordinary jobs of a more normal nature in each municipality's institutions, offices, highway authority, etc. Besides this tendency, the inter-municipal cooperations also end up with smaller grants than municipalities with their own employment secretariats. This is so because the inter-municipal budget will be determined by the least common denominator, as no municipality is inclined to spend more on the common enterprise than the other participants do. There is normally at least one municipality spending the minimum Dkr. 50 per inhabitant specified by the government, *cf.* above, bringing the other municipalities down with them. This probably explains why it appears that the budget for youth employment-measures is so much larger in the municipalities of Aarhus than in the other county. In Figure 6 all the municipalities in each county are ranked according to how much more (or less) they have spent for youth employment purposes than they were obliged to according to the law. This mandatory spending is marked by the zero-line. In the county of Storstrøm only three municipalities spent substantially more than required in 1981. It is interesting to note that they all belong to the same inter-municipal cooperation and that this cooperation disintegrated in 1982 because of disagreements between the municipalities about the proper size of the budget and the distribution of expenditures between the municipalities. However, the inter-municipal form of organization cannot explain the whole trend in the decrease of spending the county of Storstrøm. The savings have also been made possible by the new supply of special state funds for the YGP (see below). It is clear that these differences in municipal grants affect the implementation conditions for the field-workers.

At the regional level the county and the regional employment service/ Labor Market Board have been important actors. As in the municipalities, the counties have funded and planned jobs and work-experience projects together with short courses in vocational and career guidance. Besides, the county, with its Employment Committee and Secretariat, has negotiated the program conditions with central authorities and coordinated the local implementation in cooperation with the regional employment service/Labor Market Board.

Both the Employers' Association and the unions are represented on the regional Labor Market Board and on most municipal advisory committees on employment, and they are supposed to help create good relations with the labor market. That may be the case to some extent, but the most important role of these interest organizations with respect to implementation has been to hamper the development of work experience projects providing qualifications by refusing to accept such projects. Apparently both interest groups regard it as their main task to prevent 'competition distortion' rather than qualifying the youth for employment.

At the central level there have been several important actors in the process of planning, mobilization of resources, and control. Most important have been

Figure 6: The surplus spending of the municipalities for youth employment measures in relation to the mandatory spending

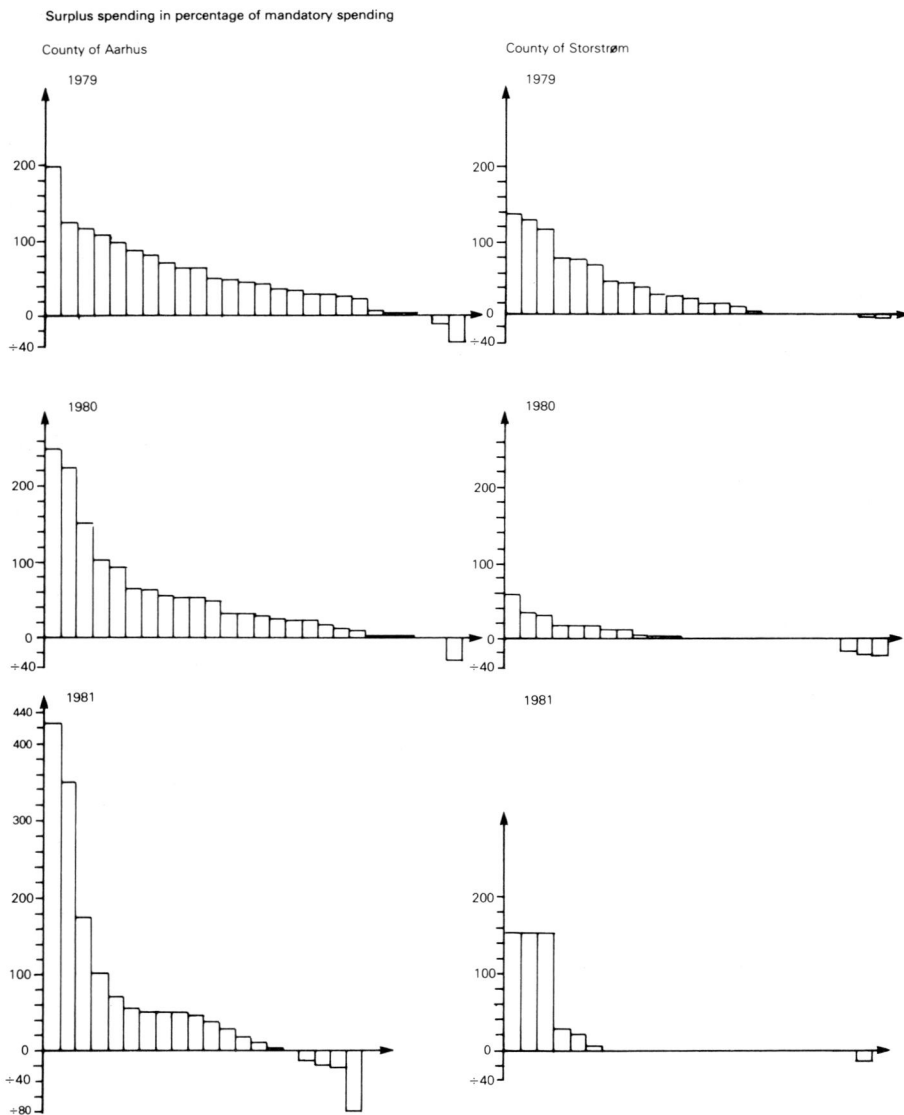

Surplus spending in percentage of mandatory spending

the ministries of Education and Labor. Within both ministries a special departmental unit for providing employment-measures developed the YGP and coordinated the implementation. Other important actors within these ministries have been the Directorate of Vocational Training under the Department of Education and the Directorate of Labor Market Training, which planned the short labor market courses, and the Directorate of Labor, which is the central authority for the employment service. The latter two directorates are subordinate to the Department of Labor.

The interorganizational network of the central and regional authorities is simplified in Figure 7. Two important dimensions of conflict can be identified: (i) the regional actors vs. the central actors; and (ii) the central special employment agencies and the regional actors vs. the two directorates for training. The regional actors have in principle been very willing to participate in the experimental program and to be pilot districts, but they have been very dissatisfied both with the state block-grant offered for the YGP (Dkr. 25 million in 1980, Dkr. 67 million in 1981) and with the planned capacity of the Vocational Training and the Labor Market Courses (short training courses). Concerning the special block-grant, the regional authorities have maintained that it was too small because the target group was larger than expected. This demand was rejected, but the ministries allowed the pilot districts to remove the absolute guarantee obligation so that the target group was only to be given jobs or training 'to the extent to which it was practically and economically possible'. Consequently, the county of Aarhus was allowed to reduce its target group by removing the shorter-term unemployed. In practice financial constraints forced the county of Storstrøm to do the same.

As to the vocational and labor market training, both dimensions of conflict are relevant. The regional actors maintained that it was necessary to increase the capacity more than planned in order to fulfill the education goals of the program. The special central employment agencies supported this demand because they were eager to implement the YG-program, whereas the training directorates were very reluctant. This reflects a traditional conflict between ordinary educational and labor market measures and employment measures. The training directorates' core clientele and main interests comprise groups of people other than the unemployed and weak target group of the YGP and other special employment programs. The interests of the core groups are supported and reinforced by the interest groups of the Employers' Association and the trade unions, who are represented in several important central committees. It is a Danish tradition that no policy concerning vocational or labor market training is made without acceptance by these interest groups.

The Directorates were very skeptical about the YGP, and they were unwilling to enhance the training capacity more in the pilot counties than in other counties. Nevertheless the Directorate of Labor Market Training accepted a large capacity increase and the other Directorate accepted a small one after the Ministers had offered them special grants for that purpose.

Figure 7: *Central and regional interorganizational networks in planning, resource-mobilization and control*

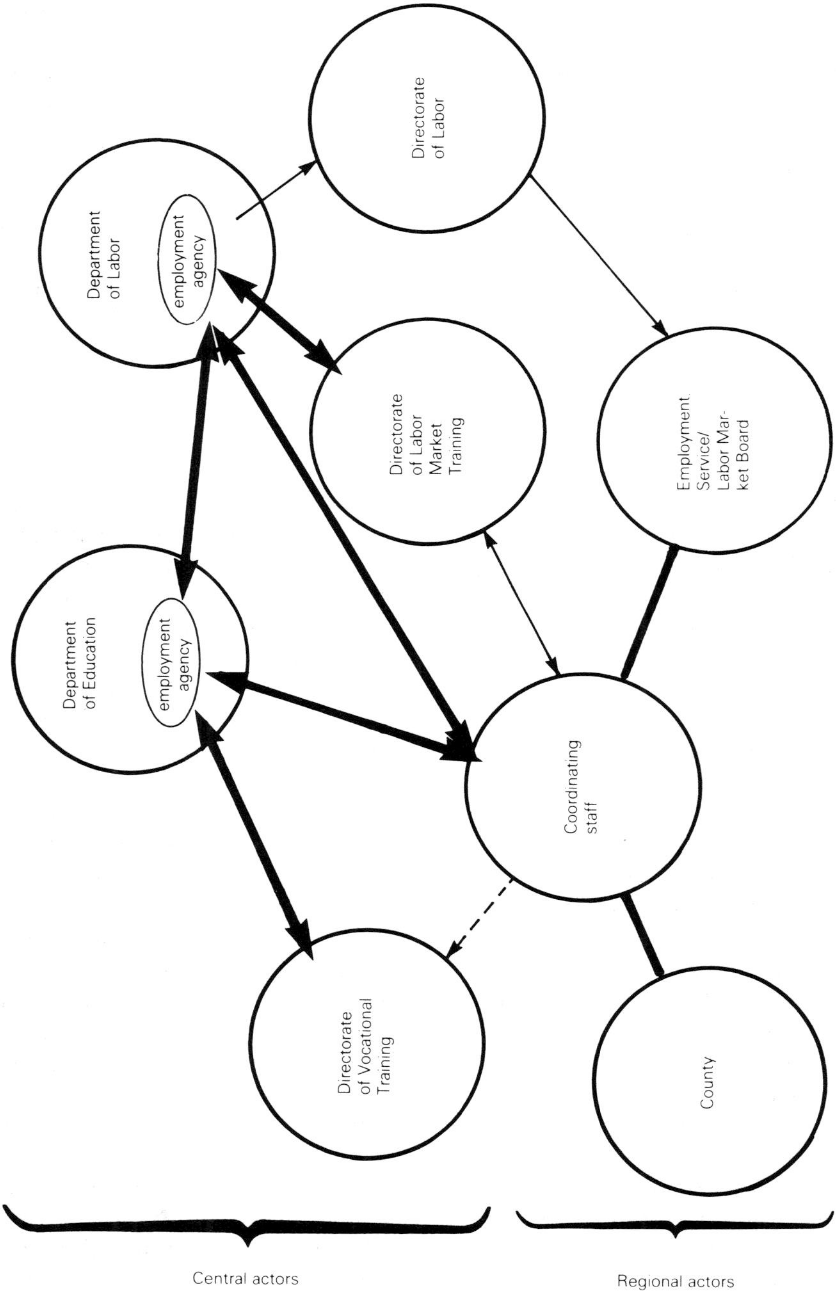

Central actors   Regional actors

Even though the negotiations in connection with state training capacity have been rather dramatic, the delivery consequences of the reluctance of the state have apparently been less significant than maintained by the regional authorities. A larger capacity would hardly have been sufficient to motivate substantially more YGP-clients for education because of the demotivating factors treated in a previous section. In fact, both the central and the regional authorities had so little information about the size of the target group and its preferences concerning types of education, training and jobs that reliable planning was indeed very difficult.

In the central-regional negotiations, the central authorities tried to persuade the counties to increase their own capacity for training assistant nurses, but in vain. The counties pressed the central authorities to increase the state capacity, but did not increase their own capacity for the most popular training with the best employment prospects.

Concluding Remarks

In this study we have used a bottom-up implementation perspective. We have constructed a model containing factors that may affect the behavior of street-level bureaucrats in solving problems according to the goals of the government. It is our hope that this model may be fruitful for studying implementation particularly of social or human services policies.

The central variables of the model — which affect the street-level bureaucrats' implementation conditions and thus help explain the extent to which the goals are reached — are: (i) the *social environment* of the implementing structure which is both the target of the policy and affects the implementation itself; (ii) the *division of labor and cooperation* in the pool of implementing organizations; (iii) the *interaction of competitive, convergent or alternative policy programs*; (iv) the *delivery-level capacity* concerning the measures and the capacity of the street-level bureaucrats themselves; and (v) the *planning, mobilization of resources and control* of the program.

The model has been applied to the implementation of Danish youth employment policy, in particular a pilot program called the Youth Guarantee program (YGP). The program has been successful in defining and reaching the target group. Eighty per cent (compared to earlier only 20 per cent) of the group have been reached, though often rather late. The program has also been successful in offering employment measures, though mostly in the public sector, which have been given a low priority in the program. However, the important goal of getting the clients into education or training has not been met. About 60 per cent of the clients return to unemployment after finishing their participation in the program.

Using the above implementation model, we have found that both the new administrative structure with its clearer division of labor and formalized cooperation and work procedures as well as the planning and mobilization of resources have been of considerable help in the implementation of the goals of the YGP, even though some mechanisms also hamper implementation. In particular, the structure and procedures and the processes of planning and mobilization of resources are responsible for the fact that a very high proportion of the target group has come into contact with the program and that it has been possible to give a temporary employment offer to almost all clients who wanted it.

The instruments and incentives of the program have, however, been insufficient to motivate the *social environment* to change its 'behavior' as expected. It has been impossible to get more than a tiny group of youngsters into further education or vocational training — which had the highest program priority — because the instruments used in searching out participants, guidance, education and training are not sufficient to motivate the youngsters. They are demotivated because of maintenance problems and insufficient economic support during further education and training and because of a justified fear of being unable to complete a vocational training course due to lack of practice places.

The capacity of practice places and jobs in the private sector has been smaller than expected. Even though both are heavily subsidized, it has been difficult to motivate employers to offer practice places and jobs. It has been even more difficult to channel the youngsters onto employment after they have completed their nine-month participation in the program since subsequent employment is not subsidized. The economic crisis of the private enterprises has affected the program by increasing the target group, decreasing the number of vacant jobs, and raising the number of competitive and qualified applicants for the existing vacancies. It has also been difficult to overcome employers' myths about possible incapability of persons who are clients of special employment programs.

The YGP has not been implemented in a vacuum and the implementation has been much affected by the interaction of different programs for employment. The YGP has suffered by having to compete for jobs with another program intended to help workers in receipt of unemployment relief, but it has also hampered implementation of other programs, such as programs for rehabilitation.

Because of their heavy workload many street-level bureaucrats have made use of various conscious or unconscious coping mechanisms such as setting priorities, passing clients on to other authorities, rationing services, standardizing clients and routinizing procedures. This phenomenon has also been shown in the studies of Lipsky and Weatherley. But it is probable that these activities, which are often distorting the original goals, have only affected implementation marginally. Apparently the most important variable is the social environment. The main implementation problem lies in the lack of sufficient incentives to encourage the alternation of the social environment.

Notes

1   This is a revised version of a paper, 'Local Implementation of Youth Employment Policy in Denmark' delivered at the 1981 Annual Meeting of the American Political Science Association, in a panel on 'The Capacity of Government to Regulate and Deliver Services at the Grass-Roots', and at a seminar of the International Work Group on Policy Implementation at University of Harvard, 1981. The article is largely based upon WINTER S. in cooperation with HADRUP S., HERMANSEN F., HUMENIUK J. and KRABSEN D., (1982) *Administrationen of ungdomsgarantiforsøget.* (The Implementation of the Youth Guarantee Program), Copenhagen, Ministry of Labor, Ministry of the Interior and Ministry of Education.

2   ELMORE R.F., (1979–80) 'Backward mapping: Implementation research and policy decisions', *Political Science Quarterly,* pp. 601–16; ELMORE R.F., (1978) 'Organizational models of social program implementation', *Public Policy,* pp. 185–228; HJERN, B. (1978) *Implementation and Network Analysis,* Discussion Paper, Berlin, International Institute of Management.

3   SIMON, H. (1947) *Administrative Behavior,* New York; HJERN, B. (1978) *op. cit.*

4   ELMORE, R.F. (1979–80), *op. cit.*, p. 603.

5   *Ibid.*

6   LIPSKY, M. (1980) *Street-Level Bureaucracy: Dilemmas of the Individual in Public Services,* New York; WEATHERLEY, R. and LIPSKY, M. (1977) 'Street-level bureaucrats and institutional innovation: Implementing special education reform', *Harvard Education Review,* pp. 171–97; WEATHERLEY, R. (1979) *Reforming Special Education. Policy Implementation from State Level to Street Level,* Cambridge, MA; PROTTAS, J.M. (1979) *People-Processing. The Street-level Bureaucrat in Public Service Bureaucracies,* Massachussetts, ELMORE, R.F. (1978) and (1979–80); *op. cit.*, HJERN, B. (1978) *op. cit.*; and HANF, K. HJERN B. and PORTER, D. (1978) 'Implementation of manpower training: Local administrative networks in the FRG and Sweden', in HANF K. and SCHARPF, F.W. (Eds.), *Interorganizational Policy-Making: Limits to Coordination and Central Control,* London.

7   See note 6.

8   ELMORE, R.F. (1979–80); *op. cit.*, HJERN, B. (1978) *op. cit.*; HJERN B. and PORTER D.O., (1979) *Implementation Structure: A New Unit of Administrative Analysis,* Discussion Paper, I.I.M., W-Berlin; HJERN B. and HULL C., (1980) *Coordination and Control in the Mixed Economy: Implementation Structures as a Way of Getting at What's Going on Out There,* Discussion Papers, I.I.M., W-Berlin.

9   WINTER S., (forthcoming) *The Implementation of a Decentralization Reform: Danish Disablement Pension Policy,* Aarhus, Institute of Political Science, University of Aarhus, in *Scandinavian Political Studies.*

10 HULL C., (1981) 'Report on the ECPR-workshop on "Implementation Seen from the Bottom Up"', *E.C.P.R. News Circular,* 40, June, pp. 44–6; HJERN, B. (1978) *op. cit.*; HJERN B. and PORTER, D.O. (1979) *op. cit.*; HJERN B. and HULL, C. (1980) *op. cit.*

11 ELMORE, R.F. (1979–80), *op. cit.*, pp. 604 and 612.

12 Thanks to Professor Jerome Murphy, Harvard Education School, who has given me valuable comments on this point.

13 LIPSKY, M. (1980) *op. cit.*; WEATHERLEY R. and LIPSKY, M. (1977) *op. cit.*; WEATHERLEY, R. (1979) *op. cit..*

Søren Winter

14 HJERN, B. (1978) *op. cit.*; HJERN, B. and PORTER, D.O. (1979) *op. cit.*; HJERN, B. and HULL, C. (1980) *op. cit.*; HULL C. (1981) *op. cit.*

15 ELMORE, R.F. (1979–80). *op. cit.*,

16 WINTER, S. (1981) *Den sociale markarbejder og de politiske mål: Faktorer der hæmmer målrealiseringen* (The Social Welfare Street-Level Bureaucrats and the Political Goals: Factors that Hamper Implementation), Aarhus, University of Aarhus, p. 5; WINTER, S. *et al.* (1982), *op. cit.*, pp. 8–14.

17 *Preliminary Note on experiments with a YOUTH GUARANTEE SCHEME, 22 November 1979, the Ministry of Labour and the Ministry of Education, Denmark, 1980.*

18 *Ibid.*, p. 7; WINTER, S. *et al.* (1982), *op. cit.*, pp. 28–39.

19 A much more detailed analysis of the implementation can be seen in WINTER, S. *et al.*, (1982) *op. cit.*

20 ELMORE R.F. (1981) *Backward Mapping and Youth Employment*, Seattle Institute for Public Policy and Management, University of Washington, pp. 4–7.

21 The reason for this limitation is purely pragmatic: to make the job manageable and because the teaching and training functions are evaluated in other evaluation studies using sociological psychological and pedagogical methodologies.

22 On 13 September 1983 $ 1 = 9.58 D.kr.

23 ELMORE, R.F. (1979–80) and (1981); *op. cit.*, and ELMORE's chapter in this volume.

24 In the county of Aarhus the employment secretariat is also responsible for follow-up activities, while this is the job of the employment service in the county of Storstrøm.

25 HJERN, B. and PORTER, D.O. (1979) *op. cit.*

26 HJERN B. and HULL C. (1980), *op. cit.*; HULL, C. (1981) *op. cit.*

27 WEATHERLEY R. and LIPSKY, M. (1977) *op. cit.*; ELMORE, R.F. (1978) and (1979–80); *op. cit.*, WEATHERLEY, R. (1979) *op. cit.*; WILLIAMS W., (1980) *The Implementation Perspective*, Berkeley/Los Angeles, pp. 94–7; LIPSKY, M. (1980) *op. cit.*; WINTER, S. (1981) *op. cit.*, pp. 16–31.

28 WEATHERLEY R. and LIPSKY, M. (1977) *op. cit.*; LIPSKY, M. (1980) *op. cit.*

29 WEATHERLEY R. and LIPSKY, M. (1977) *op. cit.*; WEATHERLEY, R. (1979) *op. cit.*; LIPSKY, M. (1980) *op. cit.*; ELMORE, R.F. (1978) and (1979–80); *op. cit.*, WINTER, S. (1981) *op. cit.*

30 WINTER, S. (1980) *op. cit.*, pp. 12–14; WINTER, S. (1982), pp. 18–19.

31 MARCH and SIMON, (1958) *Organizations*, New York pp. 185–6.

32 HANF, K., HJERN, B. and PORTER D. (1978) *op. cit.*; HJERN, B. (1978) *op. cit.*; HJERN, B. and PORTER, D.O. (1979) *op. cit.*; HJERN B. and HULL, C. (1980) *op. cit.*

Youth Unemployment in the Federal Republic of Germany: Are the West Germans Better Off?

Peter Dehnbostel and Einhard Rau

Background Data

During the 1970s the labor market crisis in the Federal Republic of Germany was interpreted as a temporary problem, primarily influenced by economic fluctuations.

Faced by an enormous rise of youth unemployment, the federal government expressed the expectation in January 1975 that youth unemployment would be reduced by measures to stimulate the economy, which would lead to economic recovery. Youth unemployment wasn't seen — at least not in the long run — as a continuous and structural problem.

In the meantime it has become obvious that youth unemployment must

Table 1: Unemployed and unemployed youth in the Federal Republic of Germany 1974–1983 (end of September)

Year	Unemployed		Unemployed youth under 20 years of age		Unemployed youth 20 to 25 years of age	
	Total (in 1000)	Rate	Total (in 1000)	Rate	Total (in 1000)	Rate
1974	556.9	2.4	69.8	3.6	88.3	3.3
1975	1,006.5	4.4	115.8	6.2	171.6	6.5
1976	898.3	3.9	102.6	4.6	154.5	6.0
1977	911.3	4.0	105.9	5.0	161.9	6.2
1978	864.2	3.8	92.0	4.4	153.9	5.8
1979	737.0	3.2	68.6	3.1	123.7	4.5
1980	823.0	3.5	81.1	3.5	143.5	5.1
1981	1,256.0	5.4	135.4	5.9	239.6	8.5
1982	1,820.0	7.5	187.2	8.7	356.0	11.5
1983	2,109.8	9.1	192.0	9.1	420.0	13.3

Source: Federal Labor Institute

be seen as an entirely structural issue. Today most predictions are that the labor market crisis and youth unemployment will last until the year 2000 and probably longer. The high unemployment rates of the last ten years — only in the early fifties and in 1967 were unemployment figures higher than 1 per cent — mainly affect younger people.

The Federal Labor Institute's official numbers continuously show new record high unemployment figures. This trend was stopped only for a very short period just before 1980, due to a temporary economic recovery (see table 1).

In most industrialized western countries, the situation is comparable to the Federal Republic of Germany.

In June of 1982, youth unemployment (as a part of total unemployment) showed the following proportions in the countries of the European Community (EC):

	%
Italy	49.3
Netherlands	45.6
Luxembourg	44.6
France	39.6
Great Britain	38.5
Belgium	34.7
Ireland	29.0
Denmark	28.9
Federal Republic of Germany	23.0
Greece	(not available)

Thirty-eight per cent of the more than 11 million unemployed in the European Community were younger than 25 years of age.

Table 2:   Total unemployment and proportions of youth unemployment in the countries of the EC (June 1984)

Country	Unemployed		Unemployed youth under the age of 25	
	Total (in 1000)	Rate	Total (in 1000)	Rate
Italy	2,914.5	12.9	1,404.8	48.2
Netherlands	815.9	14.6	317.0	38.9
Luxembourg	2.3	1.4	1.0	44.9
France	2,147.7	9.4	834.3	8.8
Great Britain	3,029.7	11.5	1,152.5	38.0
Belgium	545.7	13.4	168.8	30.9
Ireland	211.0	16.6	66.1	31.3
Denmark	244.9	9.2	60.9	24.9
Federal Republic of Germany	2,112.6	7.8	502.4	23.8
Greece	52.1	1.4	–	–
Total	12,076.4	10.4	4,507.9	37.5

Source: Statistical Office of the European Communities (eurostat.) 1984

An additional problem is long-term unemployment for young people, a problem which is growing continuously. In September of 1982, more than 37 per cent of all unemployed young people were jobless for more than twelve months. June 1984 showed the picture (see table 2).

The figures for 1982 and 1984 show — compared to the other industrialized western countries — relatively modest unemployment rates for young people. Many observers in the Federal Republic as well as in other countries are referring to the dual system of vocational education as a factor to explain the slightly better situation in the Federal Republic of Germany.

We shall explain the main ideas which constitute the dual system of vocational education. After that we shall analyze youth unemployment in the FRG in greater detail.

The Dual System of Vocational Education

The dual system of vocational education provides a connection between training in a firm (apprenticeship) and in vocational schools. In addition to the practical training, the apprentice is obliged to attend vocational school for eight to twelve hours a week. The school offers some general education as well as theoretical aspects of the vocation he or she is learning. The public school system and the privately organized system of apprenticeship share in the training of the youth.

Primarily the dual system deals with training, but beyond that it intends to introduce the young apprentice to working life and his or her future position in society.

A comparable training structure can be found in Austria and Switzerland. The dual system of vocational education for many years trains the major part of the relevant age group. Most younger people start their training between 15 and 17 years of age, directly after finishing basic or intermediate school (Haupt- und Realschule) (nine to ten years of schooling).

Those who cannot get an apprenticeship or who continue their schooling start their training some time later.

Generally speaking vocational training in the Federal Republic of Germany differentiates six fields of training: commerce and industry, trade, agriculture, public service, liberal professions and home economics.

Between 80 and 90 per cent of all apprenticeships are finished in the fields of commerce and industry and trade.

The training received in the firms can differ. It depends on the highly differentiated structures, the diverse sizes, the different products and services of the firms which train the young people. The training is more or less on-the-job training, which means that a large number of firms conduct production-oriented training with no attention to systematic and more general prerequisites of learning and training.

Efforts to systematize vocational training in the firms, and to generally improve the qualifications of the apprentices, led in 1969 to a Vocational Education Law and training regulations for several occupations. This law which was passed after many years of debates, stipulates uniform training in the firms. It regulates, among other things, the apprentice's rights and obligations, defines the instructor's necessary qualifications, systemizes the training's duration and content, formulates standards for the necessary equipment of training firms and the examinations at the end of the apprenticeship. The law's general purpose is the realization of broad and comprehensive basic vocational training and the laying of foundations for a qualified future job with all necessary skills and useful perspectives.

The training regulations for officially accredited occupations (Ausbildungs-ordnungen) are of central importance for the dual system. They are mandatory for the occupational training in a firm. They determine the content and the duration of the required training and are thus an important instrument for the realization of systematic training, independent of regional, divisional or economical peculiarities in a certain firm. Continuous adjustments to technological, social and economical changes are intended.

At the end of 1983, there were 434 offically accredited occupations in the Federal Republic of Germany. Between 1969 and 1984, 142 training regulations (for 176 occupations) had been put into effect. Approximately 900,000 apprentices were affected. That means that more than 50 per cent of all apprentices are trained according to the new regulations.

But there are still quite a number of firms — mostly in the trades — which cannot meet the training requirements as they are stated by the Vocational Education Law and the training regulations. They are too small, too specialized and/or don't have qualified instructors. But ways have been found to solve these problems. These small firms share their resources for the training of their apprentices, who get their training in different firms. Sometimes they build a joint workshop for vocational training and can thus guarantee broad not too specialized training. With such an arrangement, their training efforts can be compared with the traditional high quality training which the big firms in the FRG offer. The federal government and some state (Länder) governments encourage the installation and fund the financing of such joint workshops.

The other part of the dual system — the vocational school — is controlled by the school regulations of the different states (Länder) of the Federal Republic of Germany. The vocational school is a part of the public school system. In principle, all apprentices are obliged to visit a vocational school. The firms are obliged to grant the necessary time for schooling which takes place once or twice a week for eight to twelve hours, sometimes even in a coherent and longer time span.

Vocationally-oriented and general education courses are given at these schools. A connection to the training firms is intended. School curricula and training regulations are approved state-wide. Some states equate the vocational school's and the training firm's final examinations with the intermediate degree of the intermediate school (Realschule), which opens prospects for more advanced careers.

In general the vocational school is — compared with the training in a firm — in a relatively weak position. A major reason for this is the fact that the chambers of commerce conduct the intermediate and final vocational training examinations. The school curricula play a minor role.

The apprentice spends much more time at the firm than in the vocational school. But most important is that the supply of apprenticeships follows market conditions, which means that the individual firm decides if an apprentice will be hired and — if this is the case — which applicant will be the lucky one to get the apprenticeship.

Educational reform efforts in the early 1970s directed towards the vocational school and vocational education in general and intended to equate both parts of the dual system failed. In particular, the attempts to subsede the first year of training by a basic vocational education year (Berufsgrundbildungsjahr) were unsuccessful. Plans to integrate general and vocational education and to strengthen the role of the vocational school were blocked.

These plans were based on theoretical as well as political assumptions. Theories of vocational education boosted the abolition of the separation of vocational and general education. Politically, the plans were interpreted as ways to improve equal opportunities in the educational system as well as for future life.

Youth Unemployment and The Dual System

Being a political issue, it is obvious that opinions and assessments concerning the efficiency of the dual system differ. The present conservative government and industry point to the Federal Republic's relatively favorable position. The system has dealt quite well with the problems of unemployment, and has been able to increase the number of training positions for youth continuously in recent years. The number of apprenticeships has been raised from 1.269

Table 3: Apprenticeships and number of applicants without apprenticeships 1976–1983 (end of September)

Year	Apprenticeships	Open apprenticeships	Applicants with no apprenticeship
1976	495,800	18,100	27,700
1977	558,400	25,500	27,000
1978	601,700	22,300	23,800
1979	640,300	36,900	19,700
1980	650,000	44,600	17,300
1981	605,636	37,348	22,140
1982	631,366	19,995	34,180
1983	677,698	19,641	47,408

Source: Federal Ministry of Education and Science

million in 1970 to 1.676 million at the end of 1982. The year 1980 showed a record high of 1.715 million apprenticeships. The numbers are still increasing. In 1983 677,698 apprentices and in 1984 more than 700,000 apprentices had started their training (see table 3).

Critics of the dual system, primarily labor unions, argue against this and emphasize the failure of the traditional structure of vocational education. They criticize the lowering of training standards, useless qualifications and above all the growing number of youth who can't get an adequate vocational training. Official numbers for 1983 show that 47,408 younger people could not start training. Thirty thousand more continued school because of the shortage of training positions. The labor union's own projections for 1983 show nearly 200,000 young people without a training position and assume that the private economy is not willing or able to supply the necessary number of apprenticeships. Because of that, they doubt that the market principle is a successful means of solving the problem of the labor market, the ability to adjust demand and supply.

The year 1984, too, shows a further expansion of applicants and a still growing number of unsuccessful applicants. Preliminary statistical data point to more than 70,000 applicants who will not get a training position. This number does not include those who, because of the shortage, choose to stay in school.

It is probably right that the real unemployment figures are much higher than the officially published numbers. Statistical inconsistencies and publicly-funded arrangements for temporary training and education programs cover up the real dimensions of youth unemployment.

In view of the different assessments on the efficiency of the dual system, it is difficult to reach a final conclusion on the system's value for the necessary supply of training positions. But beyond this question, there is a consensus on two problems which are closely connected with the dual system on the one hand and the dimensions and consequences of youth unemployment on the other. These are the quality and the financing of vocational training.

The quality of training has an enormous influence on future job perspectives. Another important factor for future employment is the field in which the apprentice gets his training.

Economic developments and labor-market conditions determine the repartition of apprenticeships and training positions to the different fields (see table 4). The situation in the trades is very peculiar. A high proportion of apprentices is absorbed by the trades in times of economic crisis and high unemployment. This was the case in the 1950s and can also be seen nowadays.

In 1970, only one-third of all apprentices went into the trades and more than a half into the field of industry and commerce. In 1982 these rates expanded to nearly 40 per cent for the trades and were reduced to 45 per cent in industry and commerce. A far-reaching, serious problem arising from these circumstances follows from the fact that only a small part of all apprentices in the trades can find a job in the occupation for which they have been trained.

Table 4: Number of apprenticeships and their dissemination in different fields of training 1972–1982

Year	Apprenticeships (total in 1000)	Percentage apprenticeships in fields of training				
		Industry/Commerce	Trades	Agriculture	Public Service	Other
1972	1,301.4	55.5	33.3	2.1	2.3	6.8
1974	1,330.0	50.5	36.5	2.1	3.5	7.9
1976	1,316.6	46.5	38.8	2.8	3.3	8.6
1978	1,517.4	45.6	40.5	3.0	3.4	7.5
1980	1,715.5	45.9	40.9	2.7	3.1	7.3
1981	1,676.9	46.0	40.2	2.8	3.2	7.8
1982	1,675.9	45.6	39.7	3.0	3.5	8.2

Source: Federal Statistical Office

Table 5: Development of unemployment for bakers, butchers and pastry cooks 1979–1982

Year	Bakers	Butchers	Pastry cooks
1979	2,060	1,322	641
1980	2,611	1,572	750
1981	4,461	2,948	1,277
1982	7,796	6,014	2,504

Source: Official Newsletter of the Federal Labor Institute, March 1983

That means that the number of apprenticeships is in excess of the future need of the trades. Newly trained butchers, bakers and joiners, for example, become jobless and enlarge the group of unemployed youth (see table 1). A few examples may illustrate this kind of erroneous planning and inappropriate training which steadily increased in recent years. The number of apprenticeships for bakers, butchers and in hotel and catering industry grew enormously during these years. At the same time the numbers of unemployed butchers, bakers and pastry cooks were also steadily growing (see table 5).

The absurdity of an intensified training for these occupations is obvious. Equally important is the fact that in September of 1982, 62 per cent of all unemployed bakers and pastry cooks were under 25 years of age. These occupations even show high rates of change of occupation. They are significantly higher than average. This change is normally for the worse. In the early 1980s, more than 40 per cent of all trained bakers and pastry cooks and 50 per cent of the butchers worked in less qualified occupations. The low quality training in these occupations further complicates a positive change.

A comparable situation can be detected in agriculture and some highly sought occupations such as hairdresser and medical assistant.

It is hardly an exaggeration to state that the dual system in recent years has produced future employment and re-education problems. The extent of the inadequacy and wrong training comes from the overall unfavorable development of the demand and supply of training positions.

Table 6:   Supply and demand of training positions in firms 1976–1983 (end of September)

| Year | Supply | | Demand | | Supply/ Demand Relation |
	Number	Increase as against the year before (%)	Number	Increase as against the year before (%)	
1976	513,900	6.9	523,500	7.4	98.1
1977	583,900	13.7	585,400	11.8	99.7
1978	624,000	6.8	625,500	7.3	99.3
1979	677,237	8.5	660,024	5.1	102.5
1980	694,605	2.6	667,335	1.1	104.1
1981	642,984	−7.4	627,776	−5.9	102.4
1982	651,212	1.3	667,048	6.3	97.6
1983	697,339	7.1	725,106	9.0	96.2

Source: Federal Ministry for Education and Science, Vocational Training Reports of different years.

Until 1974, the beginning of the labor market crisis, the supply of training positions exceeded the demand by 30 to 40 per cent. But the following years showed a remarkable change (see table 6).

The worsening of supply and demand relations reduced the variety of occupational choices for many young people. That led to a more intensified drain of less qualified firms, which was further sharpened by the reduction of training positions in larger firms, factories and plants better equipped for the training of apprentices. Table 4 verifies these tendencies and the consequences which follow these developments, namely the reduction of training positions in industry and commerce and an expansion in the trades and agriculture. Many observers attribute this situation to structural inconsistencies of the dual system.

The undisputed quantitative growth of the number of available training positions could only be realized at the cost of the quality of vocational training. It has been already mentioned that dequalification leads to an increase of unemployment. From that one can draw a rather paradoxical conclusion. Unemployment and especially youth unemployment isn't only a consequence of reduced training positions but can be affected by the increase of those positions, too.

There are two main reasons for this rather strange development.

One is the demographic increase in the demand for training positions, the other is connected with the financing of vocational training. Different training costs influence the supply of positions.

The high quality training in the larger firms, in industry and big business is much more expensive than the training in the smaller shops of the trades. In times of recession, the smaller firms tend to hire apprentices as relatively inexpensive workers while industry and commerce try to economize on costs by reducing the number of apprenticeships. Is there a way to solve such a problem?

Various models and concepts have been discussed. Most important seems the idea 'of a general levy on all firms to provide funds to finance training positions in those firms that were prepared to conduct training'. (Dohnany, (1976) p. 56). In 1976, the federal government proposed legislation 'providing that if, in the previous year, the supply of apprenticeships exceeded the demand by less than 12.5 per cent a levy would be imposed on all firms that were not training and were of a certain minimum size' (*ibid.*).

The bill was rejected and even a modified bill which would have affected only a very small number of firms was, though enacted, heavily criticized by industry and the trades. The bill was suspended by the Federal Court (Bundesverfassungsgericht in 1980).

But even today there are many experts in the fields who still favor the idea of a levy as a way to raise the supply of training positions, to improve the quality of vocational training and to rectify the failures of the dual system.

Hidden Youth Unemployment

The real extent of youth unemployment in the FRG is difficult to detect. Inadequate statistics and a number of programs which provide employment for young people without vocational training and without a job distort the unemployment figures. Various institutes have calculated figures which were two to three times higher than those which are officially published.

The Federal Labor Institute is the only institution which each year provides statistical information on youth unemployment.

Legally defined, an unemployed person is without employment but available for placement.

For various reasons, the Institute's figures for training positions and unemployed are incomplete. For instance only those who state their demand for a training position at one of the 142 labor offices are registered. That means that all those looking on their own for a training position are not covered by official demand figures.

If such efforts are successful they will be covered later, together with all those who have found an apprenticeship with the help of a labor office. But those who have met with failure will never be registered.

Youth unemployment figures are likewise incomplete. A look at unemployed youth under the age of 20 registered in September of each year shows that various groups of youth are not covered by the official statistics. Here again we can detect those who look for a training position without the help of labor offices. Others live at home or work in their parent's firm.

A very important group are foreign youths, children of migrant workers. There are estimated to be up to 100,000 foreign youths without a job and not registered. Applicants for training positions are not registered as unemployed. The same holds true for unemployed who take part in vocational rehabilitation programs, temporary employment programs and further schooling.

The basic training courses financed by the Federal Labor Institute, the vocational preparation year (Berufsvorbereitungsjahr), the basic vocational

Table 7:   Participation of youth in programs avoiding unemployment 1975–1982 (in 1000)

Year	Intermediate technical school first year	Basic vocational education year	Vocational preparation year	Basic training courses	Total
1975	167	21	9	24	221
1976	171	24	20	36	251
1977	186	34	25	35	280
1978	202	47	40	32	321
1979	206	59	45	28	338
1980	204	63	46	30	343
1981	212	78	46	34	372
1982	229	83	47	35	395

Source: Federal Ministry for Education and Science

education year (Berufsgrundbildungsjahr) and the intermediate technical school (Berudfsfachschule) are popular alternatives for young people looking for a way out of the misery of unemployment (see table 7).

The table's figures show the enormous rise of participation in temporary programs between 1975 and 1982.

There can be no doubt that this expansion is a consequence of the inadequate supply of training positions. Several studies showed that the overwhelming majority of all pupils in the basic vocational education year, more than 50 per cent of all participants in the vocational preparation year and 20 per cent of the intermediate technical school's pupils had preferred a vocational training in a firm. This exemplifies the equivocal aspects of these programs. The participant's chances for a training position after they have completed these programs are rarely improved. The programs are more or less a 'dead-end street'.

The basic vocational education year was central to all plans to develop the system of vocational training. Following regulations in the 1969 Vocational Education Law, the basic vocational education year is supposed to guarantee a well-rounded basic vocational training conducted by the vocational schools, that is, independent of the efficiency measures of the firms.

The basic training was meant to improve mobility and flexibility, to provide some experience in a broader occupational field and to lay the foundations for a second and third year of more specialized training in the firms as well as in school.

In the general context of educational reform in the Federal Republic of Germany, the basic vocational education year was seen as a first step to integrate vocational and general education.

Mainly because of employer opposition, these plans could not be realized, The employers feared that the basic vocational education year would be the first step to the nationalization of vocational training and the abolishment of the dual system. These apprehensions are only conclusive insofar as the reduction of the employers' monopolisitic influence on the quantity and quality of vocational training was intended.

A kind of compromise is a modified version of the basic vocational education year which leaves — similar to the first year of vocational training in the dual system — the practical training to the firms.

About 15 per cent of all participants in the basic vocational education year (= 20 per cent of all apprentices) take part in the modified version. Only for a minor part of those is the basic year equated with the first year of vocational training in the dual system.

The original conception and idea of the basic year has, because of a number of legal, curricular and organizational modifications, disappeared. Today, its main purpose is to keep unemployed and untrained youth off the streets.

The vocational preparation year had been directed from the start against youth unemployment. Most states (Länder) of the Federal Republic of Germany make participation obligatory for those who, at the end of compulsory schooling don't begin vocational training or those who go on in school. The participants in the vocational preparation year have the opportunity to take the short-course secondary school exam (Hauptschulabschluß) during the year and to proceed to the basic vocational education year after they successfully completed the vocational preparation year. Nevertheless it cannot be interpreted as a really preparatory program. Only 30 to 40 per cent of all participants start a vocational training following the preparation year.

The Federal Labor Institute's measures for vocational preparation have existed since 1969. At first these measures were intended for handicapped youths. In the mid- and late 1970s, the measures were expanded and aimed at the reduction of youth unemployment. They were carried out by labor offices, welfare offices, employers organizations, labor unions and others. Their main goal is the preparation of younger people for vocational training and working life. Normally they run for one year. The proportion of youth who start an accredited vocational training following the preparation measures is steadily declining whereas in 1972 it had been 50 per cent, in 1982 it was only 27 per cent. So, it is no exaggeration to state that these measures as well as the vocational preparation year and the basic vocational education year are rather ineffective, due to the low quality of training.

All in all, it can be said that the government activities described above are not adequate measures to provide vocational training for young people, or at least to clear the ground for qualified vocational perspectives. Rather, they are measures to temporarily reduce the demand for training positions and means of concealing the real extent of youth unemployment.

Conclusion

We've tried to demonstrate that the official numbers of youth unemployment in the Federal Republic of Germany are much lower than in reality. The real extent of youth unemployment is not documented because of the incomplete countings and inadequate methodology. Beyond that, we've showed that the various programs for youth without work and training positions are hiding the authentic size of youth unemployment.

The fact that in 1982 the number of 187,214 officially registered unemployed under 20 years of age must be supplemented by those 395,000 which took part in the various programs (see tables 1 and 7) is proof of this. It further proves the dual system's limited capacity to provide sufficient training positions and workplaces.

It is indisputable that the dual system of vocational education has a number of advantages. Compared with other countries and other training systems, it provides a successful transfer into working life for a relatively great number of young people. Even so, is it indisputable that the dual system expanded greatly in recent years and provided many training positions. The insignificant degree of bureaucratization, independence from public funding and nearness to the reality of the industrial praxis are important benefits of the dual system.

However, growing discrepancies show the weakness of the system as well. We have described the increasing dequalification and the paradoxical situation that an increase in training positions leads to higher unemployment for young people. We blamed this development on the financing of vocational education and stressed the point that only a general levy can secure a qualified supply of training positions independent of economic recessions and upswings.

A look into the future leaves the observer sceptical. Even if the demand for training positions declines because of demographic developments during the second half of the 1980s, the main reason for youth unemployment, the general labor market crisis, will last. All projections are that structural long lasting unemployment will last until the 1990s, perhaps even until the year 2000. Rationalization, automatization and high technolgy claim new qualifications and new working conditions and it is feared that these factors will even lead to further growth of youth unemployment.

Getting control of youth unemployment demands a reform of vocational training as well as modifications of the dual system.

The abolishment of the dual system is not the point!

As we have tried to emphasize, it really has some advantages. But the necessary reform must be more than a measure against youth unemployment.

The main point is the youths' fundamental right for a high quality vocational training and future perspectives for working life. And, not least, the realization of this right is a prerequisite for the future social, political and economical developments in German society.

References

AMTLICHE NACHRICHTEN der BUNDESANSTALT für ARBEIT (ANBA) verschiedene Jahrgänge.

Ausbildungsplatzförderungsgesetz (APIFG) v.7.9.1979.In: Bundesgesetzblatt I,S.2658

ARBEITSFÖRDERUNGSGESETZ (AFG) v.25.6.1969.In: Bundesgesetzblatt I,S.582, in der Fassung des Arbeitsförderungs — Konsolidierungsgesetzes v.22.12.1981.

BAETHGE, M., u.a.: Ausbildungs- and Berufsstartprobleme von Jugendlichen unter den BEDINGUNGEN VERSCHÄRFTER SITUATIONEN auf dem ARBEITS- und Ausbildungsstellenmarkt. Göttingen, 1980.

BECKER, A.: Berufschancen nach einer Ausbildung zum Bäcker/Konditor. In: Zeitschrift für Berufs- und Wirtschaftspädagogik, Heft 9,1983, S.665–674.

BENNER, H.: Ordnung der staatlich anerkannten Ausbildungsberufe. Berlin, 1982.

BERUFSBILDUNGSGESETZ (BBIG) v.14.8.1969. In: Bundesgestzblatt I,S.1112.

BRUSIUS, I., FEHRENBACH, G.: Zur Krise des Ausbildungsmarktes 1983. In: Gewerkschaftliche Bildungspolitik. Sonderheft Ausbildungssituation 1983,S.2–5.

DER BUNDESMINISTER für Bildung und Wissenschaft: Berufsbildungsbericht 1984. Bonn, 1984

DERSELBE: Informationen -Bildung — Wissenschaft. Heft 7–8, 1984.

DERSELBE: Berufsbildungsbericht 1983. Bonn, 1983

DEUTSCHER BILDUNGSRAT: Strukturplan für das Bildungswesen. Bonn, 1970.

DEUTSCHER INDUSTRIE- und Handelstag (Hrsg.): Schule und Beruf. Für eine Revision der Bildungspolitik. Bonn, 1981.

DOHNANY, K.V. (1976) *Education and Youth Unemployment in the Federal Republic of Germany*. San Francisco.

GORDON, M.S. (1976) *Youth Education and Unemployment Problems: An International Perspective*, San Francisco.

HARTEN, H.C.: Jugendarbeitslosigkeit in der EG. New York/Frankfurt/Main, 1983.

LENHARDT, G.: Jugendliche Arbeitslose zwischen Arbeitsmarkt und Bildungspolitik. In: LENHARDT, G.: (Hrsg.): Der hilflose Sozialstaat. Jugendarbeitslosigkeit und Politik. Frankfurt/Main, 1979, S.203–283.

Presse- und Informationsdienst der Bundesregierung: Erklärung der Bundesregierung zur Jugendarbeitslosigkeit und Ausbildungsstellensituation. In: Bulletin, Nr.11 v.28.1.75 S.113–116.

RADDATZ, R.: Das duale System der Berufsausbildung — Stabilisierung und Bewährung. In: Zeitschrift für Berufs- und Wirtschaftspädagogik, Beiheft 4, 1983, S.101–109.

RAU, E.: Efforts to Integrate Training and Education: Experiences with a German Project In: Studies in Educational Evaluation, Vol. 10, 1984, pp. 49–60.

Statistical office of the European Communities (Eurostat.) (1984), Ausgabe 8, Luxembourg.

Statistisches Bundesamt: Berufliche Bildung 1982. Wiesbaden, 1982.

Steinbach, S.: (1974) *Analyse der Konjunkturabhängigkeit der betrieblichen Berufsausbildung in der BRD*, Bonn.

Part Two
Policy Directions For Adults

Introduction

Any assessment of the policy trends in employment and training efforts for adults necessarily has to address at least three basic considerations: political, economic, and social. The chapters in this section address strategies for adults with one or more of these perspectives in mind. The result is a collection of analyses that illuminate some of the key aspects of how the six countries discussed here define and implement their various employment and training policies and programs. Particular attention should be paid to the discussion of China in the context of the efforts of the five Western industrial and democratic nations. This juxtaposition of China with the other five sheds light on the underlying assumptions about how the interrelationships of social organization, government, and the economy play out in the development of policies and programs.

Political considerations are bedrock to how any country will take on issues as sensitive as the employment/unemployment problems of its adult population. What is apparent in this collection of chapters is that the political context establishes certain boundaries within which employment and training policies and programs can be considered. The litmus test of political feasibility must be passed prior to serious discussion of implementation. Willingness to support entrepreneurial activity, the decisions regarding which industrial sectors the government actively will support through intervention (and which it will not), the trends in business ownership, the political alignments of the unions, the structure of the tax codes, and the pivot of trade surpluses versus deficits all impact on how the various countries view their own situations. For each, the perception of where and why they have employment and training needs or problems is influenced by how they understand and define their condition. The political culture in the various countries, coupled with the political agenda of those currently holding political power, also shapes the perceptions of 'what is causing what'. In this context, each country defines its own problems and develops strategies to respond.

As but one example, consider the differences between Sweden and the

United States on the proper strategies for ameliorating the problems of dislocated workers. In both countries, the responses are heavily influenced by perceptions as to the appropriateness and effectiveness of government in delivering services. In Sweden, the issue is defined as a public responsibility, whereas in the United States, efforts increasingly are to make it a private sector responsibility.

A second dimension of the political context concerns the assumptions each country makes as to its own political stability and the role that employment issues plays in electoral sensitivities. It is a political axiom that those in power desire to maintain themselves in power. Consequently, where sensitivities are high and voter attention is focussed on employment issues, the response from the political group in power is likely to be rapid and highly visible. But the responses also tend to be short-term. Alternatively, in those countries that enjoy a high degree of political stability and where election patterns are more predictable, government policy may be more attuned to longer-term strategies that are part of a larger industrial policy.

Economic considerations with respect to employment and training efforts are directly influenced by the continuous need to weigh these efforts against other just and competing societal demands. Given that at some level, there is a zero-sum equation operating in the allocation of the collective resources of any society — i.e., resources put into employment and training are funds not available for medical care, education, housing construction, national defense, and so on — there is a continuous need for justification and evidence of impact. The financial austerity of recent years has forced a new scrutiny and accountability into the equation on whether an initiative should be supported.

Further complicating the economic question is that even if people agree that a goal is desirable and that resources should be allocated for it, multiple avenues or strategies are available for attempting to achieve the outcome. Most countries would not dispute the objective of furthering economic growth and job creation, for example, but the trade-offs among alternatives in employment and training efforts evoke considerable discussion. Offering tax credits, subsidizing select industries, sponsoring enterprise zones, and supporting small business development all are viable and alternative ways of allocating available resources. Nor is focussing on employment and training efforts an inevitable policy decision: It is made in light of other competing or complementary options.

The chapters in this section pay some attention to the macroeconomic policy of each country. This is because macroeconomic policy impacts on all four of the at-risk groups most likely to experience labour-market distress (Saks, 1984). These groups include: youth experiencing difficulty finding entree into the labor market, disadvantaged adults who consistently have low levels of earnings, experienced workers who are dislocated from an industrial sector where they previously had stable employment, and distressed older workers who find themselves less competitive, more prone to long periods of unemployment, and low in the queue for receiving employment and training support. Saks sees macro-economic policy impacting on these four groups of workers in two quite different ways:

> There is a division of labor in economic policy for dealing with the problems of distressed workers. There are the cyclically unemployed and underemployed and for them, *by definition*, the best program is a buoyant labor market. The other distressed workers are those who are, again by definition, structurally underemployed, unemployed, or poverty wage workers. The demarcation between these sets has been the subject of debates among economists for generations. The more recent form of the argument is over whether there is a level of overall unemployment below which the inflation rate begins to accelerate. Whether or not such a point exists, most agree that there are limits to how much overall macroeconomic stimulus can accomplish in eliminating unemployment and poverty level earnings. (p. 57)

Which leads back to a basic thesis of this volume: economic growth is a necessary but not sufficient condition to address the employment needs of all those who seek work.

Social conditions also impact on policies and programs in the employment and training area through the costs and benefits that such efforts generate. For example, what are the social costs and benefits on individual workers, on communities, and on industrial sectors of allowing a decline in certain industries or technologies? Costs and impacts are incurred by acting and by not acting. Since the 1980 to 1983 recession, the employment shifts that have taken place have had a profound impact on different industrial sectors — with some coming out dramatic winners and others dramatic losers. The degree to which employment and training programs focus either on training/retraining of workers for emergent demands or on enhancing the productivity and skill in existing occupations and industrial sectors will have no small impact on the lives of individual workers as well as on those industrial sectors themselves.

What complicates the decision making when everyone recognizes that the outcome will generate winners and losers is that the costs and benefits will not be evenly distributed among all individuals and among all sectors of the society. It is hard to maintain the semblance, let alone the reality, of distributive justice when entire industrial sectors are declining and others are growing. And although government policy may be able to modulate the degree of disparity among sectors, that is at best a stop-gap measure. The costs cannot be postponed indefinitely.

So we come full circle to needing to take political and economic factors into account when these decisions are made. The political decisions by the Reagan administration in the United States on the distribution of costs and benefits are perhaps somewhat similar to those taken in the United Kingdom by the Thatcher government, but not at all similar to those being made in Japan or Sweden. However, the economic cleavages do not necessarily follow in tandem with those political discussed above. The emphasis in the UK on broadening the base of business ownership is not shared in the US, and the Japanese and Swedes do not share the same view on the role of the public sector in taking on the responsibility for the training and placement of dislocated workers. Here Sweden is closer to UK, and the US is closer to Japan.

The end result of considering political, economic, and social issues in the assessment of country-specific employment and training efforts is that when these analyses are then juxtaposed, the cross-national patterns become somewhat clearer — if a mosaic can ever be clearly understood. Some countries are quite similar along some dimensions but quite dissimilar along others. Some share political philosophies, but translate them quite differently into actual program initiatives. Likewise, some countries experienced the economic downturn of 1980 to 1983 in comparable ways but have chosen to respond in ways not at all alike. It is in the intriguing interplay of similarities and differences that this collection of chapters offers current assessments of employment and training policies and programs in six nations.

References

SAKS, D.H. (1984) 'A research agenda for employment and training policy in the eighties', in ROBSON R.T., (Ed.), *Employment and Training R & D: Lessons Learned and Future Directions*, KALAMAZOO, MI. W.E. Upjohn Institute.

ACOT

2 5 NOV 1986

LIBRARY

Dislocated Workers and Mid-career Retraining in Three Industrial Nations: Some Cross-National Perspectives[1]

Marc Bendick, Jr.

Introduction

During the 1970s and 1980s, the problems of rapid economic change and the threats they pose to the employment of mid-career workers have occupied a central place in public policy debates in most market-oriented industrial nations. Shipyard workers in Sweden, textile workers in France, steel workers in Great Britain, coal miners in Germany, auto assemblers in the United States, and meat packers in New Zealand have each faced plant closures or large-scale reductions in force. New patterns of international trade; developments in production technology, including robotics; changes in consumer demand deriving from changes in demographics or consumer tastes — each has created serious circumstances of disruption in what for many workers had seemed relatively secure working lives (McKersie and Sengenberger, 1983; Organization for Economic Cooperation and Development, 1983).

As similar as have been the problems faced by different nations, their responses have been remarkably diverse, reflecting such factors as their cultural styles and preexisting institutions. These cross-national differences create a 'natural laboratory', allowing outside observers to derive from comparisons of their experiences lessons which may guide still other nations as they grapple with similar problems. This chapter examines three such highly diverse national responses to the problem of dislocated workers — those of Sweden, Canada, and France.

The Swedish 'Active Labor Market' Approach

The Swedish concept of the relative roles of the public and private sectors in the labor market is government-centered, with public agencies given prime or exclusive responsibility for many activities that in other nations are left to private enterprise. For example, with only a few exceptions, private employment agencies are illegal in Sweden, and Swedish law requires that all job vacancies be listed with the public labor exchange. At the same time, the private sector is very active in guiding the work of the public labor market agency. The so-called 'social partners' — business and organized labor — sit as the controlling members of the public labor market boards (AMS) at both the national and local levels. This tradition of cooperative, tripartite decision-making among representatives of government, business, and labor has deep historical and social roots in Sweden (Rehn, 1982).

Public sector employment and training activities in Sweden are noteworthy for the generous levels of financial support they command. This can be discerned, for example, by a brief comparison to the system in the United States. The annual budget of the Swedish Labor Market Board amounts to about 3 per cent of Sweden's gross national product; the comparable figure in the United States is about one-quarter of 1 per cent. In 1981, the Board spent about $450 for each member of the Swedish labor force. The comparable American figure was less than $100.

These expenditures in Sweden cover a broad range of activities, including not only training (in government training centers and on-the-job within private firms), but also job search assistance, relocation allowances, wage subsidies, work aids to encourage employment of the handicapped, 'relief work' on public projects, regional economic development initiatives, and even public subsidies to private firms to retain surplus workers rather than laying them off during a recession (for example, by placing them in company-provided training or by producing to stockpile inventories) (Ginsberg 1983).

For such activities as training, counseling, and job placement assistance, any unemployed person (or person who is in danger of becoming unemployed) is eligible, and the services are utilized by the majority of Swedes seeking work. In contrast, in more free-enterprise-oriented nations such as the United States, the public sector role in the labor market generally focusses on assistance to special needs groups, such as the handicapped or disadvantaged; this focus is achieved both by formal eligibility rules in many programs and by the often limited quality of services offered in other cases. In Sweden, publicly provided services dominate the labor market both because they are generally universally available — without income eligibility or other categorized restrictions — and because they are of high quality and recognized value.

One indication of the latter phenomenon at work in Sweden is given by the listing of job vacancies by employers with the public labor exchange. Such listing is mandatory, and about 90 per cent of vacancies are estimated to be listed. However, in the period prior to imposition of this legal mandate, some 65 per cent of vacancies were already being listed, largely because employers recognized that the public labor exchange was an effective system for finding high-quality employees.

Similar things can be said about occupational skill training provided by Swedish government training centers. These centers are staffed by well-paid, high-quality craftspersons and educators; offer in-depth, long-duration courses providing the same depth of training as pre-career students receive in regular vocational schools; utilize up-to-date equipment and state-of-the-art technology; and attract a broad range of trainees, mixing 'disadvantaged' trainees with 'mainstream' workers and the employed with the unemployed. Small wonder that a training certificate from such institutions is considered an excellent job credential and carries none of the stigma associated with public programs elsewhere in the western industrial world.

Given the range and quality of existing public labor market institutions just described, special initiatives to serve the victims of economic and technological change require only minor modifications to implement. One typical component of this modification is to move the intake function for reemployment services to the plant site itself, so that enrollment for unemployment benefits, counseling and testing, job search, and other services can be provided immediately and conveniently. As part of the Swedish tradition of tripartite cooperation, employers often provide office space (and sometimes supplementary staffing) for these efforts. A legal requirement of advance notification for any large layoff or plant closure facilitates beginning the reemployment process before unemployment actually begins. Although intake activities are brought to the plant site and adjusted to match the special circumstance of mass layoffs, workers are rapidly channeled through these intake processes into the regular stream of services offered by the Labor Market Board. Thus, for example, dislocated workers undergoing skill retraining will be trained not in a special program for them but in the regular classrooms of ongoing government training programs.

A second modification of the Swedish system for dislocated workers is that special legislation for certain industries provides them with special wage assistance to support their time spent seeking new employment. The Swedish shipyard industry, for example, is undergoing long-term decline. If a shipyard worker who is not yet laid off needs time off during the work week to interview for a new job, then the employer must release that worker for the needed time, and special government funds will pay the worker the regular wage during those hours.

Finally, the Swedish government makes special economic development efforts to recycle the plants and equipment of shrinking firms, with the idea that the new jobs generated will reabsorb some of those losing their employment. In the case of government-owned shipyards, for example, the government has offered unused factory space and equipment either free or at highly reduced prices to small enterprises (for example, small furniture companies) being founded by former shipyard workers.

However, these special efforts on behalf of those who become unemployed as part of a recognizable dislocation — such as a plant closure — are small compared to the assistance that is available to dislocated workers simply by being unemployed. Therefore, evaluative evidence concerning the effectiveness of the assistance offered specifically to the dislocated is close to nonexistent, and we must rely instead on examinations of the 'active labor market' system more generally.

On the positive side, it is clear that the quality of employment and training services offered by the public sector in Sweden is high. Programs are well funded. To work for one of the public employment and training agencies is considered an excellent career. Labor, business, and the voting public are supportive of the activities. Both for training and for replacement, the public system is the mainstream institution for the nation. The situation seems to be a self-reinforcing one that comparable institutions in other industrial nations may well envy. Excellence in service breeds public support, and public support provides the resources and the mandate to provide excellent services.

Two cautionary notes are necessary, however, to balance this favorable picture.

First, it is not obvious how much greater the total amount of investment in labor market activities is in the Swedish system, compared to that of other industrial nations. At least part of Swedish public sector activity may simply be replacing what would otherwise have been purchased by the private sector, either by employers of their employees or by employees themselves. Remember that the Swedish public employment and training system spends about $450 per year per member of the work force, whereas the American public sector spends about $100. The American Society for Training and Development (Carnevale and Goldstein, 1983) tells us that the American business sector spends perhaps $30 billion per year in training its employees, which corresponds to about $300 per year for each member of the work force. Private employment agencies in the United States enjoy annual sales of more than $250 million, which adds another few dollars per worker. Totaling public and private expenditures in the United States, we get approximately the same amount per worker as is spent by the public sector in Sweden. Of course, the level of private sector expenditure on training in Sweden is not zero; in some industries such expenditure may be as high as in the United States, or even higher. But these comparisons, while hardly definitive, serve to remind us that a larger governmental role by no means guarantees a higher total level of activity.

Of course, the shifting of responsibility from the private sector to the public sector may still be important if, within an unchanged total, resources are spent on different individuals or for different purposes. In the United States, for example, we know (Bendick and Egan, 1982) that the following occurs in the training activities supported by the private firms:

- Employees of large firms get more training than employees of small firms
- White-collar employees get more training than blue-collar employees.
- The more general education and training a worker has, the more likely the worker is to receive additional training.

- 'Disadvantaged' workers tend to be underrepresented in the hiring and training stream.

In the Swedish system, these patterns are overcome, to some extent. Extensive counseling efforts are expended to encourage participation in training by less-educated, blue-collar workers, and special pedagogical techniques are used to make training situations more comfortable for adults (Bendick, 1984). But the Swedes are candid in admitting that not all such patterns are overcome, even in their socialized system. Many of the dislocated workers experiencing the most reemployment difficulties are precisely those types of individuals who, even in the Swedish system, have been the most difficult to reach — blue-collar manufacturing workers with limited general education and low skills (Bendick, 1983a; Bendick and Devine, 1981; Bendick and Egan, 1982). Therefore, although many of the specific techniques the Swedes employ to reach such workers may be usefully emulated (Bendick, 1984), we unfortunately cannot find, even in the Swedish experience, any full answer to the problems of providing education and training for this difficult-to-serve population.

A second and related cautionary note should be sounded about the payoffs of the services provided by the Swedish system, particularly for skill retraining. There is a tendency in the Swedish system to place in occupational training any unemployed worker who cannot be immediately reemployed, in some cases regardless of whether or not the new skills to be acquired will significantly alter the worker's productivity or employability. For example, on a recent visit to Sweden, I observed a large number of workers receiving training as welders. When I remarked that this surprised me because I believed welding to be an occupation for which demand was declining, I was given two explanations for the activity. First, it was said to be preferable to have unemployed workers actively receiving training than to have them sitting idly at home while unemployed — even if the training was not very useful in the future employment market. Second, it was said that if the work force in general possesses many diverse skills, then the structure of occupations will be influenced in the direction of maintaining 'job quality'. For example, if all building maintenance workers know how to weld, then their jobs will continue to be defined as jobs requiring this special skill. Their jobs will not be reduced to routine activities with lower skill requirements, with welding farmed out to a specialist. Thus, the motivation to invest in retraining the unemployed in Sweden seems often to be sociological or psychological in nature, rather than economic; the goals frequently are to support the work ethic or to influence the nature of work, rather than to enhance an individual's immediate employability or productivity.

In saying that the objectives of such training activities are psychological or sociological rather than economic, this does not suggest that they are less important or less legitimate. However, much of the Swedish investment in training and other 'micro' labor market policies may serve such ends and should, therefore, be examined cautiously as a model for an effective, immediate-payoff reemployment strategy for dislocated workers.

More generally, the Swedish system has been criticized for excessive reliance on microeconomic labor market programs to address unemployment problems, to the neglect of macroeconomic approaches. To place unemployed workers in training or in 'relief works' (the Swedish term for public service employment or job-oriented public works) may reduce the measured unemployment rate, but it does so largely by disguising unemployment rather than actually reducing it. At least one researcher has estimated that Sweden could reduce its 'real' unemployment rate by shifting some of its emphasis away from microeconomic policies and toward macroeconomic initiatives (Johannesson and Persson-Tanimura, 1978; Johannesson and Schmidt, 1982).

The Canadian Manpower Consultative Service

The concern about the proper balance between macroeconomic and microeconomic initiatives is a central one to policy debate about dislocated workers in many nations. The traditional role assigned to government employment and training programs in, for example, the United States has been to promote the labor market opportunities of those who would remain 'structurally unemployed' (or underemployed) even in a nonrecessionary national economy. Key questions in discussions about dislocated workers, therefore, are: To what extent will workers currently on long-term or permanent layoff in economies such as that of the United States be readily reabsorbed by an economy recovering from recession? How many among the millions of workers laid off from such traditional manufacturing industries as automobiles, steel, rubber, glass, and textiles are likely to return to their old jobs or to very similar manufacturing jobs not requiring major skill retraining or career transitions to enter?

Opinions vary a great deal on this subject (Ayres and Miller, 1983; Bendick, 1983a and 1983c; Bendick and Devine, 1981; Bluestone and Harrison, 1982; Choate, 1982; Hunt and Hunt, 1983; Levin and Rumberger, 1983; Sawhill, 1983; Sheingold, 1982), and no definitive answer is possible until such an economic recovery is actually experienced. However, even the smallest estimates of the magnitude of the problem (Bendick, 1983a) agree with the larger ones in saying that there is one pool of dislocated workers who will experience significant reemployment difficulties even in non-recessionary times. These are workers unemployed as part of mass layoffs or plant shutdowns in communities already suffering very high levels of general unemployment or long-term decline. When an automobile plant or steel mill closes in a city which is traditionally a one-company or one-industry town, their laid-off employees face serious structural reemployment difficulties in their 'communities in crisis'.

For a model of how effective government assistance can be delivered to such workers and their communities, there is an innovative program in

Canada called the Canadian Manpower Consultative Service (MCS). This agency of the Canadian national government exists specifically to deliver temporary worker adjustment assistance to communities undergoing economic crisis. The MCS operations may be described as follows (Barth, 1982; Barth and Reisner, 1981; Batt, 1983; Bendick, 1983a):

- When a plant shutdown or mass layoff situation arises, the MCS becomes involved immediately and temporarily (for example, for a six-month to twelve-month period). Thus, it supplements established local labor market institutions at a time of peak demand.
- MCS's major role is that of coordinating, facilitating, and encouraging the mobilization of local resources, primarily those of local employers and local unions, into a committee. It brings in a modest amount of matching funds for administrative expenses and the services of a case officer, but local government and private resources must also be contributed.
- All workers involved in the job reduction are contacted to see if employment assistance is desired. (Typically, 70 per cent respond affirmatively.) Each person expressing interest is then interviewed individually to determine the most appropriate form of assistance.
- Those workers who need or desire career counseling, training in job search skills, retraining, or relocation assistance are referred to the publicly-run employment service.
- The major form of assistance provided to most workers — some 64 per cent of all cases — is direct placement assistance. Here, the key role that the MCS and local committee play is to bring into the open jobs in the 'hidden labor market' (i.e., those that are typically filled by word of mouth).

Throughout these activities, the hallmarks of MCS operations are a flexible and non-bureaucratic style, an emphasis on mobilizing local resources rather than importing them, a willingness to adapt to local circumstances and needs rather than to impose a prescribed set of solutions, and an emphasis on the temporariness of their involvement.

In the operation of Canada's MCS, as in the operation of the Swedish Labor Market Board, one essential element of the responsiveness of the system to the needs of dislocated workers is a mandatory advance notice of mass layoffs or plant closures. Such notice allows the public agency to begin to serve those facing unemployment prior to their actually being laid off. This early provision of services appears to be especially important psychologically, in that it reaches workers very soon after the stress of the dismissal, providing counseling, support, and a future orientation to combat the anger, frustration, and bitterness that are typical reactions (Bendick, 1983c). Contacting workers is also significantly easier before their layoff than after. Finally, early intervention is particularly important in systems, such as the MCS, that rely on local employers and unions to provide at least some of the resources for worker reemployment efforts. At the early stages of the process, companies and unions have both more interest and more resources.

A further central aspect of the MCS approach is that economic development — the promotion of existing local employers or the seeking of immigrant companies — is a major part of its portfolio of approaches to aiding communities. That is, if local circumstances dictate, MCS expertise and resources can be targeted on the creation of jobs (demand for workers), not just on enhancing the supply of workers (through placement or training). In some nations, the economic development function and the worker development functions are handled by separate state agencies, and typically in an uncoordinated fashion. The MCS pairing of the two approaches to aid communities in crisis is a useful reminder of the complementarity of the two types of activities.

The MCS also offers an interesting echo of a theme in the Swedish experience — that of serving the needs of distressed or disadvantaged individuals through the same agency that serves the 'mainstream' work force. In the MCS case, this occurs through a mandate for the agency to provide its assistance not only to communities experiencing labor surpluses from mass layoffs and plant closures, but also to communities enjoying economic expansion that happen to be labor-short. Such a dual mandate is efficient in providing for potential pairing of surplus and shortage areas and in drawing upon similar agency capabilities. It also prevents the MCS from becoming stigmatized as being exclusively associated with 'unattractive' communities and hard-to-employ workers.

Finally, it should be noted that in the MCS experience, many — certainly at least a majority — dislocated workers are assisted with job search and placement assistance rather than with skill retraining. This has been the experience both of the Canadian MCS (for which 64 per cent of service recipients receive only search and placement assistance) and of such American programs as the Downriver Community Conference Economic Readjustment Program (where some 85 per cent of service recipients receive only job search assistance). The reasons for this emphasis are numerous, but may be summarized in the assertion that most workers will eventually be reemployed in jobs requiring a skill level not particularly higher or different from what they utilized in their previous jobs. This will be true both because the skill composition of job vacancies is moving upward only slowly and because many dislocated workers are not ideal candidates for training (Bendick, 1981a and 1983c; Bendick and Devine, 1981; Levin and Rumberger, 1983). The Canadian experience suggests that reemploying dislocated workers is predominantly a matter of placement rather than of retraining.

The French 'Obligation to Spend' on Training

The fact that, for most dislocated workers, retraining is not the path to reemployment should not be interpreted to mean that mid-career retraining is an unimportant need in the labor force of a modern industrial nation. There is constant and accelerating change in the composition of output in modern industrial societies and in the technology with which it is produced. These changes, in turn, dictate that the occupational mix in the economy change constantly, and also that the skills involved within each occupation also change. However, it is important to recognize that these changes occur gradually, that most of the new skills required in the evolution of jobs are acquired incrementally, and that most retraining of mid-career workers occurs among the employed, not the unemployed. A high level of mid-career retraining among the employed is probably one of the best defenses an economy can erect against the abrupt dislocation of its work force.

Earlier in this chapter, an estimate of $30 billion per year was cited as the amount that American private employers currently expend on training their employees. Large as this number is, there is reason to believe that it is still less than the socially optimal level of investment for that economy. Due to the presence of what economists refer to as 'private market failures', the private sector acting alone persistently underinvests in the skills needed by its own work force (Bendick, 1983a and 1983c; Bendick and Egan, 1982; Stoikov, 1975). These market failures hamper both investment by employers in training their current employees and employees' investment in training themselves.

In the case of employers, the decision to invest in worker training, as with any other investment decision, depends largely on the expected return from the investment. When workers are free to move from company to company, it is risky for an employer to spend thousands of dollars to give a worker a skill in great demand, because that firm's competitor will ty to hire that worker away the minute the training is complete. When all employers together react to this fact, a situation arises in which everyone needs a skilled labor pool but nobody will pay for it.

As for employees, we do see a great deal of self-investment by workers. When a high school graduate goes to college, or when an individual takes a job despite a low wage 'because it is good experience', that is precisely what is occurring. But in an era of rapid economic and technological change, more and more workers are faced with the need to make a major investment in their own retraining at midcareer. Such bouts of midcareer formal training are difficult for workers to finance. First, they require quite a cash flow, both to pay for the instruction itself and to support the worker and his or her family while the training is proceeding. This can be a particular problem if the worker wishes to undertake retraining when unemployed, when cash flow is tightest. Second, because formal midcareer training is very expensive, individuals may be reluctant to undertake such a sizable investment when there is no certainty that it will pay off. And finally, there is a problem of information: Individuals may not be well enough informed about trends in the labor market to pick the right field in which to be trained.

The gap between what training the private sector is currently providing and the ever-increasing training needs of society may perhaps be effectively addressed in a way modeled on an aspect of French public policy. Since 1971, the French have operated a national system for financing worker training that creates an effective public-private partnership to address exactly the problems outlined. The key element of the system is what the French refer to as an 'obligation to spend', enforced by a payroll tax if that obligation is not met.

The French Further Vocational Training System was established by an agreement between employers' associations and trade unions concluded in 1970 and reinforced by laws in 1971 and 1976 (Bendick and Egan, 1982; Legave and Vignaud, 1979). As a central feature of this system, every employer of ten or more employees must make an annual contribution to the financing of training courses. Contributions are calculated as a percentage of the firm's total wage bill, with the percentage specified annually by the government in its yearly finance act (currently it is set at 1.1 per cent).

Employers may satisfy this contribution requirement in any of the several following ways:

- By financing internal training programs for their own workers, either conducting the training themselves or paying for the services of an outside training establishment through a multi-year agreement.
- By making a financial contribution to an industrywide training insurance fund, established by agreements between employers or employer associations and trade unions. These funds may be national or local.
- By making a financial contribution to programs for unemployed persons in training centers approved by the government.
- By paying their contribution into the government treasury.

Thus, if the firm chooses to train its own workers and spends at least the 1.1 per cent minimum, then its obligations are discharged. Or the firm may meet the requirement by participating in and financially supporting an industrywide training fund that serves its own employees. But the firm may as well spend on one of these forms of training, because if it fails to meet its obligations to spend, then the unspent balance of the 1.1 per cent is due to the government as a payroll tax. In practice, the majority of funds are allocated to the first of these methods, particularly among large firms; about 8 per cent of funds go to the second method, primarily among small and medium-sized firms in industries with strong trade unions. Approximately one hundred twenty thousand firms and over 10 billion French francs are involved each year; typically, one person in eight in the labor force receives some training during any year, with an average of fifty-five hours of training per trainee. Revenues may be used to finance trainees' wages during training as well as the out-of-pocket costs of the training itself.

Workers may take advantage of training opportunities under this fund for a number of purposes, including 'refresher' courses in their current occupations and advancement to higher-skill occupations. The funds may be called upon for 'adaptation' courses, in which unemployed workers switch to new fields of work, or for 'preventive' courses, in which currently employed workers convert to new occupations created by technological change. Thus, the fund becomes a valuable device both to workers (in assuring them of continued employment despite economic change) and to employers (by providing a trained labor force for emerging labor force needs).

Because the French system provides wage replacement benefits and tuition payments to workers, it tends to overcome the 'cash flow' and 'risk aversion' reasons that may prevent workers from investing in their own training. By obligating employers to expend at least a minimum level of effort on training, it addresses their reluctance to invest in training for transferable skills ('general human capital') whose benefits they may not receive. By increasing the amount of training provided to workers currently employed, it emphasizes prevention rather than cure. At the same time, by promoting the provision of training to workers by current employers, it reduces the situation of workers' undergoing training 'on speculation' in favor of training for job needs already planned for within a firm; this reduces the information and decision-making burdens on those workers, particularly blue-collar workers, who are used to a system of adapting to employers' needs and who have relatively little facility with career self-planning. Thus, such an approach may be seen primarily as addressing basic 'market failures' in the retraining market, rather than the more ad hoc needs of dislocated workers, per se.

One of the advantages of such an approach is its flexibility and decentralization of decision-making. Decisions are made by employers (with a mandatory consultation process with unions, in the case of larger firms), in light of their firms' own needs. No vast amounts of money flow into and out of the public treasury, and no government central plans or decisions constrain what a firm may do. Yet each firm has a profit incentive to use its training resources wisely, and all firms together are required to maintain a high level of sustained investment in the French work force.

The experience in France with this approach has been highly favorable in terms of increasing the total volume of resources spent on training within firms. Particularly among smaller firms — those most subject to the tendency to underinvest (Schiller, 1983) — the level of expenditures on training has increased steadily since the start of the system. Among firms of between ten and nineteen employees, for example, training expenditures as a proportion of the wage bill went from 0.47 per cent in 1972 to 0.95 per cent in 1980. The availability of an industry-wide training fund has been particularly useful in making high-quality, professionally organized training available to firms too small to run their own in-house training efficiently.

One difficulty frequently observed in the French system is that, although the total amount of investment in training has increased, a disproportionate amount continues to be spent on white-collar, professional, and managerial employees, rather than on the lower-skilled, blue-collar workers who typically experience the greatest dislocation problems. 'Management development seminars' at pleasant country resorts or English language instruction for upper-level managers are typical examples of such expenditures, which are off-target in terms of dislocation prevention. They are perhaps more appropriately described as employment perquisites for higher-level employees than hard-core skill updating. Such difficulties could be overcome through program regulation specifying targeting. It appears from the French experience that such controls would be necessary.

With that important modification, if other industrial nations adopt a similar 'employer obligation to spend' approach, they would move a long way toward addressing the midcareer retraining problems, of which dislocated workers are the visible and important tip of the iceberg. Such a proposal is by no means a political absurdity. The leadership elements of the business community should be as enthusiastic elsewhere as they are in France. Most major corporations already invest heavily in worker training. Their obligation under this system would already be discharged by their current level of activity, whereas their less active competitors (who have been stealing their staff) would be forced to carry their fair share. At the same time, the leaders of labor should be enthusiastic about a system that ensures a sustained level of resources to make workers participants in and beneficiaries of technological and other economic change, not victims of it. A higher level of general labor force training would prevent a good deal of worker dislocation by providing in-house retraining as a substitute for dislocation, and currently dislocated workers would benefit from the new entry-level employment slots that would be created as current employees move upward via training. Taxpayers stand to gain from reduced unemployment insurance and public assistance claims, and we all stand to gain from enhanced national productivity and international competitiveness.

Lessons for Future Policy Initiatives

This chapter has provided only a highly selective review of the dislocated-worker activities of market-oriented industrialized nations. Other nations besides the three examined here have their own initiatives, and the three nations discussed offer programs other than those discussed here (Wolfe, 1979). Nevertheless, the three models were selected because they are among the most provocative for policy discussions.

Of the various insights suggested by the experiences of Sweden, Canada, and France, three are of particular interest and potential utility:

- The experiences of all three nations suggest that *it is a mistake to equate mid-career retraining and dislocated worker reemployment*. Canada correctly emphasizes placement and job development over training for the dislocated: France correctly emphasizes training for the employed rather than the unemployed; and Sweden probably incorrectly overinvests in retraining the unemployed.
- All three nations in various ways *deemphasize the uniqueness of the*

employment problems of dislocated workers and tend to address them through labor market institutions serving the labor force more generally. This is a different direction from those which define dislocated workers as a distinct population and establish a separate (and stigmatizing) program for them.

● Each of the three nations, in a different way, seeks to *combine government, business, and labor resources and roles in addressing the dislocated worker problem, rather than devising a 'government-only' approach.*

Such broad themes embody the main lessons of the experiences of these nations.

Note

This chapter is based in part on research supported by the German Marshall Fund of the United States. An earlier version appeared in *Displaced Workers: Implications for Educational and Training Institutions*, edited by Kevin Hollenbeck, Frank C. Pratzner, and Howard Rosen, Columbus, Ohio National Center for Research in Vocational Education (1984) pp. 189–308.

References

AYRES, R.U., and MILLER, S.M. (1983) *Robotics, Applications and Social Implications*, Cambridge, MA, Ballinger.

BARTH, M. (1982) 'Dislocated workers'. *The Journal of the Institute of Socioeconomic Studies*, 7, 1, spring, pp. 23–35.

BARTH, M.C., and REISNER, F. (1981) *Worker Adjustment to Plant Shutdowns and Mass Layoffs*, Washington, DC, ICF, Inc.

BATT, W.L., Jr. (1983) 'Canada's good example with displaced workers'. *Harvard Business Review*, 83, 4, (July-August) pp. 6–22.

BENDICK, M. Jr. (1981a) *Assisting Coal Miners Dislocated by Sulfur Emissions Restrictions: Issues and Options*, Washington, DC, The Urban Institute.

BENDICK, M. Jr. (1981b) *Plant Closure and Worker Layoff Procedures in the United States*, Washington, DC, The Urban Institute.

BENDICK, M. Jr. (1983a) *Government's Role in the Job Transitions of America's Dislocated Workers*, Testimony before the Committee on the Budget and the Committee on Science and Technology, US House of Representative, 9 June.

BENDICK, M. Jr. (1983b) *Reemploying Dislocated Workers — Five Strategies for Pennsylvania*, Testimony before the House of Representatives Committee on Appropriations, Legislature of the Commonwealth of Pennsylvania, 9 March.

BENDICK, M. Jr. (1983c) 'The role of public programs and private markets in reemploying workers dislocated by economic change'. *Policy Studies Review* 2, 4, May, pp. 715–33.

BENDICK, M. Jr. (1984) 'The Swedish 'Active Labor Market' approach to reemploying workers dislocated by economic change'. *Journal of Health and Human Resources Administration*, 6, 3, February.

BENDICK, M. Jr., and DEVINE, J.R. (1981) 'Workers dislocated by economic change: Do they need federal employment and training assistance?'. *Seventh Annual Report: The Federal Interest in Employment and Training*, Washington, DC: National Commission for Employment Policy.

BENDICK, M. Jr., and EGAN, M.L. (1982) *Recycling America's Workers: Public and Private Approaches to Midcareer Retraining*, Washington, DC, The Urban Institute.

BLUESTONE B. and HARRISON, B. (1982) *The Deindustrialization of America*, New York, Basic Books.

CARNEVALE, A.P., and GOLDSTEIN, H. (1983) *Employee Training: Its Changing Role and an Analysis of New Data*, Washington, DC, American Society for Training and Development.

CHOATE, P. (1982) *Retooling the American Work Force: Toward a National Training Strategy*. Washington, DC, Northeast-Midwest Institute.

GINSBERG, H. (1983) *Full Employment and Public Policy: The United States and Sweden*. Lexington, MA, Lexington Books.

HUNT, H.A., and HUNT, T. (1983) *Human Resource Implication of Robotics*, Kalamazoo, MI, W.E. Upjohn Institute for Employment Research.

JOHANNESSON, J. and PERSSON-TANIMURA, I. (1978) *Labour Market Policies in Transition — Studies about the Effects of Labour Market Policy*, Stockholm Labor Market Board.

JOHANNESSON, J. and SCHMIDT, G. (1982) 'The development of labour market policy in Sweden and Germany: Competing or convergent models to combat unemployment?', *European Journal of Political Research*, 8, pp. 387–406.

LEGAVE, C. and VIGNAUD, D. (1979) *Descriptions of the Vocational Training Systems: France*, Berlin, European Centre for the Development of Vocational Training.

LEVIN, M., and RUMBERGER, R.W. (1983) *The Educational Implications of High Technology*, Palo Alto, CA, Stanford University.

McKERSIE, R.B., and SENGENBERGER, W. (1983) *Job Losses in Major Industries. Manpower Strategy Responses*, Paris, Organization for Economic Cooperation and Development.

Organization for Economic Cooperation and Development (1983) *Positive Adjustment Policies. Managing Structural Change*, Paris, OECD.

REHN, G. (1982) *Cooperation between the Government and the Social Partners on Labour Market Policy in Sweden*, Stockholm, Swedish Institute for Social Resarch.

SAWHILL, I. (1983) *Creating Jobs: Options for the 98th Congress*, Testimony before the Committee on the Budget, US House of Representatives, 8 February.

SCHILLER, B. (1983) 'Corporate kidnap of the small business employee', *The Public Interest*, 73, summer, pp. 72–87.

SHEINGOLD, S. (1982) *Dislocated Workers: Issues and Federal Options*. Washington, DC, Congressional Budget Office.

STOIKOV, V. (1975) *The Economics of Recurrent Education and Training*, Geneva International Labour Organization.

WOLFE, M. (1979) *Adjustment Policies and Problems in Developed Countries*, Washington, DC, The World Bank.

Dislocated Workers in the United States: Assistance, Amelioration and Prevention[1]

Lois-ellin Datta

Dislocated workers are long-time workers who lost their jobs because there was no need for their skills in the place where they used to work. Dislocated workers are not a new phenomenon in the United States (see, for example, Borus, 1964; Hammerman, 1964; Palen, 1966; Pichler, 1967); the attention they have received in the past few years is.

This chapter is concerned with dislocated workers, dying businesses, and distressed communities. It is concerned also with US policies aimed at preventing such problems and with programs intended to alleviate the distress. Three points are made. First, the current problem of dislocated workers is not much of a national problem, as national problems go. It may be receiving considerable attention not so much because of its present size but because many believe that it could get worse. Second, the most promising remedies for the current problem require considerable effort on the part of government, communities, business and labor unions, ministering to the stricken. Third, the most promising remedies for the future may not be in group action; rather, they seem to reside in a shift in perspective about worker responsibilities. This may run counter, however, to an incoming tide of belief that workers should develop a long-term allegiance to their employer if productivity and quality are to rise, a belief that would argue for policies based more on shared risk, shared benefit distributions.

The next sections of this chapter present these arguments in more detail.

Part 1

Today: Dislocated Workers

The United States has a mobile work force. About 20 per cent of the work force change their status annually. Many who had not been looking for jobs previously start looking, and many of these find jobs. Many who had been employed change jobs, particularly among younger workers. Some who had been employed lose their jobs and cannot find others, but keep looking. And some who had been employed leave the workforce.

It is the last three groups with which we are concerned. In all three groups there are two types of changers: workers who change their status voluntarily, and workers who change involuntarily. Within this last sub-set, there are again two types of involuntary changers: those who lose jobs which someone else then fills and those who lose jobs because their skills are no longer needed. The latter are the 'redundant', 'displaced' or 'dislocated' workers: those whose previous jobs are no longer available to them or anyone else.

Data on dislocated workers are slippery. First, there are more benefits (and social support) for a worker who is laid off than one fired. Management sometimes can exercise considerable discretion in deciding which job is surplus, using early outs to deal with older or less productive workers. Second, some period of unemployment between being laid off on one job and hired on another are used in some estimates of the size of the dislocated worker population but in not others. Third, laid off workers who are not eligible for unemployment compensation or other benefits may not be picked up in the reporting system. These and other factors contribute to considerable variation in counts of displaced workers (see for example, Cawkell, 1983; Jenkins and Montmarquette, 1979).

Kohlberg (1983) reports,

> Dislocated workers are people who are unemployed and unlikely to return to their previous occupations because their skills have become obsolete or because of structural changes in smokestack industries. The typical dislocated worker is a male, 40 years old or older, a union member, and the head of a household; although he usually has no more than a high school education, he has been able to maintain a middle-class salary for most of his working life. No agency presently keeps count of displaced workers, but in the spring of 1983 various independent survey organizations reported between half a million and two million unemployed as a result of dislocation.

Bendick (1983b) has testified, however, that only 1 or 2 per cent of the 11 million unemployed in the United States in 1983 were dislocated, a figure closer to 100,000 to 200,000. The differences in part reflect the number of workers who were ever laid off, many of whom found jobs fairly soon, (within, for example, eight weeks) and those unemployed for longer periods of time (for example, twenty-six weeks or longer).

The workforce always has had such workers, although their numbers have fluctuated. Individual businesses and industries always have been more or less successful, and if unsuccessful, their employees have lost their jobs, as the saying goes, through no fault of their own. The economy in general has been more and less successful, and, if unsuccessful, a great many workers lose jobs at one time. At the depth of the US Depression in the 1930s, about one-third of the total workforce were unemployed.

The costs of such unemployment are high (Shostak, 1980). There are direct budgetary costs to employers and governments; for example, in payouts for unemployment benefits. For workers whose unemployment coverage runs out and who then become eligible for other programs, there are the costs of public assistance in cash and in kind. There also are indirect economic effects: the services and goods which could be produced by these workers are irretrievably lost (Bale, 1976; Barth, 1982) as are the costs of employer-provided training. And there are other effects (Ignani, 1983; Wegmann, 1983). Although magnitude and direct causality are disputed, the weight of evidence is that these include some degree of stress related illnesses, increases in abuse of spouses and children, and deaths (Ferman and Gordus, 1979). And, as Elder (1975) has shown, there may be inter-generational effects of these stresses in the children and in their children when men and women have played the game by the rules — worked hard, stayed loyal to a company, sank deep roots in communities — and lost.

Parnes and King (1977) using data from a longitudinal survey covering 1966 through 1971, found that many middle-aged men who had served at least five years with their prior employees and who had involuntarily lost their jobs reported a long-run loss of income and occupational status; adverse health effects; a sense of powerlessness, and loss of initiative. Compared to controls matched for personal and occupational characteristics in 1966 who did not involuntarily lose their jobs, many of the displaced workers had not caught up — economically or psychologically — when followed a minimum of two years after their job loss even though 40 per cent had found some other work within a week. Jacobson and Thompson (1979) measured earnings losses due to displacement as the difference between actual earnings after displacement and projected earnings in the absence of displacement. The case survey method yielded data from a variety of industries (for example, steel, meat packing, aerospace, TV receivers, textiles, shoes) and samples ranging from about thirty to about 700 workers displaced between 1960 and 1970. They estimate that displaced women tend to leave the workforce; men, to remain in it. Losses were greatest in unionized industries with low quit rates and a high proportion of males. Over a five year period, the economic costs to the workers are estimated to be twice the average yearly earnings for those remaining in the work force, and about four times the average yearly earnings for all displaced workers. Transfer payments (for example unemployment insurance) are estimated to reduce the income loss by about 12 per cent. The researchers emphasized, however, that general economic conditions, size of the local labor market and worker tenure substantially affect the size of the earnings losses. Magaziner, discussing these and other data, (1983) concludes,

A substantial number of the newly unemployed have health and social problems that are aggravated by the tensions and insecurities connected with a loss of role and a fear that the community is collapsing. Crime often increases as some workers let off their tensions; health problems increase as others bottle up their anxieties and fears. An increased death rate is also associated with unemployment since most suicides in the United States are by out-of-work males in their middle to later years. (p. 34)

More indirect costs to industries and businesses may be high also: successful companies subsidize the unemployment insurance costs of unsuccessful companies when unemployment insurance rates rise; the companies losing workers may pay lump sum benefits and severance costs; they may lose trained workers needed later if the factories reopen; they bear the costs of new recruiting, hiring and training; expensive equipment depreciates without yielding returns.

And lastly, communities experience both direct and indirect costs. Demands for community-supported social services may rise suddenly; businesses may face mounting unpaid bills; demand for goods and services decrease; the bottom drops out of the housing market; and, as those who can do so get out, increasingly those who stay need more and can give less — the elderly, the handicapped, the unskilled (Buss, 1980, C&R Associate, 1978; Hansen, 1981).

As Magaziner (1983) notes, 'Ripple effects are felt across the entire economy as people stop making purchases, fail to pay their bills or dump their homes onto the market. Local governments lose revenue precisely at the time when demands for social services increase.'

The findings of earlier studies were confirmed in two national studies. One examined the status of workers 20 years of age or older whose jobs were abolished or plants shut down between January 1979 and January 1984 (US Department of Labor, 1984). Of 5.1 million workers who had been at their jobs at least three years before they were displaced, 60 per cent were reemployed, 25 per cent were looking for work, and about 15 per cent had left the labor force — mostly women and older men. About 45 per cent of those reemployed, however, were earning less in their new jobs than in the ones they lost. In another study, the US General Accounting Office found that about 67 per cent of 342,000 workers who received trade adjustment benefits were rehired by the same employer shortly after they were laid off; the Office recommended limiting benefits to those who could not find jobs after a longer period of unemployment (1980).

According to the Department of Labor (1984) displacement struck differentially by industry and region. Workers in manufacturing, primarily durable goods, and in the East North Central and Mid-Atlantic regions were disproportionately affected. More likely to be dislocated, they also were least likely to be reemployed: the East North Central area had about one-third of all displaced workers who were unemployed, and about half had been without work for more than six months.

Bendick and Devine (1980) compared the relative impact of declining region, occupation and industry using all workers unemployed as of March

1980 on the number of weeks of unemployment. Multiple regressions showed that being from a region with unemployment exceeding 8.5 per cent added two weeks to the average of eleven weeks of unemployment; being from a declining occupation had a relatively small effect (adding half a week); and being from a declining industry had no measurable impact, data that emphasize the effect of regional economic conditions relative to occupation or industry specific factors.

Despite the large increase in a short time, as problems go, dislocated workers are a fairly small proportion of the total work force relative to the attention they have received. It is estimated, for example, that 75 per cent of those affected find work within six weeks and that only about 10 per cent still are unemployed after six months. For March 1980, the highest estimate of displaced workers unemployed for more than eight weeks was about 900,000: less than 1 per cent of the entire US labor force and less than 14 per cent of all unemployed. The smallest estimate was about 0.1 per cent of the total labor force and less than 2 per cent of all unemployed (Bendick and Devine, 1981). Furthermore, some observers believe that as economic conditions in the US improve generally, these dislocated workers may be among the first to benefit, a prediction sustained by the more rapid rate of reemployment reported for this group as the economy has improved during 1984.

This is not to understate the distress of individuals who have worked all their lives, done a good job, and find themselves jobless, dependent, in danger of losing everyone and everything they worked for. The pain of separated families, families living in cars on the edges of strange towns, of men and women who have tried everything they know to find work and cannot is terrible and real. (See, for example, Brooks, 1983; Clark and Nelson, 1982; Clark and Nelson, 1983; Lublin, 1983; Matthews, 1983b.) But we must look even beyond this individual suffering to understand why this problem, more than others, has gotten so much attention.

The reason, it is argued, is that many believe that the problem is 'you today, and me tomorrow': that is, there is more involved than economic swings. This 'more' may have the potential for affecting very many people.

More of 'Us' Next Time?

Why would a business fire a long-term, loyal, steady worker whose work was satisfactory? There are three reasons (Mellen, 1979):

1 The economy is in a general shift, and an individual business is caught in this shift. The economy expands and contracts, and some workers are unlucky enough to be caught in a period of contraction, although (in this explanation) many workers still remain employed (see, for example, Bendick, 1983b).

2 Technology has changed and the worker's skills are rendered obsolete.

For example, IBM has closed all its punched card plants in the US; the once ubiquitous punched card has gone the way of the slide rule and so have the punched card makers (Perkins, 1984). In this explanation, the worker's old skills will not be needed again, although many of the skills may be tranferrable to other work and the worker might be retrained (see, for example, Coleman, 1980; Ayres, 1983).

3 The industry of which the worker is part is caught in the long-term, major shift. Other countries have become more competitive. The product is not obsolete, nor are the worker's skills — but the company or the industry is no longer competitive. Greenhouse (1984), for example, reports that the US machine tool industry's orders are stuck at half their 1979 levels, that the industry is operating 60 per cent of capacity and that imports are now accounting for 40 per cent of the market, twice their 1979 levels, The industry's analysts and executives, he observes, are concluding that the contraction is likely to be irreversible, and the industry has petitioned the President to limit imports to 17.5 per cent of the domestic trade (see, Bluestone, Harrison and Baker, 1981; Littman and Lee, 1983; Stein, 1983).

How seriously should these concerns be taken?

Economic shifts

Few can doubt that there are broad economic currents affecting the overall economy: the famous tide that lifts all boats as conditions improve or drops them when conditions deteriorate. At issue is whether these shifts in the future are likely to be more frequent, more extreme, or more long-lasting, any one of which would predict that more workers are likely to be dislocated (Bailey *et al.*, 1983). There are factors which would predict greater instabilities: for example, expansion of multi-national corporations and organizations aimed at controlling prices through controlling supplies, such as OPEC, can mean rapid, major changes in critical resources such as oil should the controlling organizations decide this is in their best interests. There are, however, other factors which would predict no greater instabilities than we have experienced: for example, the growth of other multi-national organizations such as the World Bank whose interest may run counter to destabilizing forces and who have the capacity to modulate some of the larger swings. Without denigrating the importance of economic shifts as causes of worker dislocation, in the balance there do not seem to be compelling reasons to expect *greater* shifts than at present as a major reason for more serious problems in the future (Bendick, 1981, 1982b and 1983).

Technological changes

Technological changes are rapid, and there is reason to expect that the pace will continue to increase. Although these changes may yield a net increase in jobs in the new industries, they undeniably dislocate workers in the old industries (Feingold, 1983). The development of high-speed, large capacity computers has affected the conduct of virtually every aspect of our business and industrial life and much of our personal life also, changes that have created thousands of new jobs but made thousands of others unnecessary. Some believe that the biological developments in genetics are likely to affect food production and distribution as profoundly as developments in physics, chemistry and engineering affected communications. There are enormous consequences if this be true for economic and political realignments. As an example, the United States depends on food exports for a large part of its international trade. But if, through bioengineering, most nations can become self-sufficient for most dietary needs, the value of food as an item of international trade and a source of power could disappear.

In more immediate terms, the future is here for many in the United States, who already need to run fast to stay in the same place as demands of jobs change, and need to run even faster to get ahead. The problems affect younger workers — since schools are often some years behind industry in access to latest technologies — and older workers, who may be less willing to invest in learning and in whom employers may be less willing to invest. While opinions differ about the extent of dislocation that will be the result of any single new technology, (Cawkell, 1983; Collier, 1983; Modern Office and Data Mangement, 1980), such change is a major reason to expect dislocation and displacement to increase.

Competitiveness

With regard to decreased competitiveness affecting individual plants or certain industries more in the future than at present, the situation may get worse before it gets better (Bale, 1976). This is not to say that competitiveness is a new issue. Jefferson spent years in France trying to obtain recognition for the United States as a nation. One obstacle was that Jefferson was instructed to do so without agreeing to relax the protective tariffs imposed by the United States on the import of French woven material while getting the French to give up the tariffs they imposed on the import of the United States tobacco (in order to increase the profitability of French agricultural ventures in the Carribean). Nonetheless, as a nation we have prided ourselves on being able to be competitive by superior productivity. In some areas, it is clear we already are far from competitive, a result that has been attributed variously to lack of investment in modernization after World War II (an investment forced on Japan and Germany whose factories were largely destroyed); management practices that were less effective than those of the Japanese; greater greed on the part of management; and greater greed on the part of labor.

It seems too soon to determine how successful we will be in recompeting for many of our traditional markets (Eizenstat, 1984), although it is not too soon to recognize that if poor management practices, employee avarice or employer greed are major factors, all lose. At present, however, this type of plant closing and consequent extensive reduction in the workforce seem to account for many of the dislocated workers, and providing assistance, a price that may have to be paid for freer trade with less protectionism (Bale and Mutti, 1978; Stein, 1983).

Overall both uncertainties in the ability of the United States to maintain a strong competitive position in many of its traditional businesses and industries, and technological change mean that in the near term, at least, we may anticipate that more — rather than fewer — workers will be dislocated.

Demography

This expectation is bolstered by the demographic profile in the US. Even if none of the factors discussed above were salient, more older workers in the future will be dislocated due to demographic changes (Ehrbar, 1983). The US workforce will age as life span increases, as the 'baby boom' after World War II becomes older, and as economic pressures encourage workers to be earners for longer periods in their lives. By the year 2000, when the post-war population bulge reaches about 55 years of age, almost any closing or lay-off affecting populations in the same proportions within age groups as it does now will create huge absolute numbers of middle-aged, probably hard-working and stable people, men and women, workers in their prime, who have played the game and lost . . . unless the rules of the game are changed.

The next section considers some changes in the rules of the game.

Part II

Programs and Policies in the US: Considering the Options

Three types of interventions will be discussed. The first, which has received the greatest attention, is aimed at assisting workers presently affected by lay-offs and plant closings. The second, which is receiving increasing attention, is aimed at managing new lay-offs and plant closings in ways that minimize the problems for workers, employers and communities. The third type are longer-range strategies, intended to prevent large scale problems.

Assisting dislocated workers

Dislocated workers have been seen as the deserving poor. As Murray (1984) observes,

> I am asked to consider the case of a man who has worked steadily for many years and, in his fifties, is thrown out of his job because the factory closes. Why should I transfer money to him . . . provide him

with unemployment checks and, perhaps, permanent welfare support? The answer is not difficult. I may rationalize it any number of ways but at bottom I consent to transfer money to him because I want to. The worker has plugged along as best he could, contributed his bit to the community, and now faces a personal disaster. He is one of my fellows in a very meaningful way — 'There but for the grace of God . . . . ' and I am happy to see a portion of my income used to help him out. (p. 197).

Many strategies have been initiated for assisting dislocated workers. Although these will be discussed separately, they often are used in combination (see Kohlberg, 1983 for thirty-one brief descriptions of such programs).

— Reassignment to different jobs within the same plant or location based on analysis of readily transferrable skills;
— Reassignment to different jobs within the same plant or location, with employer provided training;
— Relocation of the worker within the company to the same job at a different site, to a related job, or to a different job with employer provided training;
— Career counseling and outplacement assistance, including assistance in preparing resumes, operation of a job search and job placement effort, and follow-up assistance in social services, counseling and support during the transition;
— Initiation of worker self-help networks and job clubs to provide support, assistance and guidance both during the immediate transition periods and when long-term unemployment creates additional stresses; and
— Retraining programs operated by third parties that may provide counseling and placement assistance but which center on improving basic skills and training in new skills.

Support for these programs and services comes from several sources. First, at the local level, some labor/management contracts have retraining clauses in them, requiring management to offer no-cost training if workers so choose. Job security is becoming nationwide a major bargaining issue. Retraining provisions are increasingly widespread and recently, it has been proposed that collective bargaining be required before management closes a plant. Support for job security entitlements is increasing also at the state level. Siegel (1984) reports that some states have taken considerable initiative in this direction. Legislation being considered by Connecticut, for example, would provide special assistance to employees who want to buy a firm about to be closed. A Connecticut Business and Industry Association has developed a six-point approach to be followed voluntarily so that employers fulfill greater responsibilities to workers affected by lay-offs. Massachusetts is considering legislation that would support retraining, continuation of fringe benefits such as health insurance, and development of advance pledges by firms on provisions in case of a shut-down. And the Federal government, through the Job Training Partnership Act, Title III, of 1984, has set aside $223 m for retraining programs for dislocated workers to be operated by the private sector. These most recent initiatives are in addition to the numerous provisions in various pieces of special legislation going back many years that have protected the income and cushioned lay-offs among workers such as loggers and railroad firemen (Beauregard, Van Horn and Ford, 1983).

It is too early to say how successful these strategies may be; evaluations are limited in both quantity and quality. The results of these studies suggest, however, that some individuals have been helped, and the programs may contribute to the high percentage of laid-off workers who find new jobs within a few weeks. There are, however, already reports indicating that these approaches may be successful for a more limited subset of laid-off workers than was hoped. Bale and Mutti (1978), for instance, found that retraining programs were only minimally effective, leading to a major distributional effect and income loss for those workers who had to accept jobs in industries where they received lower pay than in their earlier occupation. Some of the reasons why the programs may help a smaller number of dislocated workers than anticipated are economic; some psychological (National Alliance of Business, 1981; National Commission on Employment Policy, 1981; Rives and West, 1979 and 1980).

— When the bottom drops out of the real-estate market, many workers can not afford to relocate. Their homes are their most valuable possession, and they can not get enough money for their house in a depressed housing market to buy another one in a more prosperous community. Samuelson (1980) has noted that older people are less likely to move than younger. Of the 500,000 workers who received Trade Adjustment Assistance Act help between 1974 and 1979, only 2700 took available out-of-town job search money and only 1700 actually relocated. Samuelson's conclusions are reinforced by Bendick (1982a) who believes that government assistance should not be focussed on relocation. And Magaziner (1983), considering why dislocated workers relocate as a last resort, observes,

> ... in many people's worklives, there is a large, legitimate element of conservatism and inertia, factors that are some-times described as company and community loyalty. Many workers are willing to make substantial sacrifices in terms of physical comfort, lifestyle and economic rewards to stay with the same firm rather than move to another job. Fellow workers, familiar surroundings, and known work patterns and status all help to create a comfortable atmosphere. Work places are, at the bottom, communities. People generally do

not like to sever community ties, particularly when they have developed friendship and status relationships, patterns of recreation and shopping, financial ties and family and social responsibilities in the region. (p. 33)

— Many are highly paid and highly skilled; they have to enter a new skill area at entry levels, and thus must adjust to earning a great deal less money as well as to being a junior person at a senior age and to being — as a just-hired worker — vulnerable to new lay-offs at a time in life when they often have family commitments requiring a regular income. Boggs and Buss (1983), for example, studied the participation in training programs of steelworkers unemployed after the Youngstown steel plant closing. The workers were not interested in education, according to the researchers, because most could find other jobs, many were waiting for a reopening of the plant, and still others felt steelmaking was their way of life and would not consider other kinds of work. Yeager (1973) concluded that long periods of unemployment among 5000 workers laid off by three defense firms between 1963 and 1965 resulted from ' . . . perfectly rational search strategies in which workers expected the government to bail the firm out of financial trouble so that displaced personnel could be recalled. These false expectations of recall increased the severity of the layoff because they gave displaced workers an incentive to remain unemployed in the local labor market.' (p. 98). While these observations cannot be generalized to more distressed economic conditions, Yeager found that the period of unemployment was about twice as long when bailouts were expected than when recall expectations were lower.

— Some skills, often those most in demand among job paying wages close to those laid-off workers previously earned, are not that easy to learn: many older workers have not been learners for many years and are resentful and unsure of themselves as learners, and at least some of the retraining programs have been put together hastily without adequate checks of what real jobs are available, adequate training materials, adequate teachers, or adequate preparation for the learners. Burns (1982) for example, studied training provided to 150 displaced workers following the Chrysler plant closing in the summer of 1979. He found that the institutions providing training were concerned primarily with increased enrollment while the participants were concerned primarily with the extended funding allowance available for the training period. The training was hastily put together and conducted. Although some participants perceived the program as being beneficial, many did not gain employment (56 per cent found jobs, mostly younger males). Burns' findings have been echoed by Choate and Epstein (1982), Mcgowan (1983), Mathews (1983a and 1983b). Retraining appears to be valuable for some, but not many workers, at least as it has too often been practiced — on a crash basis. The most successful immediate assistance approach seems to be help in job search and outplacement. Bendick (1983a and 1983b), who has analyzed the 'disabilities of affluence' that distinguish so strikingly the dislocated from the disadvantaged worker, strongly recommends that for most displaced workers only career management and job search help be provided, together with encouragement for temporary job search clubs. Concerned with the displacement evident in CETA (and continued in JTPA allocations) from the disadvantaged to the dislocated, he argues that education should be provided only to the illiterate who lack high school level basic skills or for workers already employed. Such workers would, he concludes, move on if they had advanced training, creating vacancies less skilled dislocated workers could fill.

It seems fair to say that observers across the spectrum of political opinion conclude that some supports impede rather than promote individual adjustment to plant closing. Murray (1984) who might be considered hardline, would seem to agree with Bendick:

> Let us return to the case of the middle aged worker, who loses his job, wants desperately to work but can find nothing. He receives unemployment insurance, hating every penny of it. He would seem to be 'completely involuntarily' in his situation and his search for a job unaffected by the existence of unemployment insurance. In fact, however, his behavior ... *is* affected by the existence of unemployment insurance. For example, the cushion provided by unemployment insurance may lead him to refuse to take a job that requires him to move to another town, whereas he would take the job and uproot his home if he were more desperate. (p. 213)

Not surprisingly, alternatives to ameliorating the suffering and economic loss to worker, employer and community are sought, since increasing the desperation of the older worker is an unpalatable remedy.

Managing lay-offs

The well-publicized problems with crash programs has turned attention to better management of lay-offs. Approaches being tried include:

— Labor-management agreements that spell out worker rights and responsibilities in case of closing, covering such issues as minimum advance notice, relocation management, and extension of some benefits;
— Notification to labor and government at the very earliest time when plant closings or lay-offs are seen as a possibility (Cipparone, 1981); and

— Joint labor-management planning for the lay-off, brokered and supported by skilled third parties, to counsel workers, find jobs, and ease the transitions, starting as soon as there is any reason to believe lay-offs are ahead.

Perhaps paradoxically, more is known about the effectiveness of these amelioration approaches than about assistance strategies, primarily because they have been implemented since 1963 in Canada (Batt, 1983; Swift, 1984). The Canadian system, the Manpower Consultative Service (MCS), is supported by the central government and managed in the provinces. Field workers — usually retired, highly successful, respected former executives in local industries — are responsible for maintaining close contact with businesses and industries in their territory to learn at the earliest possible time of impending closings. They initiate meetings with management and labor, urging them to form a joint committee to anticipate the size of the lay-offs and the nature of the worker skills available. The committee, with technical assistance from the field worker, creates a large private sector network in the immediate region in order to avoid relocations, an approach that is said to be successful in most cases in absorbing the release of workers. Through services the committee determines are needed, workers receive counseling, outplacement assistance and follow-up assistance aimed at creating a controlled 'seepage' into the community and minimizing the need for retraining. While the program has not been systematically evaluated, it is claimed to be not only effective but inexpensive, averaging less than $100 per affected worker. The MCS 1984 budget was $4 million; the total staff, sixty-six employees. MCS has been credited with helping firms as large as Ford Motor Company of Canada, as well as smaller businesses, handling problems such as lay-offs, closings and technological change. It is cited frequently in comparative studies as offering the most lessons from which countries such as the United States can learn (Stein, 1983). Bendick (1982a and 1983c) in particular praises its program of economic development assistance to communities and mainstreaming social services through coordinating available help rather than creating new programs and segregating dislocated workers.

Prevention

A number of strategies have been proposed for the longer run. These include:

— Reduction in the duration and extent of unemployment benefits, on the grounds that many workers are unable to face the reality of the changes and are sustained by unemployment insurance for so long that they are still further behind in terms of age, lost opportunities and work skills than when they started. McLennan (1983), for example, reports that state trust funds are in poor financial condition, due to overextension of the program. He believes policies need to change in order to help workers adjust more rapidly to job loss and to target greatest benefits to those facing greatest hardship from unemployment. Among the changes he recommends are: (i) increasing the relation between a firm's unemployment experience and the unemployment insurance tax it pays; (ii) requiring all states have ten-day minimum waiting period; (iii) paying unemployment insurance only after a worker completes a job search seminar; (iv) taxing all unemployment insurance benefits to reduce disincentives to work; (v) facilitating reemployment; and (vi) providing greater assistance to permanently displaced, highly experienced workers (see also Bendick, 1983d.)

— Establishing both expectations and an infrastructure that makes learning a life-long enterprise, with workers expecting they will have to invest their own time and resources throughout their working lives (as they do now in preparing to enter the labor market) in maintaining their current skills and developing new ones. The US tax code permits deductions for training needed to remain employable in one's present position. New proposals include creating incentives for continual worker self-investment in training for new jobs. Recently, enrollments in community colleges have boomed. Not a little is attributed to self-initiated and often self-supported preparation for new careers by blue, pink and white collar workers who are taking responsibility for being ready quickly — and on their own terms, at their own time — to shift occupations (*Higher Education Daily*, 1984).

— Developing individual training accounts, along the lines of IRAs, to be drawn on (without tax penalty) only for retraining purposes (Hook, 1984). The workers, it is argued, will be better users and purchasers of training with their own funds. One model often cited is the 'GI Bill' whose effectiveness is attributed to its voucher-like balance of flexibility and accountability: veterans selected themselves what training they wanted, and from whom, but had only their entitlement and no more to 'spend' on their education and training. Another model often discussed is the French Further Vocational Training System (Bendick, 1982 and 1983c): Employers' annual contributions are used to finance voluntary training courses for life-long learning. One serious problem for preventive purposes is that proportionately few skilled technical and blue collar workers take advantage of these opportunities. This is similar to some United States experience with employer supported life-long learning programs offered by some companies: participants are not those most likely to be affected by dislocation.

Other strategies aimed at prevention on a still larger scale have been proposed.

— Encouraging greater productivity through incentives such as Employee Stock Ownership Plans, believed to mobilize worker pride and to capitalize on self-interest in having a profitable plant (Stern, Wood and Hammer, 1979).

— Greater use of protective tariffs and development of more home markets in traditional industries such as automobiles and steel.
— Greater investment in research and development to maintain an overall competitive edge in ideas that will compensate for the loss of international trade due to higher tariffs needed to protect traditional industries domestically.

Again, it is too early to tell how effective these would be. While argument from international experience requires caution, incentives for workers to reduce loyalty to companies and feel more dependent on themselves for their futures at ages where job mobility has been difficult may run counter to belief that increased productivity depends in part on greater loyalty of the worker to the company. The strategies aimed at major shifts in locus of responsibility for maintaining individual skills and readiness for new jobs certainly have much that is consonant with trends toward voluntary retraining already evident in US higher education enrollments. Enshrining this trend in policies aimed at reducing working dependency on individual companies conflicts, however, with trends toward policies encouraging greater worker identification of their economic well-being with that of their employers.

There may be a more balanced alternative: mutual risk, mutual responsibility. Foulkes and Whitman (1984), for example, conclude that job security enhances loyalty to companies, confidence and trust in management, less resistance to technical change, lower staff turnover and better employee relations, attitudes which can contribute to higher productivity. They report that thirty leading companies in the United States already operate with a no lay-off policy, including Xerox, General Food, Control Data, Hewlett-Packard and Bank of America. These policies require, however, stable demand rather than cyclical demand, and careful planning — in forecasting demand and productivity, in hiring, and in career counseling. As McKenzie (1979 and 1982) argues, restrictions on business mobility need to be examined closely, since the price of worker security may be a highly inefficient flow of capital (see also Arnold, 1980; Boyle, 1982; Raines, Berson and Gracie, 1982). Bolt (1983) has observed that policies that may be needed to make greater job security work include quid pro quos from both labor and management:

— commitments on the part of business and industry to shape their product and marketing strategies to enhance security: fewer large but unpredictable customers whose contracts may require hiring and firing a lot of people;
— commitments from management to reduce pressures on earnings by limiting debt and dividends;
— commitments from labor to participate in work flexibility, accepting reassignments and retraining: reassignments, for example, from production to marketing and sales when business is bad; and

— commitments from labor to accept incentives aimed at building longer-term investment in employer success such as stock options and profit sharing rather than short term benefits.

Given the strong evidence that the duration of unemployment is substantially greater in regions with high unemployment rates, there is relatively little attention in discussions of worker displacement to strategies aimed directly at regional economic well-being, recovery and growth in contrast to strategies focused on the individual worker and individual employer. Arguably, regional policies would be most humane and consistent with what is well-established concerning the characteristics and behaviors of displaced workers (in contrast to policies aimed at increasing desperation in order to promote relocation). There is no dearth of such approaches. Examples include requirements that a minimum amount of all monies available for new federal contracts be awarded in areas with unemployment rates above the trigger levels and support of regional economic planning commissions such as the Appalachian Regional Commission, as well as more informal but widespread and usually successful efforts to target military spending and special projects in Congressional districts impacted by unemployment. While a review of regional economic development policies is beyond the scope of this paper, it seems important to emphasize that such policies, if they could be effective prospectively, would seem to have notable potential for prevention.

Summary

The problem of dislocated workers today is serious, but public anxiety seems out of proportion to the numbers, unless the concern is regarded as partly anticipatory. Reasons to expect matters would grow worse were considered and it was concluded that for three reasons — two speculative and one simple arithmetic — they would. Speculatively, technological change which displaces workers will increase and so will lay-offs and closings associated with non-competitive positions in businesses and industries not affected by technological change. Most seriously, by arithmetic, as the post-World War II baby boom ages, any lay-offs affecting older as well as younger workers will pick up far more older workers than at present. Finally, three types of strategies aimed at the dislocated worker were reviewed: assistance, amelioration and prevention.

Assistance is receiving greatest resources and policy attention but there is reason to believe that such aid, while certainly humane and helpful to some, does not assist many. Amelioration has been tried extensively in Canada. Where circumstances are similar — particularly with regard to the absorptive capacity of communities — some analysts firmly believe it could be similarly effective here. Prevention policies now under discussion, involving more worker anticipation of the need to be retrained and more initiative in preparing for retraining, have the advantage of consistency with a surge of voluntarily initiated training and education for job switching purposes. They may have the disadvantage, however, of decreasing still further the mutual responsibility and investment of the employer and the worker in each other's prosperity that may be an important component of greater productivity.

Thus, despite the attractiveness of solving the future problem by defining it as part of life-long learning the responsibility for which is primarily the worker's, the most promising policy course may be to seek mutual responsibilities and mutual support, particularly those encouraging worker investment in the success of the business and employer investment in the security to the workers, and to explore regional economic development policies.

Notes

1   The views expressed here are those of the author and no endorsement by the United States General Accounting Office is intended or should be inferred.

References

ARNOLD, M.T., (1980) 'Existing and proposed regulation of business dislocations', *Journal of Urban Law*, 57, winter, pp. 209–55.

AYRES, W. (1983) 'Testimony on the Impact of Robotics on Employment', Hearing before the Sub-committee on Economic Goals and Intergovernmental Policy of the Joint Economic Committee, Congress of the United States, Ninety-Eighth Congress. Washington, D.C., Joint Economic Committee, 18 March 1983.

BAILEY, M.N., BURTLESS, G., POWELL, M.R., Jr. and SEMERAD, R.D. (1983) 'Unemployment', *Brookings Review*, 2, 1, Fall, pp. 28–31.

BALE, M.D. (1976) 'Estimates of trade displacement costs for US workers', *Journal of International Economics*, 6, pp. 245–50.

BALE, D. and MILLER, D. (1976) *The Effects of Adjustment Assistance on Trade-Displaced Workers: A Case Study*, Bozeman, Montana, Department of Agricultural Economics and Economics, Montana State University, January.

BALE, M. and MUTTI, J.H. (1978) 'Income losses, compensation and international trade', *Journal of Human Resources*, 13, 2, Spring, pp. 278–85.

BARTH, M.C. (1982) 'Dislocated workers', *Journal of the Institute for Socioeconomic Studies*, pp. 23–5.

BATT, WILLIAM L., Jr. (1983) 'Canada: A good example with displaced workers', *Harvard Business Review*, 61, 8, July-August, p. 6.

BEAUREGARD, R.A., VAN HORN, C.E. and FORD, D.S. (1983) 'Government assistance to displaced workers: An historical perspective', *Journal of Health and Human Resources Assistance*, Fall, pp. 166–83.

BENDICK, M., Jr. (1982a) '*Workers dislocated by economic change: Toward new institutions for midcareer worker transformation.*' Washington, D.C., Urban Institute, February.

BENDICK, M., Jr. (1982b) 'Employment training and economic development' in PALMER, J.L. and SAWHILL I.V. (Eds.) *The Reagan Experiment*, Washington, D.C.,

Urban Institute.

BENDICK, M., Jr. (1983a) 'Reemploying dislocated workers: Five strategies for Pennsylvania'. Statement before the House of Representatives Committee on Appropriations, Legislature of the Commonwealth of Pennsylvania, Washington, D.C., Urban Institute, 9 March.

BENDICK, M., Jr. (1983b) 'Government's role in the job transitions of America's dislocated workers'. Statement before the Committee on Science and Technology and the Committee on the Budget, US House of Representatives, 9 June.

BENDICK, M., Jr. (1983c) *Dislocated Workers and Mid-career Training in Other Industrial Nations*, Washington, D.C., Urban Institute, August.

BENDICK, M., Jr. (1983d) 'The Swedish "active labor market" approach to reemploying workers dislocated by economic change'. *Journal of Health and Human Resources Administration*, 6, 2, Fall, pp. 209–24

BENDICK, M., Jr. and DEVINE, Jr (1981) 'Workers dislocated by economic change: Do they need federal employment and training assistance?', *National Commission for Employment Policy Seventh Annual Report*, Washington, D.C., National Commission for Employment Policy.

BLUESTONE, B., HARRISON, B. and BAKER, L. (1981) *Corporate flight: The Causes and Consequences of Economic Dislocation*, Washington, D.C., Progressive Alliance.

BOGGS, D.L. and BUSS, T.F. (1983) 'Retraining and educating displaced workers: the Youngstown case', *Journal of Health and Human Resources Administration*, 6, 2, Fall, pp. 240–57

BOLT, J.E. (1983) 'Job security: Its time has come'. *Harvard Business Review*, December.

BORUS, M. ELIOT. (1964) 'The Economic Effectiveness of Retraining the Unemployed: A Study of the Benefits and Costs of Retraining the Unemployed Based on the Experience of Workers in Connecticut'. Doctoral dissertation, Yale University.

BOYLE, M.R. (1982) 'Plant closings: Options for economic adjustment', *Economic Development Commentary*, 6, Fall, pp. 17–23.

BROOKS, G. (1983) 'Left behind'. *Wall Street Journal*, p. 1 (W), p. 1 (E) 5 August.

BURNS, D.C. (1982) 'A Case Study of Trade-Adjustment Assistance Sponsored Community College Training Following the Lyons/Muir Chrysler Plant Closing'. Doctoral dissertation, University of Michigan.

BUSS, T. (1980) *Public Policies for Communities in Economic Crisis: A Selected Bibliography of Current Research on Plant Closings*. Monticello, Ill., Vance Bibliographies.

C&R ASSOCIATES. (1978) *Community Costs of Plant Closings: Bibliography and Survey of Literature*, Report to the Federal Trade Commission.

CAWKELL, A.E. (1983) 'Information technology and work', *Journal of Information Science*, 6, pp. 123–35.

CIPPARONE, J.A. (1981) 'Advance notice of plant closings: Toward national legislation'. *University of Michigan Journal of Law Reform*, 14, winter, pp. 283–319.

CHOATE, P. and EPSTEIN, N. (1982) 'The work force of the future', *Nation's Business*, 70, 11, November, pp. 58–60.

CLARK, M. and NELSON, J. (1982) 'Northwesterners out of work: The human costs of unemployment'. *Ideas for Action in Education and Work*, 7, November.

CLARK, M. and NELSON, J. (1983) 'Northwesterners out of work: The effects of job dislocation'. *Ideas for Action in Education and Work*, 8, May.

COLEMAN, S. (1980) 'Australian unions condemn technology report'. *Computerworld*, 8 September, p. 16.

COLLIER, D.A., (1983) 'The service sector revolution', *Long Range Planning (UK)*, 16,

6, December pp. 10–20.

CORRIGAN, R. and STANFIELD, R.L. (1984) 'Casualties of change', *National Journal*, 11 February, pp. 20–58.

CRAYPO, C. and DAVISSON. W.I. (1983) 'Plant shutdown, collective bargaining, and job and employment experiences of displaced brewery workers', *Labor Studies Journal*, 7, winter, pp. 195–215.

EHRBAR, A.F. (1983) 'Grasping the new unemployment', *Fortune*, 107, 16 May, p. 106.

EIZENSTAT, S.E. (1984) 'Industrial policy: Not if, but how', *Fortune*, 109, 2, 23 January, pp. 183–5.

FEINGOLD, S. NORMAN, (1983) 'Tracking new career categories will become a preoc-cupation for job seekers and managers', *Personnel Administrator*, 28, 12, December, pp. 86–91.

FERMAN, L.A. and GORDUS, J.P. (1979) *Mental Health and the Economy*. Kalamazoo, MI, Upjohn Institute.

FOULKES, F.K. and WHITMAN, A. (1984) *Full employment, product/marketing strategies*. Boston, MA, Human Resources Policy Institute, Boston University.

GREENHOUSE, S. (1984) 'A survival fight in machine tools', *New York Times*, 8 July.

GORDUS, J.P. (1981) *Plant Closings and Economic Dislocation*, Kalamazoo, MI: Upjohn Institute for Employment Research.

HAMMERMAN, H, (1964) *Case Studies of Displaced Workers: Experiences of Workers After Layoff*, Washington, D.C., Bureau of Labor Statistics, (Report Bo BLS-BULL-1408)

HANSEN, G.B., BENTLEY, M. and SKIDMORE, M. (1981) *Plant Shutdowns, People and Communities: A Selected Bibliography*, Logan, Utah, Utah Center for Productivity and Quality of Working Life, Utah State University, May.

HEARN, F., MERTENS M., and FARICELLIA J. (1983) 'An American tragedy: Act two', *Dissent*, 30, spring, pp. 183–9.

Higher Education Daily. (1984) 'The Unemployed: New faces on campus', 27 July, p. 5.

HOOK, J. (1984) 'Individual training accounts eyed to assist the dislocated', *Congressional Quarterly*, 7 April, pp. 781–2.

IGNAGNI, K. (1983) 'Translating employment statistics into human terms', in KOHLBERG, W.H. (Ed.) *The Dislocated Worker*, Washington, D.C., National Alliance of Business, pp. 164–7.

JACOBSON, L. and THOMPSON, J. (1979) *Earnings Loss Due to Displacement*, Alexandria, VA., The Public Research Institute. CRC 385, August.

JENKINS, G.P. and MONTMARQUETTE, C. (1979) 'Estimating the private and social opportunity cost of displaced workers', *Review of Economics and Statistics*, 61, 3, August, pp. 342–53.

KOHLBERG, W.H. (Ed.) (1983) *The Dislocated Worker: Preparing America's Workforce for New Jobs*, Washington, D.C., National Alliance of Business, December.

LITTMAN, D.A. and LEE, M-H. (1983) 'Plant closing and worker dislocation', *Economic Review*, Fall, pp. 2–18.

LUBLIN, J. (1983) 'The age barrier', *Wall Street Journal*, 2 August, p. 1 (q), P. 1 (E)

MCKENZIE, R. (1979) *Restrictions on Business Mobility*, Washington, D.C., The American Enterprise Institute.

MCKENZIE, R.B. (Ed.). (1982) *Plant Closings: Public or Private Choices?* Washington, Cato Institute.

MCKERSIE, R.B., GREENHALGH, L. and JICK, T.D. (1981) 'The CEC: Labor-management cooperation in New York', *Industrial Relations*, 20, 2, spring, pp. 212–20.

MAGAZINER, I.C. (1983) 'The rationale for a US industrial policy', *Journal of Contemporary Issues*, 11, 1, pp. 29–44.

MATHEWS, J. (1983) 'Quiz shows most ill-equipped for course: Retraining '83', *Washington Post*, 7 November, p. A1.

MICK, S.S. (1975) 'Social and personal costs of plant shutdowns', *Industrial Relations*, 14, 2, May, pp. 204–6.

Modern Office and Data Management, (1980) 'Keeping abreast of changes with a different kind of workforce'. September pp. 24–5.

MURRAY, C. (1984) *Losing Ground: American Social Policy, 1950–1980*. New York, Basic Books Inc.

National Alliance of Business. (1981) 'Worker adjustment to plant shut downs and mass lay-offs: An analysis of program experience and policy options', August.

National Commission on Employment Policy (1981a) 'The role of CETA in providing services to non-disadvantaged, displaced workers', October.

National Commission on Employment Policy. (1981b) 'Federal interest in employment and training: Seventh annual report', Washington, D.C.

PALEN, J.J. (1966) 'The displaced worker: The social and economic effects of the Studebaker shutdown'. Doctoral dissertation, University of Wisconsin.

PARNES, S. and KING, R. (1977) *Middle Aged Job Losers*, Columbus, Ohio, Center for Human Resource Research, Ohio State University.

PERKINS, J. (1984) 'IBM punch card plant will close'. *Washington Post* 2 July.

PICHLER, J.A. (1967) 'The influence of shutdown provisions upon the adjustment patterns of displaced workers'. Doctoral dissertation, University of Chicago.

RAINES, J.C., BERSON L.E., and GRACIE D. McI., (Eds) (1982) *Community and Capital in Conflict: Plant Closing and Job Loss*, Philadelphia, Temple University Press.

RIVES, J.M. and WEST, J.M. (1979–80) 'Reemployment of displaced workers'. *Economic Forum*, 10, winter, pp. 73–81.

RIVES, J.M. and West, J.M. (1980) 'CETA program and displaced workers', *Aging and Work*, Fall, pp. 221–7.

ROTTENBERG, S., 'Reply', *Industrial and Labor Relations Review*, pp. 284–8.

SAMUELSON, ROBERT. (1980) 'On mobility', *National Journal*, 16 August, p. 1366.

SHOSTAK, A. (1980) 'The human cost of plant closing', *American Federationist*, 87, August pp. 22–5.

SIEGEL, J.S. (1984) 'Some positive aspects of plant closing laws', *New England Business*, 6, 7, 16 April, pp. 73–5.

STEIN, L. (1983) 'Trade adjustment assistance as a means of achieving improved resource allocation through freer trade: An analysis of policies for aiding the import-injured in the USA, Canada and Australia', *American Journal of Economics and Sociology*. 41, 3, July, p. 243.

STERN, N., WOOD, K.H., and HAMMER, T.H. (1979) *Employee Ownership in Plant Shutdowns*, Kalamazoo, MI, Upjohn Institute.

SWIFT, D., (1984) 'Resurrection: A federal department cuts the red tape to set workers back on track', *Canadian Business*, February pp. 29–30.

US Congress, Senate Committee on Labor and Human Resources (1979) *Plant Closings and Relocations*, Hearing, 96th Congress, 1st session, Washington, D.C., GPO.

US Congress, Senate Committee on Labor and Human Resources (1980) *Employee Protection and Community Stabilization Act of 1980*, Hearing, 96th Congress, 2nd session on S. 1609, Washington. D.C., GPO.

US Congress, Senate Committee on Labor and Human Resources (1981) *Workers and The Evolving Economy of the Eighties*, Hearings, 96th Congress, 2nd session, 17–18 September 1980, Washington, D.C, GPO.

US General Accounting Office (1980) *Restricting Trade Act Benefits to Imports Affected Workers Who Cannot Find a Job Can Save Millions*, Washington, D.C., U.S. Government Printing Office, 15 January.

WEGMANN, R.G. (1983) *Reemployment Assistance for Laid-Off Workers: Information Series No. 258*, Columbus, Ohio, ERIC Clearinghouse on Adult, Career and Vocational Education.

YEAGER, J.H. Jr., (1972) 'Unemployment in the Defense Industry: An Analysis of the Unemployed Worker's Job Search Strategy and the Manpower Policies the Firm'. Doctoral dissertation, Texas A & M University, December.

ACOT

2 5 NOV 1986

LIBRARY

Manpower and Development in Japan: A Study of the Japanese Education and Training System

Ken Inoue

Introduction

The three basic resources necessary for economic development are financial resources (money), physical resources (material) and human resources (manpower). Although all three are closely related and mutually dependent in the process of economic development, manpower appears to be the most fundamental resource. This is because it is human beings that cultivate land, exploit natural resources, create the means of production and save surplus products for future investment. A country with rich natural resources and ample financial resources cannot necessarily achieve steady economic development if it does not have enough manpower to utilize and develop them. On the other hand, a country with well-educated manpower has a chance to obtain economic success, even if it has poor natural resources. Japan, which does not have significant natural resources, is an obvious example of economic development in which manpower has played a crucial role.

This chapter consists of three main sections: (i) education and training in a Japanese company; (ii) Japanese management and manpower; and (iii) work-

Table 1: Distribution of Labor Force and GDP

	Labor force (1980) (%)	GDP (1982) (%)
Primary industries	10.9	4
Secondary industries	33.6	42
[manufacturing]	(23.7)	(30)
Tertiary industries	55.4	54
[public sector]	(3.6)	(n.a.)
TOTAL	100	100

Note: Total number of the labor force is 55,811 thousand, and it includes 'others'. Total amount of GDP is $1,061 billion.
Source: Ministry of Labor, World Development Report 1983.

ers' participation and economic development. The first section deals with education and training programs in industry organized by both the government and companies. In the second section, in order to understand the management policies of the in-company education and training, we will examine the characteristics of Japanese management in the employment, promotion and wage systems. The third section analyzes workers' participation as a resource of economic vitality of Japanese companies by focussing on labor participation in management, suggestion system, and company-wide quality control. Finally, some effects of Japan's manpower management policies will also be examined.

Education and Training in a Japanese Company

This section aims at examining the in-company education and training system.[1] As indicated in table 1, 85 per cent of the Japanese labor force is engaged in the private sector of secondary and tertiary industries, and they produce more than 90 per cent of total GDP. Manufacturing industry employs 24 per cent of the labor force and produces 30 per cent of the Gross Domestic Product (GDP). Since most of the labor force is working in companies, it is meaningful to examine their education and training system in order to understand the role of manpower in Japan's economic development. In the following we will first briefly look at (a) government policies for skill acquisition in a company, then, examine (b) the education and training system in a company.

Government Policies for Skill Acquisition in a Company

The Vocational Training Law, which represents the government's vocational training policies has two origins, namely, skilled workers training and vocational guidance.[2]

The government began to be concerned about in-plant skilled workers training in the late 1930s, mainly because of the military requirement. In 1939, the ordinance of skilled workers training in factories and workshops was enacted, and large factories were obliged to train skilled workers with a government subsidy. Although the law was abolished at the end of World War II, the idea of in-plant skilled workers training was retained in a newly-enacted Labor Standard Law of 1947. It is important to note that the Labor Standard Law regulated in-company vocational training from the viewpoint of criticizing apprenticeship. This is because in the pre-war period, there was severe exploitation of young workers under the name of apprenticeship. Especially in the small and medium size companies where feudalistic human relations still widely remained, apprentices were overworked and forced to do tasks unrelated to skill acquisition such as household matters. Therefore, the Law aimed to establish a modern skill acquisition system in a company. This is the origin of authorized vocational training in an enterprise(s) regulated by the present vocational training law.

Another origin of the present vocational training policies is vocational guidance which started in the 1920s. In order to cope with the unemployment problem, the government established vocational training institutions, since there was a shortage of skilled workers even at a time of mass unemployment. In 1947, after World War II, the Employment Security Law was enacted to give the unemployed vocational training in public institutions. This has developed into the present system of public training institutions administered by the Ministry of Labor.

These two training programs, namely, skilled workers training based on the Labor Standard Law, and vocational guidance based on Employment Security Law, were unified into the Vocational Training Law in 1958, just before Japan started its high economic growth (the Law was completely revised in 1969 in order to meet Japan's rapid economic development). The Law requires the Minister of Labor to prepare the basic scheme of vocational training which indicates the fundamental direction of the policies for vocational training and skills certification (Article 5), and each prefecture governor is to prepare the prefectural scheme of vocational training based on the basic scheme (Article 6).

The first and the second basic scheme based on the revised Vocational Training Law were planned for 1971–75 and 1976–80 respectively, and the third scheme (for 1981–85) has now been implemented. The aims of the most recent basic scheme of vocational training, which is subtitled 'Preparation for career training system', are: first, basic vocational training should be provided for young persons who are going to start working, according to their ability and aptitude. It is necessary to strengthen the relation between school education and public vocational training. Second, training for currently

Table 2: Authorized in-company vocational training institutions

	1978	1979	1980	1981
Number of Employers				
Single	262 (0.3%)	257 (0.2%)	263 (0.2%)	305 (0.2%)
Association	99,425 (99.7%)	143,682 (99.8%)	152,581 (99.8%)	179,091 (99.8%)
TOTAL	99,687	143,939	152,844	179,396
Number of Institutions				
Single	262 (28.2%)	257 (25.9%)	263 (26.5%)	305 (28.3%)
Association	667 (71.8%)	734 (74.1%)	730 (73.5%)	771 (71.7%)
TOTAL	929	991	993	1,076

Source: Ministry of Labor

employed workers should be strengthened, because we can expect structural change in industries, technological innovation, extension of working career, and demand for self-development.

In order to cope with this situation, education and training organized by employers has to be developed, and supported by public vocational training. Third, occupational capability redevelopment training should be provided, especially for persons leaving the changing occupations and women intending to work. Fourth, the evaluation system for vocational capability should be provided according to each stage of the working career, and the skill certification system must be expanded. Fifth, Japan should play an important role in international technical cooperation through vocational training.

Authorized in-company vocational training is performed by single enterprises or an association of enterprises. The former is implemented by relatively large companies, and the latter by relatively small companies. Table 2 indicates the number of authorized in-company vocational training institutions and the number of employers organizing the training institutions. From this table, we can observe the following points. First, the percentages of the number of single employers, which are relatively big enterprises, are only 0.2–0.3 per cent. However, they share 26–28 per cent of the total authorized vocational training institutions. Second, 99.7 or 99.8 per cent of employers who organize authorized vocational training institutions are performing the training as associations. This fact implies that almost all enterprises which use the authorized in-company vocational training system, are relatively small companies.

It is important, however, to note that the total number of enterprises in Japan is more than 5.8 million in 1978. Therefore, the percentage of enterprises which have authorized in-company vocational training institutions individually or as an association is only 1.7 per cent of all enterprises. Almost all companies are performing employees' training in another way, rather than using the authorized vocational training system. We will examine this in the next section.

Education and Training System in Japanese Companies

Although the purpose here is to examine the in-company education and training system, it is important, first of all, to clarify the difference among companies. Roughly speaking, Japanese companies are classified into two groups by their size, namely, large companies, and small and medium companies. According to the Fundamental Law of Small and Medium Enterprises, small and medium companies are defined by the number of employees or the amount of capital. In the case of manufacturing business, for example, small and medium companies are defined as those with less than 300 employees or less than Y 100 million of capital. Table 3 indicates the share of large, small, and medium enterprises classified by industry. From this table,

Table 3: Share of the number of large companies and small and medium companies

	Small and medium (%)	Large (%)	Total number (%)
Mining	99.5	0.5	6,817 (0.1)
Construction	99.9	0.1	495,345 (8.5)
Manufacturing	99.5	0.5	841,132(14.4)
Retail, wholesale	99.6	0.4	2,865,596(49.0)
Finance, insurance	99.5	0.5	75,261 (1.3)
Real estate	100.0	0.0	213,331 (3.6)
Transport, etc	99.5	0.5	115,096 (2.0)
Electricity, gas, etc	97.5	2.5	5,305 (0.1)
Service	98.6	1.4	1,231,708(21.1)
TOTAL	99.4	0.6	5,849,321 (100)

Note: Small and medium means companies with less than 300 employees exept wholesale
(less than 100), retail (less than fifty) and service (less than fifty).
Source: Prime Minister's Office

we can observe that more than 99 per cent of enterprises are small or medium companies in any industry. Although in the following part of this chapter, we will mainly concentrate on companies in the manufacturing industry, it is important to note that the number of manufacturing companies comprises only 14.4 per cent of all companies while in terms of the numbers of workers, it comprises 29.6 per cent.

Table 4 shows shares of the number of businesses, number of workers, amount of gross and net product among small, medium and large companies in the manufacturing sector. From this table, we can observe the following points. First, although the number of large companies are only 0.5 per cent of all companies, they produce nearly half of the products. Second, although small companies share 87.2 per cent in number, their share of gross product is only 12.6 per cent. These differentials among companies affect their in-company education and training performance.

Table 5 shows the difference of education and training performance between large enterprises, and small and medium enterprises. We can observe from this table that 42.0 per cent of large companies have regular and

Table 4: Shares of manufacturing companies classified by size

Size by number of employees	Small (less than 19) %	Medium (20–299) %	Large (300+) %	Total number/yen
Number of companies	87.2	12.3	0.5	841,132
Number of workers	73.5		26.5	12,509,000
Amount of gross product	12.6	40.1	47.3	¥ 162 trillion
Amount of net product	16.1	41.0	42.9	¥ 56 trillion

Source: Prime Minister's Office (first two rows); Ministry of International Trade and Industry
(last two rows)

Table 5: Education and training performance during 1979 in manufacturing companies

	Large (%)	Small and medium (%)
Regularly and systematic	42.0	6.3
Systematic training as necessary	47.8	39.0
Support for individual training	5.6	28.5
Not systematic, obtain by experience in job	3.5	25.3
Others	1.0	1.0

Source: Small and Medium Enterprise Agency, 1980

Table 6: Index of expenditure per worker for education and training

Size of company	30–99	100–299	300–999	1000–4999	5000+
Index	20.4	31.2	52.5	61.0	100

Source: Small and Medium Enterprise Agency, 1983

systematic education and training programs, while in the case of small and medium companies, only 6.3 per cent have them. This is mainly because of the difference of financial capability of education and training.

Table 6 indicates the index of the expenditure for education and training per worker classified by the size of company. It is obvious from this table that the smaller companies are, the less they spend for employees' education and training. Small companies which have between thirty and ninety-nine workers can spend only 20.4 per cent of the amount spent by large companies which have more than 5000 workers for workers' education and training. Although we will examine the system of in-company education and training in the following part of this section, it is important to remember such differentials among companies as we have observed so far.

First of all, it is important to note the following three points about the education and training system in Japanese companies. First, the system covers almost all levels of employees in a company, from blue collar workers to white collar workers, new employees to old employees, clerical staff to general managers. Second, therefore, under the life-time employment system in Japan, this means a life-time education and training system for all workers. All employees in a company continuously take various types of education and training at each stage of their working career until they retire. For the company, this system means that education and training for employees are a long-term investment in the future development of human resources (for example, suppose 18-year-old school leavers work until they are 60, the range of the investment in their initial training is forty-two years). Third, Japanese companies use the term of 'education and training' in a broad sense. For example, when some of the managers state that a company is a DŌJŌ (literally, traditional training place where one practices the way of martial arts) of life, it means every activity in a company is a part of education and training

Table 7:   *Methods of self-development for the management*

	Large (%)	Small and medium (%)
Reading special newspapers and magazines, watching T.V. etc.	72.2	59.0
Attending various study seminars	78.1	58.0
Having study meeting with other employers in the same business	38.0	36.5
Taking consultation from specialists	32.4	31.9
Attending special educational institutions	10.2	6.5
Others	4.3	2.6
Do not do anything	5.6	11.8

Note: Because of multi-answers, total is not 100 per cent
Source: Small and Medium Enterprise Agency, 1983

for employees.[3] Concretely speaking, they include not only on–the–job training and study seminars, but also formal and informal meetings at any level, company communications, purchasing specialized magazines, moral stories from the President, and private counseling, etc. Even recreation such as parties, festivals and short trips organized by a company are sometimes regarded as a part of education and training.

Let us start by looking at the main method of education and training in companies. Tables 7 and 8 show the methods of education and training for managers and employees respectively, in manufacturing industry. From table 7, we can observe the following points. First, large companies use any methods for managers' self-development more often than small and medium companies. Second, in the case of large companies, 'attending various seminars' is the most popular method (78 per cent), whereas, in the case of small and medium companies, 'reading special newspapers and magazines, and watching T.V., etc.' shows the highest percentage (72 per cent). Third, the percentage of 'do not do anything' in small and medium companies is almost double that in large companies.

From table 8, we can observe the following points. First, on–the–job education and training is the most popular method of employees' education

Table 8:   *Methods of education and training for employees*

	Large (%)	Small and medium (%)
On-the-job education and training	87.0	82.8
Attending study seminar in public training institutions	53.9	41.1
Attending seminar in a company	73.5	36.5
Attending study seminar in private training institutions	64.8	28.3
Having study seminar with other companies in the same business	8.4	17.9
Working temporarily in the related companies	15.7	16.2
Attending formal schools such as univ. and special training schools	29.8	4.6
Others	2.7	0.6
Do not do anything	0.6	1.0

Note: Because of multi-answers, total is not 100 per cent
Source: Small and Medium Enterprise Agency, 1983

and training both in large, and small and medium companies (87 per cent in large companies and 83 per cent in small and medium companies). Second, in the case of large companies, so called off-the-job training, such as attending seminars in public or private institutions, or in a company is also actively performed, but not in the case of small and medium companies. Third, in the case of small and medium companies, 'Having a study seminar with other companies in the same industry' is regarded as a more important method of education and training than in the large companies.

These differences between large, and small and medium companies are mainly derived from the differentials of financial capability of companies as we examined before (table 6). We should also, however, note that there is a difference in the needs of manpower between large companies and small and medium companies. Generally speaking, the former require manpower who have special knowledge and can make managerial policies or planning of R & D, while the latter require those who have leadership in production and sales.

We will roughly classify these methods into on-the-job education and training, and other institutional training, and briefly examine them in the following.

On-the-job education and training is a very important method of employee education and training in company. It has the following features: first, on-the-job education and training can be performed individually based on one's educational needs and personal character. Second, through on-the-job education and training, one can learn the knowledge and skills which are directly related to one's job. Third, on-the-job education and training can be performed anytime and anywhere. In the case of on-the-job training in Japanese companies, however, we should not miss another crucial role, namely the formation of human relations in a company. The following story is introduced as an ideal example of on-the-job education and training in one of the manual books of in-company education.

> In some company, Mr A, a division manager, intended to educate one of his staff, Mr K, to be a good salesman. One evening in a very cold winter, Mr K came back from his business. He looked depressed and reported to his boss, Mr A 'I am sorry, but C shop is hopeless, I think we had better give up'. After listening to his report quietly, Mr A told him strictly 'I understood you made every effort, but I think your explanation was not enough. Please go to C shop again.' and taught him the knack of sales kindly. Although Mr K was very hungry and tired, he went back to C shop with some criticism against Mr A. However, this time he succeeded in his sales at last, after explaining in the same way as he was taught by Mr A. Mr K was very happy and went back to the company, thinking of the situation where he would report his success to Mr A next morning. To his surprise, Mr A was waiting for him in the company, although it was so late. When he had a late supper with Mr A, he felt something warm between them. He

understood that Mr A was very strict to his business but warm to his staff. Since then, Mr A put his complete trust in Mr K.[4]

As shown in this example, the objectives of on-job-training are not only teaching some specific skills and knowledge but also building tight human relations between staff and their chief.

Institutional training can be defined as vocational education and training based on a systematic curriculum for a certain period in a certain class.[5] We can classify the institutional training into four types by its organizer; (i) institutional training organized by a company; (ii) institutional training organized by an association of companies; (iii) institutional training organized by formal educational institutions; and (iv) institutional training organized by specialized management institutions. The first type is the most popular method of training after on-the-job training in large companies (see table 8 above). The second type is performed mainly by small and medium companies. The third type include a program to send employees (or employers themselves) to formal educational institutions (for example, universities, special training schools and miscellaneous schools), public vocational training institutions (for example, vocational training schools, and skill development centers) or other public study seminars organized by companies, associations, prefectural or municipal governments. The fourth type is performed by a specialized organization such as Japan productivity centers, Union of Japanese Scientists and Engineers. In the following section, we will concentrate on the first type, namely, institutional training organized by a company, since other types of institutional training are usually used as a supplement to the first type.

Consider the in-company institutional training system of Nippon Steel Corporation, which is one of the largest companies in Japan. We may say this system represents a typical education and training system of Japanese large manufacturing companies. The in-company institutional training system is composed of two types of education and training, namely, specialized education and training, and stratified education and training. The former includes programs for white-collar employees and for blue-collar employees in which some special skills or knowledge are sequentially instructed. Employees in any position take this program according to their needs. For example, computer training, foreign language courses and safety training are typical programs of specialized education and training. The latter system is horizontal, i.e., all the employees in the same positions get the same training.

Japanese companies hire new graduates very carefully and selectively, paying attention to their future potentiality rather than specific vocational skills or knowledge. Since Japanese companies have such a long-term perspective, initial education and training for new employees is very important. Generally speaking, a one or two week intensive program is provided for all new men and women. Most of the large companies have their own training center, where all trainees stay for the whole period of training. Although the basic purpose of this orientation program is an introduction to the company and giving basic knowledge of business, the most important objective is to motivate new employees to work in that company. The fundamental philosophy of the company, which is usually highly society-oriented, is discussed by the president or the executives, and new employees are urged to establish an attitude of mind as full-fledged members of society and the company. Other attitudes such as pride, self-esteem, sense of duty and responsibility are also emphasized.

It is also important to note that one of the most required virtues in Japanese companies is a sense of harmony and teamwork, since all employees work in the same company for the rest of their life. In order to promote this sense, for example, some companies oblige all new employees to stay in the company dormitory for at least their first year. A retired ex-employee of the company becomes the superintendent of the dormitory and takes care of both the private and public life of new employees, and once a year, the President of the company is invited to the dormitory festival.

Stratified education and training programs continue for new employees until they become middle-level manpower. The main objective is to promote employees' conciousness and understanding of their role in the company rather than teaching specific knowledge, which is learned in specialized education and training courses or on-the-job training. Together with ordinary lecturing and seminars, several imported methods such as role playing, sensitivity training, transaction analysis and case method are often used. Some companies use institutional training for the purpose of providing the opportunites to meet the executives and other employees, and develop their personality by knowing other people.

In regard to managers' education and training, the main objective is to understand the whole system of the company from the managerial point of view. They often have informal meetings with managers in other divisions or departments to discuss managerial problems. Another important objective of managers' training is to learn how to guide their staff and raise their morale. They are required to have many formal and informal meetings with their staff. For example, in one company, general managers are to have lunch with every staff member on his or her birthday. They also organize recreation activities for their staff such as sports games, hiking and parties. The staff's family are also invited to understand the company. They expect to develop a total human relationship with their staff through these activities. An ideal manager is regarded as a person who can get the full confidence of his staff, and this is an important objective of managers' education and training, as well as learning some specific knowledge and skills of management.

From the examination so far, we can summarize the following two points. First, Japanese major companies perform long-term and systematic education and training for all employees. Second, the main objectives of education and training are not only learning specific knowledge and skills but also improving employees' moral and human relations. We will examine, in the following section, why Japanese companies can perform such long-term, systematic and human relation oriented education and training. This is closely related to the so-called Japanese style of management.

Japanese Management

A great number of studies about the Japanese management system have already been done both in Japan and abroad. This is mainly because Japan's high economic growth in the 1960s and relatively good economic performance in coping with two oil crises in the 1970s attracted strong worldwide interest in her management style. If we look at the studies written in English, quite a few works have been published since Abegglen's *The Japanese Factory* of 1958. Their methodologies of approach to Japanese management have wide ranges such as the structural approach, functional approach, cultural or psychological approach, and historical approach.[7] However, it is not our purpose to examine all of these studies here. Our main concern is to understand what kind of management system Japanese companies have for the formation and utilization of manpower.

The purpose of this section is to suggest that Japan's management system for manpower is one of 'internal accumulation type' rather than of 'external procurement type'.[8] In the following section, we will analyze this point from two aspects of the Japanese style of management, namely, (a) employment and promotion system; and (b) wage system.

Employment and Promotion System

Basic policies of the internal accumulation type of manpower management are, first to hire capable new graduates, second to educate and train them intensively in a company, and third to keep them in the same company for the whole period of their working careers. We have already examined the first and second point in the previous sections. It is important, however, to remember that in hiring new graduates, Japanese companies are concerned about their general ability and potentiality rather than specific knowledge and skills, and in training them, special emphasis is put on the improvement of human relations as well as teaching vocational knowledge and skills.

The third point is the so-called life-time employment system, which is widely recognized as one of the basic characteristics of Japanese management. However, it is important to note that there is no legal obligation in this system. In other words, life-time employment is merely a *custom* of Japanese companies and neither employers nor employees have any obligation of life-time employment. Employers can dismiss their workers anytime (although an announcement is required) and workers can also leave their company anytime. Therefore, there must be some reasons why both employers and employees in Japanese companies try to keep the life-time employment system.

Let us first examine the case of employees. Life-time employment gives stability to a worker's life and he can make a steady career plan on the basis of the security of his employment. Aged workers, especially, tend to prefer staying in the same company where they have worked. Second, because Japanese companies adopt a seniority wage system, the longer workers stay in the same company, the higher salary they can get (we will examine the details in the next section.). Third, in Japan it is very difficult to leave one company and get a better job in another company, because most of the companies, especially the large ones, hire only new graduates as regular staff. Fourth, traditional ethics in Japanese society require that once one gets a job in a company, one should not easily change to another company.

Employers also have reasons to keep the life-time employment system. First, they can undertake long-term manpower planning. When they make a large investment in education and training, it is essential for them to be sure that their employees will stay for a long period in the company. Second, by providing many years of education and training, employers can adapt their workers to the tradition of the company, and expect high morale and loyalty. Third, it is difficult to recruit skilled and experienced workers from the labor market outside of the company, since capable workers are trained in a company and stay there. They are also prudent in hiring workers from other companies, since it often causes friction between new and old employees. Keeping harmony among workers is one of the most important roles of management. Fourth, employers also have traditional ethics that require they should not easily dismiss their workers, since both employers and employees regard their company as a kind of family. Employers' paternalism and employees' loyalty are two of the most significant cultural factors of Japanese management, and the life-time employment system is reinforced by this.

Based on this life-time employment system, employees in a Japanese company form an internal labor market inside the company, which is distinguished from the ordinary external labor market. This internal labor market has the following characteristics. First, it is a closed system, in which there is only one entrance and one exit. Employees enter this market at the beginning of their working careers and exit at the time of their retirement. Second, it is a competitive market, in which every employee is in race for promotion. Although seniority and academic qualifications determine the initial conditions in this market, those in similar age and academic qualification groups have equal opportunities for promotion. They are very often transferred among departments during their working careers, and the company gradually examines their merits and aptitudes. The most capable men among the white collar workers, who win the long promotion race in this internal market, become the executives of the company. Blue collar workers also have an opportunity for promotion up to foreman. This is called the internal promotion system. Third, this internal labor market is flexible in job allocation. The company freely transfers its employees in this market according to its needs. This means that as long as the company accumulates enough human resources in this market, it can flexibly cope with the changing economic situation by dynamic mobilization of its own manpower.

Figure 1 summarizes these characteristics mentioned above, and compares this system with that of external procurement. It is important, however, to note that these characteristics are only tendencies of Japanese companies and do not exist in a pure sense. Generally speaking, the larger the company, the more they have these tendencies. We should also note that the most important factor of this internal accumulation type of manpower management is to keep the mobility of all employees in a company. This means that in Japanese companies, the type of post has a very loose relation with the worker's qualification. In the case of European or American companies, which have an external procurement type of manpower management, job content and responsibility are clearly defined together with the necessary qualification for the person who is applying for the post. Therefore, everyone who has this qualification (both inside and outside the company) can apply for the post, and the company hires the person for this particular job. Workers have to get their qualifications at their own expense, say, by going to training school, but if they have the qualifications, they can apply for a post at any company. We may say that these companies employ not the worker himself, but his qualification, namely, his specific vocational knowledge or skills. Therefore,

Figure 1: *Internal accumulation type and external procurement type*

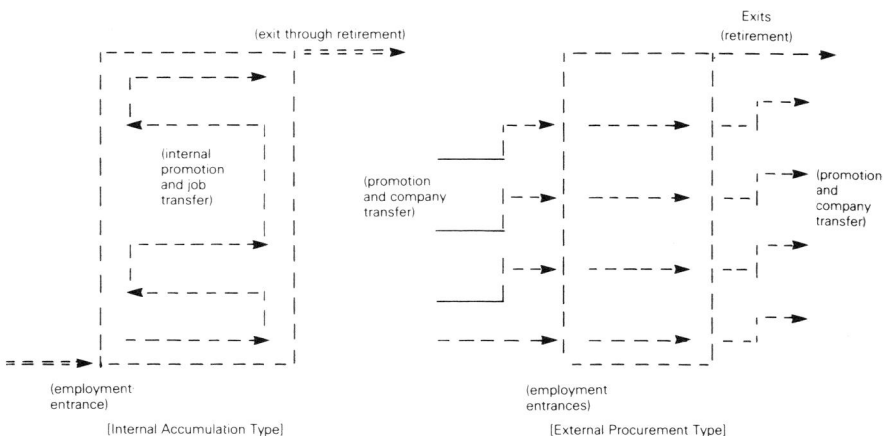

[Internal Accumulation Type]

[External Procurement Type]

when the post becomes redundant, the company does not try to transfer the worker into another post, but immediately lays him off.

Japanese companies, however, look at employees' potential and train them as flexible manpower at company expense. Since they pay the cost of their employees' education and training, when the post become unnecessary, they try to transfer the worker into another post. In other words, Japanese companies keep training their workers so that they can mobilize them at any time in any way, since they are the only human resources the company can use immediately. Therefore, in Japanese companies most of the posts do not require specific qualification, and the job content and responsibility of the post are not clearly determined. We may say that none of the newly employed graduates know their specific duties in a company when they are hired. All of them are expected to have the potential to do any type of job, and the company trains them to do so. The flexibility of manpower is a strong advantage of Japanese companies.

Workers' Participation and Economic Development

In the previous sections, we analyzed the characteristics of education and training in Japanese companies and their management policies for the utilization of manpower. The purpose of this section is to examine how Japanese companies have been able to develop Japan's economy in relation to this management style. Although Japan's economic success can be explained by reasons other than companies' management policies (for example, institutional reforms after World War II, appropriate government leadership, and favorable international environment), we will concentrate on the utilization of manpower in Japanese companies and in particular, workers' participation.

We use the term 'workers' participation' in a broad sense, which includes at least the following three points. First, workers' participation means each worker's positive commitment to his/her job. He performs his duty not only because he has to, but also because he can get self-fulfilment through his job. The best results are expected from a worker when he actively involves himself in his job. Self-esteem and pride in doing his duty are important factors. Second, workers' participation means every worker's voluntary commitment to the job. Not only white-collar but also blue-collar workers should actively participate in production and management of the company according to their duties. Third, workers' participation includes workers' cooperation. An employer cannot achieve his aim without the positive cooperation of his employees, nor can employees improve their production and working conditions without their employer's understanding. The more they cooperate, the better results they can get.

Participation is the key to utilize human resouces, because it motivates workers and enables them to maximize their ability both as individuals and as a group. One of the most important factors of the success of Japanese companies is this workers' participation. In the following part of this section, we will examine the three aspects of workers' participation, namely, (a) labor participation in management; (b) suggestion system; and (c) company-wide quality control. Finaly, we will consider some effects of these management policies and workers' participation on Japanese economic development.

Labor Participation in Management

Labor participation in management usually includes collective bargaining, labor-management joint consultation, ownership sharing, profit sharing, and workers' participation in the board of executives. Although it is not our purpose to describe all of these systems, we should note the following points as characteristics of Japanese labor-management relations.

First, almost all Japanese companies adopt the so-called enterprise union-ism. As shown in table 9, 94 per cent of total unions are enterprise unions. Since all the members of a union are, at the same time, employees of the company, the interests of labor and management can be matched relatively easily. After the first oil crisis, for instance, Japanese unions accepted the relatively lower level of wage increase compared with the higher inflation rate. This is mainly because unions adopted a long-term point of view, and gave priority to the security of employment rather than wage increase. As a result, Japan was able to avoid mass unemployment and a dramatic downturn in the economy.

Second, the internal promotion system also contributes to labor participation in management. In Japanese companies, it is common that a worker stays in a company first as an employee, then as a leader of the union, and again becomes an employee of the company. The post of union leader is considered a good opportunity to learn labor-management relations, and those who have held the post are usually promoted to management positions. The union representative may even become a member of the board of directors.[9]

Third, we should also note the decision-making system of Japanese companies, which is known as the RINGI system (literally, it means discussion through reporting to one's superior). Since, as we saw in the previous

Table 9: Number of unions and their members classified by type of union (1975)

	Number of unions (%)		Number of members (one thousand) (%)	
Enterprise unions	65,337	(94.2)	11,360	(91.1)
Industrial unions	1,775	(2.6)	682	(5.5)
Craft unions	720	(1.0)	169	(1.4)
Others	1,501	(2.2)	259	(2.0)
TOTAL	69,333	(100)	12,472	(100)

Source: Ministry of Labor, 1980.

section, each worker's job content and responsibility are not clearly prescribed in Japanese companies, decision-making is performed collectively involving many workers in the company. Under this decision-making system, most of the decision plans are first provided by ordinary employees or lower managers. They have several formal and informal discussions with other managers at the same level whose sectional interest may be related to this decision, and consensus among them is sought. Once they reach consensus, the decision plan is raised to the senior managers' level. They repeat almost the same process and accumulate their ideas and consensus to the plan. In this way, the decision plan goes through a hierarchy of the company up to general manager, executives, or the President, according to the significance of the decision. Although the final decision is taken by the top management, it is the result of many workers' consensus. Especially for lower level workers, this system provides an opportunity to participate in decision-making. Therefore, once a decision has been adopted, all the workers who are familiar with the decision cooperate and the objective can be achieved smoothly.

Fourth, labor participation in management is also supported by the community-oriented mental attitude of Japanese workers and managers. Under the Japanese management system which we have examined so far, both management and workers begin to feel that they are living in the same community and sharing their life and fortune with each other. They often regard their company as a big family and this emotional relationship promotes the sense of participation.

Suggestion System

The suggestion system aims to collect workers' ideas and opinions about their job and company, and improve the company's system and productivity. As shown in table 10 almost three-quarters of all companies have the suggestion system, and more than 80 per cent of workers are involved in it. In the case of large companies, the corresponding percentage is more than 90 per cent. This nationwide suggestion system is coordinated by the Japan Research Associa-

Table 10: Suggestion system

Size of company by number of employees	No. of establishments involved (%)	No. of workers involved (%)
5000+	91.9	94.5
1000–4999	80.9	83.5
300–999	70.8	73.4
100–299	66.2	68.5
TOTAL	74.1	82.2

Source: Ministry of Labor, from Inagami, (1983) p. 32

Table 11:   Trends of the suggestion system

	1973	1975	1977	1979	1981
Number of companies	141	189	229	372	465
Total number of suggestions (thousand)	3,322	4,942	5,748	13,499	32,223
Average number of suggestions per company (thousand)	23.6	26.1	25.1	36.3	69.3
Average number of suggestions per employee	4.5	4.7	5.6	7.2	14.2
Adoption rate (%)	68.0	72.3	69.3	70.0	70.0
Implementation rate (%)	92.3	72.5	90.2	93.1	92.6

Sources: Inagami, (1983) p. 34

tion for the Suggestion System, which was established in 1958. Suggestions mainly concern improving work methods, saving materials and energy, improving the working environment, and updating equipment and machinery.

For employees, the suggestion system provides opportunities to realize their ideas and improve their working conditions. For employers, good suggestions lead to increased productivity. They can also expect a raise in workers' morale, when their suggestion is adopted. Table 11 indicates the trend of the suggestion system. We can observe the following points from this table. First, the total number of suggestions has increased from 3.3 million in 1973 to 32.2 million in 1981, an almost tenfold increase in eight years. Second, accordingly, the average number of suggestions per company and per employee have also increased. While the former was 23,600 in 1973, it reached 69,300 in 1981. The latter has also increased from 4.5 in 1973 to 14.2 in 1983. Third, on average for this period, 70 per cent of all suggestions have been adopted, and the implementation rate has reached 88 per cent.

It is also reported that the yearly cost of suggestion activities was Y 3.77 million on average of the data of 301 companies, and total economic benefits derived from the suggestions was estimated at Y 34.18 billion. Therefore, the rate of return of the suggestion system ([benefit-cost]/cost) reached Y 30.41.[10]

Company-wide Quality Control

The most unique system of workers' participation in Japanese companies is 'small group activities'. It is said that more than ten million workers are involved in small group activities.[11] This figures implies that almost one-fifth of all Japanese workers including all industries organize small groups spontaneously in their workshop. These small group activities are formed on the basis of the Japanese management system and group-oriented cultural background, and support the vitality of the companies and Japan's economic development.

Although there are various types of small groups such as recreation circles, safety circles, suggestion circles, ZD (Zero defects) circles and JK (JISHU KANRI, voluntary control) circles, etc., we will concentrate on QC (quality control) circles here, and examine them in relation to company-wide quality control. Quality control was originally one of the management techniques imported from the United States after World War II. However, under the leadership of the Union of Japanese Scientists and Engineers (JUSE), quality control activities have developed into a unique system in Japanese companies, and nowadays the techniques of Japanese quality control are exported worldwide. We may safely say that quality control activities have played one of the most important roles in Japan's export promotion.

Ishikawa, one of the most famous experts of quality control, mentions the following six points as the unique characteristics of Japanese quality control: company-wide quality control, education and training for quality control, quality control circle, nationwide promotion activities, evaluation system of quality control, and utilization of statistic skills.[12] We will briefly examine the first three points in the following.

Company-wide quality control (CWQC)

Company-wide quality control means at least the following three points.[13] First, everybody in a company participates in quality control activities. It is the crucial point of CWQC that everyone at any level, from the President and executives to blue-collar workers and salesmen, are to be involved in quality control. Second, therefore, every department of the company must participate in the quality control. Quality control can be applied not only for the production line, but also any other department such as planning, sales, personnel management, etc. Sectionalism among departments must be removed. Third, CWQC aims at total quality control of all company activities. It controls not only quality of goods, but also quality of prices, time, and services, etc.

Education and training for quality control

It is said that quality control starts and ends with education, and everyone in a company must be educated in CWQC. This is partly because quality control is based on statistical analysis of data, and requires that everyone has a basic knowledge of statistics. However, a more important reason for education and training is that quality control is one of the management philosophies to change the quality of the company itself, and therefore, systematic and repeating education is essential to understand and implement this new philosophy. These education and training programs are mainly conducted by the JUSE. Its 'basic course' has been held more than sixty times since it was started in 1949. Duration of the course is six months, and in each month there are five days of lectures and case study. Every attendant is required to collect data from his own plant every month, and solve problems by learning basic skills of quality control. Graduates of the course organize a QC program in their own company based on JUSE's program with the assistance of external consultants, and disseminate the knowledge and skills to other members of the company.

QC circle

According to *Fundamental of Quality Control Circles* edited by the JUSE, a QC circle is defined as 'a small group which carries on continuously as a part of company-wide quality control activities, self development and mutual development, control and improvement within the workshop, utilizing quality control techniques with all members participating'.[14] Aims of QC circle activities are to contribute to the development and improvement of companies, to create better workshops based on humanism, and to realize the full potential of employees through the development of their ability.

As shown in this definition, a QC circle is a small group organized by the spontaneous participation of all workers in a workshop. As shown in table 12, the number of QC circles registered in JUSE reached 115,254 and the number of participants is more than one million in 1980. It is estimated that the number of unregistered circles is almost ten times that of registered circles. It is remarkable that such a great number of workers are spontaneously forming QC circles. This is mainly because the QC circle aims at self-development and mutual development of workers. Workers are participating in the circle not because of the direct economic benefit (most of the circles have a meeting before or after working hours without any payment), but because they can

Table 12: Registered number of QC circles

Year	Number of QC circles	Number of participants
1962	23	—
1964	1,051	—
1966	7,307	90,829
1968	17,416	212,134
1970	33,499	388,543
1972	51,615	551,643
1974	65,477	664,458
1976	78,395	774,012
1978	94,787	903,471
1980	115,254	1,062,759

Source: Inagami (1983) p. 31

improve human relations in a workshop and get self-fulfillment through their job. The following episode explains this point.

> A study group from abroad visited one of the radio manufacturing factories in Japan. After listening to the report of a female worker, who made a suggestion about her job, one of the foreign visitors asked her 'Don't you think the suggestion about improvement in the manufacturing process is the duty of a specialist, not of ordinary workers like you? It seems that you did what is not your business'. However, she answered that 'Although my job is a small part of production, I know this job best in the company. I noticed something wrong in my job process and suggested the improvement. As a result, the number of sub-standard articles decreased one third. Did I do something wrong?'.[15]

As shown in this example, QC circles give workers a pride in their job, and develop their potential. It is said that QC circles bring back the essence of working as a human activity to workers who have been alienated in the progress of automation. Although there is some criticism that QC circle activities are another way of exploiting workers, this seems to be from a minority.[16] As long as small group activities such as QC circles are based on workers' spontaneous participation, they will develop further.

Some Effects

Lastly, let us briefly examine some effects of these manpower management policies in Japan. Apart from economic growth rate and the amount of GDP we can mention the following points.

First, Japan's rate of unemployment is very low, compared with other countries. As indicated in table 13, Japan's rate of unemployment was only 2.4 per cent in 1982, which is the lowest rate in the OECD countries. One of the main reasons for this low rate lies in the internal accumulation type of management policies such as life-time employment.

Table 13: Rates of unemployment in selected OECD countries (%)

	1970	1975	1980	1982
Japan	1.1	1.9	2.0	2.4
USA	4.8	8.3	7.0	9.5
UK	3.1	4.7	6.9	12.7
FRG	0.8	3.6	3.0	6.1
France	2.4	4.1	6.3	8.0
Italy	5.3	5.8	7.4	8.9
Canada	5.6	6.9	7.5	10.9

Source: OECD, 1983.

Table 14:   *Index of workdays lost in labor disputes classified by countries*

	Number of workdays lost (average of 1978–1980)	Number of employees (1978)	Number of work-days lost per employee
Japan	1.0	1.00	1.0
	(1,096,000)	(38,760,000)	(0.028)
USA	31.9	2.32	13.9
UK	15.7	0.59	26.5
FRG	1.5	0.57	2.6
France	2.3	0.45	5.1
Italy	16.5	0.37	44.4

Note: Figure in brackets indicate ACTUAL numbers for Japan.
Source: The Japan Institute of Labor, 1983.

Second, Japan's labor-management relations are relatively stable com-pared with other countries. Table 14 indicates the workdays lost in labor disputes in selected countries. As shown in the table, the number of workdays lost in Japan is the lowest both in total days and days per worker (one thirty-second of the number of workdays lost in U.S.A. and one forty-fifth of the number in Italy).

Third, Japanese companies have to cope with technological innovations without causing serious problems such as unemployment. This is because in introducing new technology, Japanese companies can transfer their employees from obsolete posts to new posts by giving them training. Since workers' employment and wages are secured regardless of their current job, they do not object to the introduction of new technology such as industrial robots. On the contrary, they often welcome it, because they know that as long as they get proper training, they can use this new technology, to release them from hard physical working. According to the government's investigation, the introduc-tion of robotics resulted in surplus labor in 31 per cent of companies, and reduced working hours per person in 25 per cent of companies. In regard to the wages of workers who were transferred, 12 per cent of companies increased their salary and 87 per cent did not change. Only 1 per cent reduced their salary.[17]

Fourth, the quality of Japanese products has become remarkably good, and therefore, productivity is increased. Table 15 shows the data presented at the US-Japan semiconductor seminar in 1980. From this table, it is obvious that there is a significant difference in quality between Japanese and American products. Furthermore, quality control leads to reductions in production cost, because it decreases the rate of sub-standard articles significantly. The increase in quality and decrease in cost has resulted in the strong competitive power of Japanese companies in an international market.

Fifth, Japan has achieved a relatively egalitarian income distribution. Table 16 indicates the income distribution in selected countries. As shown in this table, the share of the lowest 20 per cent of people in Japan is 8.7 per cent,

Table 15:   Comparison of quality between Japanese and American semiconductors

Companies	X	Y	Z
J1	0	0.01	89.9
J2	0	0.019	87.2
J3	0	0.012	87.2
A1	0.19	0.09	86.1
A2	0.11	0.059	63.3
A3	0.19	0.267	48.1

Notes: X   :   Rate of sub-standard articles at the time of purchasing.
        Y   :   Rate of trouble after 1,000 hours' usage.
        Z   :   Index of the evaluation of quality.
        J1, J2, J3 are Japanese companies' products.
        A1, A2, A3 are American companies' products.
Source: Karatsu, (1981) p. 7

Table 16:   Income distribution

	Lowest 20%	Second quintile	Third quintile	Fourth quintile	Highest 20%	Highest 10%
Japan	8.7	13.2	17.5	23.1	36.8	21.2
Canada	3.8	10.7	17.9	25.6	42.0	26.9
France	5.3	11.1	16.0	21.8	45.8	30.5
FRG	7.9	12.5	17.0	23.1	39.5	24.0
USA	4.6	8.9	14.1	22.1	50.3	33.4
Italy	6.2	11.3	15.9	22.7	43.9	28.1
UK	7.0	11.5	17.0	24.8	39.7	23.4
Sweden	7.2	12.8	17.4	25.4	37.2	21.2
Finland	6.8	12.8	18.7	24.9	36.8	21.2

Source: World Bank Development Report 1984.

which is the highest rate among the selected countries (and among all the other countries for which the data are available), [18] and the lowest 40 per cent (lowest 20 per cent and second quintile) is also the highest (21.9 per cent). On the other hand, the highest 10 per cent of people share only 21.2 per cent, which is the lowest together with Sweden and Finland (also among the world), and even the highest 20 per cent share the lowest percentage (36.8 per cent). It appeared from this fact that Japan has the most egalitarian pattern of income distribution. Although the reasons for this egalitarian distribution can be explained by many factors such as institutional reforms and tax policies, the Japanese education and wage system are two important factors. More than 90 per cent of people go to upper secondary school and the rate of attendance at university also reaches more than 30 per cent. Although there is wage differential between upper secondary leavers and university graduates, the gap is not very big. Furthermore, because of the seniority wage system, every worker's salary is gradually increased according to his age. These systems taken together prevent workers' income from differentiating very dramatically, one from another.

Acknowledgement

This chapter is excerpted from a larger report by the same title and prepared for the World Bank, August 1984. Grateful acknowledgement is made to the World Bank for its assistance in facilitating the publishing here of this chapter.

Notes

1　We will concentrate on the contemporary period. In regard to the in-company education and training since the Meiji period, see LEVINE, S.B. and KAWADA, H. (1980) *Human Resources in Japanese Industrial Development*, Princeton, Princeton University Press.
2　The concrete meaning of vocational guidance in Japan is to assist the unemployed workers to acquire skills by providing vocational training for them.
3　For example, Nihon Zoki Seiyaku Ltd. See NIHON, K.G.C.K.S., (Ed.) (1978) *Chuken Kigyo no Jinzai Ikusei*, Tokyo, Daiyamondo-Sha, p. 53.
4　Manteru Ltd, *Ibid*, pp. 145–6.
5　SUMIYA and KOGA, (Eds) (1978) *Nihon Shokugyo Kunren Hattenshi: Sengo-hen* Tokyo, Niho Rodo Kyokai, p. 336.
6　Daikure Ltd. See NIHON, KG, C.K.C. (1978) *op cit*, p. 139.
7　For example, LEVINE, S.B. (1958) *Industrial Relations in Postwar Japan;* COLE, (1971) *Japanese Blue Collar: the Changing Tradition;* DORE, R.P. (1974) *British Factory — Japanese Factory: the Origins of National Diversity in Industrial Relations;* (1981); PASCALE & ATHOS, (1981) *The Art of Japanese Management;* (1981) OUCHI, *Theory Z: How American Business can meet the Japanese Challenge;* SCHONBERGER, R.J. (1982) *Japanese Manufacturing Techniques: Nine Hidden Lessons in Simplicity.*
8　I owe the concept of 'internal accumulation types' to TANAKA, M. (1979) *Shogai Koyo Kakumei*, Tokyo, Daiyamondo Sha.
9　For example, Sankei Newspaper made an agreement to grant the union the right to send its President to the Board of Directors and then have a say on personnel appointments concerning directors in charge of labor problems. See Japan Institute of Labor, (Ed.) (1979) *Japanese Industrial Relations Series No. 2: Labor Unions and Labor-management Relations*, Tokyo.
10　INAGAMI, T. (1983) *Japanese Industrial Relations Series No. 11: Labor-management Communications at the Workshop Level*, Tokyo, Japan Institute of Labor
11　UEDA, T. (Ed.), (1982) *Shoshudan Katsudo Suishin Manyual*, Tokyo, Swin Gijutsu Kaihatsu Senta.
12　ISHIKAWA, K. (1981) *Nihonteki Hinhitsu Kanri*, Tokyo, Nikkogiren, pp. 52–3.
13　*Ibid.*, p. 128.
14　In regard to in-company education for quality control, see NIKKAGIREN, (1981) *Hinhitsu Kanri*, 32, 7, and NIKKAGIREN (1982) *Hinhitsu Kanri,* 33, 10.
15　KARATSU, (1981) *TOC Nihon no Chie*, p. 144.
16　For example, MUKAIGASA & TOGITA (Eds), (1980) *Kojochosa: Kyodai Kojo to Rodosha Kaikyu*, Tokyo, Shin Nihon Shuppansha.
17　Japan Small and Medium Enterprise Agency, (1983) *Chusho kigyo Hakusho*, pp. 294–5.
18　See World Bank, (1984) *World Development Report 1984*, Washington, DC, pp. 272–3.

References

COLE, (1971) *Japanese Blue Collar: The Changing Tradition*, Berkeley, University of California Press

DORE, R.P., (1973) *British Factory — Japanese Factory: The Origins of National Diversity in Industrial Relations*, London, George Allen & Unwin.

INAGAMI, T., (1983) *Japanese Industrial Relations Series No.11: Labor-management Communication at the Workshop Level*, Tokyo Japan Institute of Labor.

ISHIKAWA, K., (1981) *Nihonteku Hinshitsu Kanri: TQC towa Nanika* (Japanese Quality Control: What is TQC?), Tokyo, Nikkagiren.

JAPAN INSTITUTE OF LABOR (Ed.) (1979) *Japanese Industrial Relations Series No. 2: Labor Unions and Labor-management Relations*, Tokyo.

JAPAN SMALL AND MEDIUM ENTERPRISE AGENCY, (1980, 1981 and 1983) *Chusho Kigyo Hakusho* (White Paper of Small and Medium Enterprises), Tokyo, Japanese Small and Medium Enterprise Agency.

LEVINE, S.B., (1958) *Industrial Relations in Postwar Japan* Urbana, University of Illinois Press

LEVINE, S.B., and KAWADA, H., (1980) *Human Resources in Japanese Industrial Development*, Princeton, Princeton University Press.

MUKAIGASA and TOGITA (Eds), (1980) *Kojo Chosa: Kyodai Kojo to Rodosha Kaikyu* (Factory Investigation: Big Factory and Proletariat), Tokyo, Shin Nihon Shuppan-sha, 1980.

NIHON, K.G.C.K.S. (Ed.) (1978), *Chuken Kigyo no Jinzai Ikusei: Seikoshita 66 sha no Jireishu* (Manpower Formation in Medium Companies: Examples of 66 Companies), Tokyo, Daiyamondo-sha.

NIKKAGIREN (Union of Japanese Scientists and Engineers), *Hinhitsu Kanri* (Quality Control), 32, 6 and 7 (1981), 33, 10, (1982), Tokyo.

OUCHI, W., (1981) *Theory Z: How American Business Can Meet the Japanese Challenge*, Reading, MA Addison-Wesley Publishing Company.

PASCALE, R. and ATHOS, A.G. (1981) *The Arts of Japanese Management*, New York, Simon and Schuster

SCHONBERGER. R.J., (1982) *Japanese Manufacturing Techniques: Nine Hidden Lessons in Simplicity*, London, The Free Press.

SUMIYA and KOGA (Eds) (1978), *Nihon Shokugyo Kunren Hattenshi 〈Sengo-hen〉: Rodorvoku Toya no Kadai to Tenkai* (History of Japanese Vocational Training 〈Postwar period〉, Tokyo, Nihon Rodo Kyokai.

TANAKA, H., (1979) *Shogai Koyo Kakumei: Nihonteki Koyo no Saiken o Mezashite* (Career Employment Revolution: Toward the Reconstruction of Japanese Employment), Tokyo, Daiyamondo Sha.

UEDA, T. (Ed.) (1982) *Shosyudan Katsudo Suishin Manyuaru* (Manual for Promoting Small Group Activities), Tokyo, Shin Gijutsu Kaihatsu Senta.

WORLD BANK, (1984) *World Development Report 1984*, Washington, D.C., World Bank

Economics of Worker Education in China

Ann Orr

Introduction

Producing skilled workers and technical personnel for enterprises in order to raise economic growth and development has been a continuing task for the Chinese economy. The formal age-based system of vocational/technical education in China has not developed steadily since the 1950s and remains underdeveloped compared to other developing economies. While the formal vocational/technical education system grew substantially in the 1950s, by 1970 enrollment had declined to pre-1949 levels and was only rehabilitated in the late 1970s. By 1982, enrollment in the system had recovered to pre-1970 levels. Enrollment at the secondary level, however, only constituted 3 per cent of all secondary level students which was substantially below that of other developing countries (World Bank, 1983).

Traditionally, enterprises in China have assumed an imporant role in the education and training of the work force. A wide-ranging system of worker education outside the formal age-graded school system and primarily financed by enterprises was developed in the 1950s. Workers in an enterprise were given free access to enterprise-run schools where both basic and vocational education were provided. Enterprises have also traditionally relied heavily upon internal education and training programs as a source of skilled workers, technicians, engineers and managers since the acute shortage of such skilled personnel occurred during the rapid industrialization of the 1950s (Hoffman, 1974; Colletta, 1982). This system has been gradually restored since the disruptions of the Cultural Revolution and has been assigned an important role in China's educational development plan to produce the skills and to improve the overall quality of the work force needed to attain the goals of rapid modernization.

The system consists of schools ranging from junior middle school level vocational training to post-secondary technical colleges operated directly by enterprises, ministries overseeing an industry, or local government agencies. Schools in this system are designed to provide vocational and technical education to workers of enterprises and the initial cost of the education is borne by the enterprise. This cost is in various forms: the cost to the enterprise of running the school, tuition for schools not directly run by the enterprise and, since the worker continues to receive wages, the value of the worker's production that is foregone while in training.

The renewed emphasis on enterprise-financed education and training is being promoted at the same time that fundamental reforms in the basic structure of the urban economy in China are planned (Beijing Review, 1984b). The underlying objective of these reforms, adopted by the Central Committee of the Chinese Communist Party, is the creation of a market-oriented economic system in China. This will significantly alter the economic environment in which enterprises operate. Under these reforms, the functions and responsibilities of enterprises are to be separate and distinct from those of the government. Each enterprise is to become an independent economic entity solely responsible for its own profitability and economic survival. Financial reforms are directed at increasing cost- and profit-consciousness among enterprises by providing them the incentives of retaining after-tax profits. Market forces are to be relied upon to guide the decisions of the enterprise in product planning, marketing and pricing.

The reforms extend the decision-making power of large- and medium-sized state-owned enterprises in virtually all areas of human resource management: recruitment and hiring, wages and bonuses, promotion and the utilization and allocation of their work forces. Currently, enterprises recruit workers whom they are required to employ for life. Wages are set nationally and promotions are primarily based on seniority. Inter-occupational wage differentials are small and unrepresentative of productivity differentials among workers with different skills. Promotions are effectively out of the control of individual managers and enterprises are limited in the number of promotions they can grant. Reforms in these areas are directed at increasing the mobility of workers, allowing enterprises more authority in the hiring, promotion and termination of workers and in linking pay to performance, responsibility and productivity. Labor mobility combined with expanded autonomy in the utilization and compensation of labor by enterprises is expected to improve the efficiency in the allocation of labor both within and among enterprises.

The relationship between the reformed wage and employment systems in Chinese enterprises and the system of enterprise vocational and technical education was not explicitly recognized or addressed in the economic reforms. In the new environment created by these reforms, the expense of developing skills through education and training becomes an investment by the enterprise in the human capital (skills) of the workers and a component of current operating costs. Decisions regarding the provision of vocational education and training become economic decisions involving comparisons of the costs of alternative means of producing skills with the benefits to be derived in the form of increases in worker productivity and higher profits. Greater competition among enterprises for skilled labor and increased worker mobility, however, increase the risk to the enterprise of the trained worker seeking higher pay elsewhere and thus the loss of the benefits of their investment. Therefore, while the reforms are expected to increase the efficiency in the allocation of labor and non-labor resources in industrial production, they potentially undermine the current system of enterprise education and training that is considered vital in fulfilling the skill requirements for the rapid modernization of industry.

The central question which China must resolve if it is to rely on a strategy of enterprise-based education and training in the economic environment created by the current reforms is how to coordinate the systems of wages and employments with the system for providing the amount and type of training necessary for modernization. The systems must be seen as mutually suppor-tive and part of a consistent strategy to meet the overall objective of skill development.

In establishing an efficient system of skill development at the enterprise level, the following set of issues must be addressed: (i) What is to be the distinction between the responsibilities of government and enterprises for worker education? The experience of market economies, for example South Korea, suggests that without legislative requirements or strong economic incentives enterprises cannot be relied upon to provide either basic education or vocational/technical education which produce skills that are transferable among enterprises. The burden of financing such education will then fall upon the individual and/or the government; (ii) What is the appropriate pattern of wage differentials between workers with different skills and, as skills are accumulated, over the tenure of a worker? (iii) What is the necessary duration of employment of a worker in the enterprise that financed training which allows the enterprise to collect the benefits of its investment in the worker's training? (iv) What should be the scope of authority of individual enterprises to hire and promote workers and to adjust wages and conditions of employment in order to balance the costs and returns to the investments in worker education and training.

This chapter analyzes the features of an enterprise wage and employment system in a market economy which supports the provision of education and training by the enterprise. The theory of investment in human capital provides the framework for the interpretation of the economic implications of both the current system and the reforms for worker education and training in China. The theoretical discussion considers cases representative of some features of the Chinese economy and labor market in order to derive the implications for a wage and employment system consistent with China's system of enterprise education.

Theoretical Framework of Enterprise Education and Training

The theoretical model of a competitive labor market has been expanded to analyze the labor markets for workers with different skills (Becker, 1975).

Workers can increase their productivity by learning new skills or perfecting and mastering old ones through investments in both schooling and on-the-job training (OJT) and experience.

Both the enterprise and worker have an incentive to participate in OJT. Following their completion of training, the worker's productivity rises above what it would have been in the absence of training and raises the worker's wages. The future receipts of the enterprise generated from the sale of the greater output of the trained worker also rise, however, and the excess of future receipts over future wage payments measures the return to the enterprise of providing training. The amount of investment in skill development is thus an economic decision for the enterprise and worker based on a comparison of the expenditures and returns to training.

Two types of training are distinguished in the theoretical analysis of investment in OJT: general training and specific training. General training raises the productivity of a worker in many enterprises besides the one providing it. Because their productivity is increased in many other enterprises, competition among enterprises for these workers causes their wages to rise by the same amount that their productivity is increased. That is, enterprises providing general training must pay the trained worker a wage equal to what the worker could obtain in another enterprise or risk having that worker leave the enterprise.

Because the trained worker captures the returns to the training, the generally trained worker is presumed to pay for that training mainly in the form of wages below what the worker could earn in an alternative occupation during the training period. Worker wages over time reflect the pattern of investment, below their potential productivity during the training period and rising after the completion of training to reflect their higher productivity.

Since generally trained workers possess skills which can be purchased by the enterprise in the labor market, long-term attachments between employer and employee are unlikely to be found.

Enterprise-financed training in general skills is observed, however, in two market conditions relevant to the Chinese economy. One is a situation of imperfect capital markets, where workers are unable to finance their training expenses out of saving or bank borrowing. This situation is found in some developing economies where earnings are at such a low level that reductions in earnings to finance training are not feasible. In this type of market situation, enterprises are observed to make investments in the general training of the work force. The higher wages allow the workers to make the investments that raise their productivity. The gains to the enterprise from such investments are greater if the trained worker remains with the enterprise.

A second market situation occurs in labor markets which are not perfectly competitive or where significant impediments to labor mobility exist. The former situation usually occurs when one enterprise is a major employer in a market and, therefore, alternative employment opportunities for trained workers are limited. As a result of the reduced risk of losing a trained worker to a competition the enterprise is given an incentive to finance the training of its work force. The latter situation can arise from legislative restrictions on mobility or prohibitively high costs of migration. The reduced risk of a trained worker seeking alternative employment opportunities can also result in enterprise-financed general training. In this case, restrictions on labor mobility, however conducive to enterprise-financed training, introduce inefficiencies into the economy because workers are not necessarily employed in their most productive occupations.

Specific training is training that raises the worker's productivity more in the enterprise which provides the training than in other enterprises. The skills are of little value outside the enterprise and often there is no competitive labor market in which the skill of a specifically trained worker is traded. An example of this type of training is the skill needed to operate a machine used uniquely by an enterprise.

The productivity of the specifically-trained worker within the enterprise providing the training follows the same pattern as that of the generally-trained worker, relatively low during the training period and rising sharply after the completion of training. Since specific training is not useful outside the enterprise, the productivity of the specifically-trained worker in another enterprise and the wage the worker can command in the market are unchanged.

Unlike general training, investments by the worker in specific training are made at the risk of losing the return on the investment because of a lay-off or other termination of employment by the enterprise. The enterprise also incurs a risk of losing the return on its investment in specific skills because of the possibility that the trained worker will leave and impose a 'capital loss' on the enterprise. As a result of the risks of losses to both parties, the costs and returns to specific training are shared by the enterprise and worker (Oi, 1962).

In an environment where specific training is important to reducing turnover of workers will be the concern of both enterprises and workers. Long-term employment contracts serve to ensure the continued employment of the worker in the enterprise and are often found in enterprises and industries with a high degree of specific skills. Pension programs which link retirement payments to length of service with an enterprise provide additional incentives to the worker to remain with the enterprise and induce enterprises to undertake investments in specific training.

Overview of the System

Enterprise education in China is now an important supplement to the formal education system and the current era places demands on the system of enterprise education to produce skilled and technical personnel needed for the modernization of industry.

As a result of the underdeveloped system of formal vocational/technical education, enterprises have the additional burden of providing pre-service secondary level vocational/technical education to new workers in order to obtain the desired number of semi-skilled and skilled workers. The scarcity of technicians produced by the formal technical education system has also created a need in enterprises to resort to upgrading workers to technicians through internally-financed education at the post-secondary level. While illiteracy is no longer a major problem among workers, there is still a need for remedial education in basic and technical subjects for workers as a result of the disruption in education during the Cultural Revolution. In 1981, a program to upgrade the general educational level of young workers who entered the work force since 1968 (approximately under 35 years old) to junior middle school level was launched and scheduled to be completed by 1985. Later, this supplementary education program was extended to intermediate technical education. This is no small task as this group of workers comprised over 66 per cent of the industrial work force in 1982 (Population Census Office, 1983). There is also the goal of upgrading the technical knowledge of those key production workers whose knowledge has become outdated or who have never had an intermediate level of technical education. Such upgrading and retraining are aimed at enlarging the pool of skilled production workers in industry which is necessary to the modernization of production.

Currently, the majority, 78 per cent, of industrial workers have less than a senior secondary school education and within this group, only a little more than half have a junior middle school education. The proportion of industrial workers with post-secondary education is only 2 per cent (*ibid.*). With such a dearth of educated and skilled workers, the task of worker education and training remains tremendous in the next decade.

The autonomy of the enterprise in this area is currently limited, as is the case in other enterprise functions. Education and training programs in Chinese enterprises are subject to the approval of various governmental agencies overseeing the education activities of the enterprise. As a result, the education provided to workers may not be consistent with the skill needs of the enterprise. The administrative structure of worker education above the enterprise level is elaborate, with a National Committee for Worker Education at the highest level, which parallels and works jointly with the Ministry of Labor and Personnel and the Ministry of Education. The actual oversight of enterprises is shared by the agencies of these organizations at the local level and the local agencies of the technical ministry responsible for the industry of the enterprise. This is illustrated by the case of large iron and steel enterprise. Cadres selected by the enterprises for training at one of the metallurgy schools run by the Ministry of Metallurgy have to be approved by the Ministry. The fields of specialization, number of new students admitted and the allocation of students among specializations in the enterprise's secondary and post-secondary technical schools have to be approved by the provincial bureau of higher education. The provincial committee for worker education administration oversees the supplementary general and technical education of young workers and worker technical schools and spare-time schools. The local labor bureau oversees admissions and fields of instruction in vocational schools.

Within the organizational structure of enterprises, committees and departments are jointly responsible for worker education at the enterprise level, with these responsibilities divided into several tiers according to the nature of the education and training. Generally, the lowest organizational unit — the workshop — is responsible for education most directly related to the production activities of the enterprise such as the pre-service training of production workers, OJT of workers and the maintenance of the operating skills of production workers. Education of skilled workers or technicians, cadres and the supplementary general education of younger workers is the responsibility of the worker education committee or the worker education department at the enterprise level. The structure varies with the complexity of worker education demands on the enterprise.

The extent of worker education activities also varies with the size and technical demands of the enterprise. For example, the Anshan Iron and Steel Company, the largest integrated company in China with over 200,000 workers, directly runs an elaborate system of sixteen schools ranging from the level of a skilled worker school to a technical university. The cumulative proportion of workers participating in education and training is as high as 54 per cent in three years and the enterprise-run schools accept students from other enterprises (Beijing Review, 1984a). By contrast, in a much smaller enterprise in the textile industry, with just over 3000 workers, there is a great dependence on external educational facilities and teacher resources and the rate of participation in training is much lower. Classes are conducted in borrowed classrooms, workers are sent to specialized education courses and T.V. courses run by the local textile bureau and cadres are sent to outside universities for advanced education and training. Beside basic pre-service training, supplementary education mandated by the government for younger workers and short specialized training courses, there is no systematic education and upgrading of intermediate and senior workers (grade 4 and above).

Programs

A very large component of pre-service and in-service training in China is general training, in the terminology of human capital theory. The enterprise finances the training by directly providing the training or by paying for the tuition. In the case of pre-service training, workers finance it by foregoing regular wages they would have received had they not been in training. In the case of in-service training, which usually takes workers away from production but pays them their regular wage, the enterprise incurs an additional cost. The worker, on the other hand, does not invest in this training.

Pre-service training in Chinese enterprises is generally provided to new production workers in semi-skilled and skilled jobs. Semi-skilled workers are trained to the minimal level of skill required to perform a specific job independently. These workers are junior middle school or senior secondary school graduates with no vocational/technical education. Training lasts three to six months depending on the requirements of the job. Trainees are paid the lowest grade of basic wage but do not receive any bonus. This type of training is very similar to pre-service training in industries in market economies in Asia, such as South Korea. The duration of the training is short and the scope is narrowly focussed on the demands of a specific job.

Apprentice training lasts from six months to two-three years, depending on the job, during which only living expenses and a supplement for food are paid. Some apprenticeships are used to train semi-skilled workers but are usually training programs for skilled workers. Some enterprises also recruit students for their own technical schools, to be trained skilled workers and employed by the enterprise upon graduation in jobs ranging from electricians to welders to carpenters to shoemakers. The curriculum usually lasts three years and is at the senior secondary school level and applicants are at the least junior middle school graduates. Training in these technical schools involves substantial classroom teaching. In many cases, the first year or two are devoted to basic education and technical subjects and the third year to practical training in the factory. During the first two years workers are paid a subsistence stipend and in the third year, are paid the lowest wage (grade 1) in wage scale.

In-service training to upgrade semi-skilled workers to skilled workers and middle level technicians is just being revitalized. In a very large enterprise in heavy industry, workers with over two years of seniority are eligible to apply to the secondary and post-secondary technical schools run by the enterprise where the curricula are usually two-four years. These workers are, at a minimum, junior middle school graduates and are selected by examination. Upon successful completion of the curriculum they are reemployed by the enterprise. A similar curriculum lasting about two years trains middle level technicians at the senior secondary technical school level in the textile industry. During training, workers are paid their wages but do not receive the bonus distribution even though they are released from their duties at the factory. The direct expenditures for training are paid by the enterprise.

Other types of technical upgrading for production workers are more fragmented and short-term. One enterprise plans to train key production workers for about six months to raise their technical level to the equivalent of senior secondary vocational/technical school. Workers are sent to short specialized training courses after work or, in some enterprises, technical classes lasting up to two hours are given during shift changes. Informal maintenance and upgrading of operating skills are provided on-the-job at the workshop level. These forms of skill upgrading do not appear to be regularly scheduled or planned over the tenure of the worker, but are provided on an 'as-needed' basis.

A system has yet to be in place in most enterprises to implement technical education activities on a regular basis. In those enterprises which have progressed further, there are hints of the system to be evolved. In one large building material enterprise, education and training functions are included in the economic responsibility system of the various units of the enterprise. These functions are measured in terms of the rate of participation in training and the amount of time spent in training by workers in these units. Worker training plans in a shipyard in Shanghai include a new emphasis on training of grade 3–5 workers in its secondary technical school (Risler, 1983). These plans were developed under a directive from the State Council of the People's Republic of China aimed at upgrading the skills of experienced workers in skilled jobs. This training will prepare workers for qualifying examinations to be promoted to grades 4 through 6 which are being planned by the government.

Another form of in-service training, which cannot be separated from skill upgrading, is training for new technology. The means of training include classroom training and as well as OJT. The duration of training is brief and much more narrowly defined than upgrading education. In the Shanghai Petroleum General Works, for example, when a new, highly automated piece of equipment was bought from abroad, workers had to be trained to operate it. They were trained by the manufacturer of the equipment in the operational techniques required for the equipment in technical classes in the spare-time college and senior secondary technical school. They were also given OJT with the new equipment. During the annual overhaul of the equipment, they observed the installation and maintenance procedures (Beijing Review, 1982). The successful absorption of such short-term training is dependent on a sound technical education among the workers. In many Chinese enterprises, the necessary educational foundation for the successful adaptation to new technology is missing, so that upgrading of the general level of worker training is an integral part of training for new technology.

Wage Structure

Wage scales in China are set nationally for three broad categories of occupations: blue-collar workers (semi-skilled and skilled), white-collar and technical personnel, and cadres and administrators in government organizations. Enterprises have no authority to deviate from these wage scales. The distinguishing feature of these wage scales is the small differentials between blue-collar workers and technical and managerial staff. The higher productivity of more skilled and educated workers is not linked with higher wages. This could reduce incentives for workers to acquire skills and cause enterprises to misallocate labor. With respect to enterprise training and education, the inflexibility of wages prevent enterprises from structuring different wage profiles for workers with different amounts of training in order to capture their returns to training. Rather, their return is guaranteed by life-time employment of workers.

There are eight grades in the scale for workers with a 17 per cent differential between each grade and a ratio of 3 to 1 between grade 8 and grade 1. The white-collar and technical personnel scale has seventeen grades with smaller grade differentials of about 10 per cent and a ratio of 9:1 between the highest and the lowest grade. There are twenty-four grades in the cadre scale with the ratio of the highest to lowest grade of about 12:1[1] (Ma, 1982).

There are variations around these scales to take into account differences in cost of living, different industries and different skill or physical requirements between different jobs in the same broad occupational category. Wage scales for different jobs in a large textile enterprise illustrates differentials by skill requirement within the worker wage scale. The wage scale for operatives only went as high as grade 7 while wages for more skilled electrical workers were about 6 per cent higher at each comparable grade and could go as high a grade 8. Therefore, except for workers in the top wage grade, the differential between semi-skilled and skilled jobs is small.

Workers are, in principle, promoted up the wage scale with increased seniority, skill and qualifications. In practice, enterprises have almost no authority in wage promotions according to these criteria, as the rate of promotion within an enterprise is determined by the government. As part of enterprise reforms initiated in the last several years, enterprises have been given the authority to promote 1 per cent of their work force annually. This has been increased to 3 per cent since May of this year (*Economic Daily*, 5 December 1984.) This authority is so restrictive that there are enterprises which choose not to exercise it. From the point of view of the worker, this rate of promotion makes the probability of being promoted so remote that it does not constitute a realistically attainable reward.

Promotions in recent times have only been 'wage adjustments' given across the board by government in 1971, 1977, 1979 and most recently in 1983. A construction material enterprise gave an adjustment of one grade to 40 per cent of its work force in 1977 and 1979, and to almost all workers in 1983, a pattern representative of promotions in China in the last decade. Even though the enterprise had devised a system of evaluation of the education and skill of workers, it was not given permission to use it in determining the choices for promotion in 1983. The government's intent in wage adjustments in recent years has been to end the erosion of real urban wages that ocurred in the late 1960s and 1970s while maintaining wage differentials between workers with different years of seniority. This, combined with small wage differentials across occupations, has created a strictly seniority-based wage system bearing little relationship to worker characteristics, such as education and training, ability and skill, which directly affect worker productivity.

Recent reforms in promotions include experimentation with 'floating' promotions, which do not adequately reduce the rigidity in long-term wage increases over the tenure of the worker. A worker evaluated as worthy of a promotion is given a wage increase of one grade on a probationary basis for one-two years. This increase is converted to a permanent promotion pending sustained good performance during the probationary period. While floating promotions can raise the wage grade of a worker on a one-time basis, they do not provide the basis of a system of productivity linked promotions in the long-run and do not bypass the restriction of the promotion rate allowed by the state.

A much more dramatic experimental reform in Guangdong Province allows enterprise directors to promote up to 30 per cent of the work force annually if the enterprise can realize higher profits than the preceding year. This margin of authority to promote is much more in line with increasing the flexibility of enterprises to upgrade worker skills and provides the basis of creating a wage profile of workers that corresponds to productivity over his working life. This reform is too new to be evaluated for its effectiveness and the potential for inflexibility due to government intervention remains as candidates selected for promotion by enterprises are subject to approval by the local labor bureau.

The most far-reaching wage reforms have been implemented in special economic zones and are likely to be the basis on which national reforms in the wage system will be developed (Beijing Review, 1984c). The new system in effect pays a 'minimum income' to each employee which guarantees a minimum standard of living while providing incentives for substantially higher total wages linked to higher individual and group (enterprise) produc-tivity. Thus, total wages consist of four components: basic wage, subsidies, job wage and floating wage. On average the basic wage and subsidies comprise 31 per cent and 10 per cent, respectively, of total wages while the job and floating wages comprise 37 and 22 per cent, respectively, of total wages. The first two components which are not linked to productivity comprise only about 40 per cent of total wages. The other two components which are productivity-linked comprise a larger proportion — 60 per cent — of total wages. The job wage reflects the degree of skill, responsibility, qualifications and working conditions of the job and has fifteen grades with about 5:1 ratio between the highest and the lowest. It is this component that will motivate workers to acquire more skill and qualifications which lead to higher productivity. From the perspective of the enterprise, it links productivity of labor to the cost of labor. The floating wage is equivalent to the bonus in the current system and rewards performance at a given skill level but is also dependent on the profitability of the enterprise. A new system of evaluation and promotion is also being instituted to promote qualified employees to more skilled and responsible jobs, which would lead to higher wages.

The incentives established by this wage system are designed to raise and reward productivity. As human capital theory suggests, the job wage and floating wage components allow enterprises to vary total wages of workers over their career to encourage and reward investments in training. There is currently little information on the relationship of wage structures and differen-tials to skill acquisition in these Chinese enterprises.

Recruitment and Tenure of Employment

The lack of wage incentives created by the seniority-based promotion system is aggravated by some of the other features of the Chinese employment system, namely recruitment, the life-time employment system and the restriction on labor mobility.

Although the allotment of new blue-collar workers to be hired each year is handed down to the enterprise by the labor bureau which oversees it, within the allotment the enterprise has the authority to recruit by examination but is limited to the pool of job-seekers in the local area. In principle, the examination process can be used to select the best qualified workers. In actuality, there is substantial pressure on the enterprise to accept applicants who are less than qualified. One source of pressure is current workers who feel that, when employment is difficult to find, the enterprise should provide employment for their children. Another source of pressure is the generally poor quality of education of job-seekers in this occupational category. Enterprises can only expect to obtain a fraction of the ideal type of worker in terms of education (usually junior middle school and senior secondary level) and ability, however selective they may try to be. The entrance examination can in fact be used to determine job assignment among those selected. In some enterprises, workers with high scores are assigned jobs with higher skill requirements but differences in wages between different types of blue-collar jobs are small, especially at the lower grades. Under this system of recruitment, it is not feasible to compensate for the lack of selectivity of the promotion system by being highly selective in recruiting young workers with the kind of motivation and educational background that would maximize the success of technical training.

The commitment of the Chinese government to provide employment to all able-bodied men has been unchanged since the 1950s. Currently, permanent workers in an enterprise are legally entitled to employment and cannot be dismissed except for the commission of a very serious crime. As a result, dismissals can almost never be used as a disciplinary measure.

Voluntary turnover is also extremely rare, as most enterprises hire only at the entry level of an occupational category and, until very recently, hiring has been channeled through government labor bureaus. Graduates of post-secondary technical school and above continue to be assigned by the Ministry of Labor and Personnel to enterprises. A policy of strict control over geographical mobility further restricts job mobility. As a result, workers are unable to use job mobility to obtain higher wages or more favorable working conditions. From the perspective of the enterprise, the immobility of the work force has its advantages, at least with respect to workers in which it has invested in training. Since technical skills are still scarce, the lack of inter-enterprise mobility guarantees the enterprise the productivity of the trained worker throughout his working life in the absence of wage-promotion incentives. From the perspective of economic efficiency, however, the distribution of skilled workers is less than optimal.

Two major reforms in the employment system have been the experimentation with the use of contract employment in lieu of life-time employment and, more recently, experimentation with increased mobility of skilled workers and professional and managerial personnel.

Contract employment is only used among new entrants to the labor force and even among this group, only a small proportion are currently employed under this system. The objective of this system is to give enterprises the flexibility to dismiss workers who are not performing up to standard. The compensation for workers is that their wages can be negotiated up to 15 per cent higher than the standard wage at their grade. Workers are offered contracts only after pre-service training and examination. The length of the contract, wages and job performance criteria are the major items negotiated. This system of contracts basically divides a worker's tenure at an enterprise into renewable short-term employment contracts. Upon the expiration of a contract term, which ranges from one to five years, both parties have the option not to renegotiate the contract and terminate the relationship. The worker is free to seek employment elsewhere and risks becoming unemployed or getting a higher wage and better working conditions. This experimental system, if implemented according to the intent of the reform, will create much greater flexibility in the employment system and a more direct relationship between productivity and wages. The rigidity of the promotion system remains to be changed for the overwhelming majority of workers under the old system; in particular, the large cohort of workers in their twenties and thirties who are prime candidates for upgrading of skills.

The second experimental reform is the new authority given to individual enterprises to recruit independently for skilled and technical personnel to meet their labor needs. Such decentralized recruiting can even span provincial and municipal boundaries, subject to approval by the Ministry of Labor and Personnel (MOLP). Thus far, not surprisingly, this method of recruiting has been used primarily by enterprises in geographically remote regions or in small and medium cities where skilled and technical labor are relatively scarce. Although centralized assignment of technical and professional labor is still the norm, this reform is taken seriously enough by the MOLP to issue guidelines for this type of recruitment (State Council, 1984). Some of the guidelines, such as requiring municipal or provincial labor bureau approval and MOLP approval for recruitment across administrative boundaries can potentially neutralize the increased mobility of skilled labor. Enterprises are also told not to offer wages higher than 'appropriate' in order to bid away a worker from his original job, which is the crux of the system of efficient allocation of labor.[2]

The implications of worker mobility for enterprise investment in worker education are profound. While the cost of high turnover of unskilled workers has been found to be very low, high turnover among scarce skilled workers trained by the enterprise tends to be very costly. In the face of greater worker mobility enterprises will have to have the authority to structure their wages over the worker's tenure in order to ensure a return on their investments in worker education. Variable length contracts may be an important instrument in ensuring enterprises and workers of their desired return on their investments. In the absence of authority to adjust wages and employment contracts to their investments in training, there will be little incentive for enterprises to make investments in training. This may also result in a system of vocational education and training which would more closely resemble the system in many market economies where little enterprise education takes place.

In some Chinese enterprises that have experimented with the contract system, some unwanted turnover of skilled workers, such as electricians and those who work with electrical equipment, has already occurred. The complaints of enterprises have emphasized the loss of skilled workers who are trained for six months to one year and who subsequently receive informal OJT, but leave after a contract period of two-three years for higher wages in self-employment or another enterprise. This is a classic case of an enterprise paying for the cost of general training of workers, but not paying the prevailing (market wage) for a trained worker (Becker, 1975). The enterprise attracts too many trainees and too few trained workers. This problem can be alleviated by reducing wages during the initial years of the contract period so as to shift some of the cost to the worker and increasing wages to meet prevailing wages in later years.

Conclusion

The economic environment that will be created by economic reforms in China demands changes in the enterprise education and training system if the skills needed for modernization are to be produced. Currently, enterprises provide a large component of basic and vocational/technical education that, in other economies, is normally provided in the formal school system. With little distinction between the functions of enterprises and government and limited worker mobility, the provision of education and training by enterprises was a response to social and economic needs. To the extent that enterprises were concerned with a return to their investments in education and training, the immobility of workers guaranteed them receipt of the benefits of higher productivity.

In the reformed environment, enterprises will calculate the extent to which the resources used to provide education, both basic and vocational/technical, directly benefit them and are likely to be reluctant to continue to provide it on a broad scale. Rather, enterprises will view the provision of education as an investment and will only make such investments if a return is guaranteed. A shift in the provision of basic education can be expected to occur away from enterprises and toward individual workers and/or the government. Individuals can be expected to make their basic education and training decisions based on a calculation of the return to their investment measured by wage differentials between skills levels. In the absence of social externalities and serious market imperfections, the market will guide individuals and enterprises to the appropriate amount of education and training. If imperfections exist, such as labor immobility or the inability of workers to finance the initial cost of training, and/or social benefits are expected to be derived, then the government and enterprise provision of education and training is an alternative means of producing skills.

In the reformed environment, competition and mobility ensure that wages reflect worker productivity. When workers receive substantial amounts of education and training within enterprises, wage profiles over the tenure of the worker must be structured by each enterprise individually to reflect the amount and type of education and training being provided. Career wage profiles of higher skilled workers must increase to reflect the acquisition of skills so that the worker has an incentive to take training in the skills needed by the enterprise. Wage differentials between skilled and unskilled workers should reflect the relatively higher productivity and contribution to the enterprise of the skilled worker. Should wage differentials not reflect relative productivities, workers can be presumed to leave the enterprise and seek employment in the enterprise where the skill is most highly rewarded.

Where specific training is important, wages must be structured so as to maintain the employment and commitment of the trained worker to the enterprise for a period sufficiently long to allow the enterprise to capture the return to their share of the training investments. Substantial variation in the amount and type of training provided can be expected to exist across enterprises in China. Where relatively extensive training is provided, a correspondingly longer period of employment with the enterprise will generally be required.

Since the economic reforms have not been fully implemented in China, the special economic zones provide the closest approximation to the market conditions which are likely to prevail in the reformed economy. In these zones, wages have adjusted to reflect productivities and workers have been relatively mobile in seeking the highest reward for their skills. The wage system provides the potential flexibility for enterprises to structure their wages to reflect productivity. Examination of the experiences of those enterprises where specific training is important would provide further insights into how the economic reforms might affect skill development.

Acknowledgement

This chapter is excerpted from a larger report prepared for the East Asia and Pacific Projects Department, The World Bank, January 1985. Grateful acknowledgement is made to The World Bank for its assistance in facilitating the publishing here of this chapter.

Ann Orr

Notes

1   The occupational-wage structure of a combustion engine enterprise in Beijing (Tung, 1982) illustrates wage differentials in effect, by education and skill. A blue-collar worker with one-two years of experience (grade 2) was paid about 40 yuan per month while a very skilled blue-collar worker (grade 7–8) made 90–107 yuan a month. The ratio of the latter to the former was a least 2.5:1. A technician was paid 80 yuan and workshop cadres earned 70–80 yuan. The ratio between the wages of these lower technical and managerial workers and a novice production worker was about 2:1. Engineers were paid 100–120 yuan — about two-and-a-half to three times that of novice production workers. Therefore, wage differentials between technical and managerial staff and production workers were small. Directors and deputy directors of departments were paid 140–160 yuan and up and the chief engineer and factory directors were paid 220 yuan. Wages in these very high echelons of managers were only three-and-a-half to five-and-a-half times the lowest wage in the enterprise.
2   This has not stopped enterprises from offering what appears to be very attractive conditions of employment, judging from some of the employment announcements in the newspapers. Most jobs offer a contact of employment of three years or more. There are many offers of a one grade increase over the qualified applicant's current wage, housing for the family, employment for the children and in some cases, to change the household registration of spouses and children who are registered in rural areas to the city of the new employment. This last provision is important as only registered residents of urban areas are entitled to government price subsidies in the purchase of fuel, cooking oil and grains.

References

BECKER, G., (1975) *Human Capital: A Theoretical and Empirical Analysis, with Special Reference to Education*, 2nd edn. Cambridge, MA, National Bureau of Economic Research.
Beijing Review, (1982), 3.
Beijing Review (1984a) 16 January.
Beijing Review (1984b), 4.
Beijing Review (1984c) 3 December.
COLLETTA, N., (1982) *Worker-Peasant Education in the People's Republic of China: Adult Education During the Post-Revolutionary Period*, World Bank Staff Working Papers, No, 527, Washington, DC.
Economic Daily, (1984) 12 May.
HOFFMAN, C., (1967). *Work Incentive Practices and policies in the People's Republic of China, 1953–65*, New York, State University of New York Press.
HOFFMAN, C., (1974). *The Chinese Worker*, New York State University of New York Press.
MA, H. (Ed.), (1982), *Modern Chinese Economic Dictionary*, Beijing Chinese Academy of Social Sciences.
OI, W., (1962). 'Labor as a quasi-fixed factor of production, *Journal of Political Economy*, December.

Population Census Office, (1983). *Major Figures by Ten Percent Sampling: Tabulations on the 1982 Population Census of the People's Republic of China*, Beijing, Population Census Office.

RISLER, M., (1983) 'Tendencies in vocational and adult education in the people's Republic of China', unpublished.

State Council of the People's Republic of China (1984). *Announcement* No. 6.

TUNG, R., (1982). *Chinese Industrial Society After Mao*, Lexington, MA, Lexington Books.

World Bank, (1983). *China: Socialist Economic Development, Vol. III: The Social Sectors, Population, Health, Nutrition and Education*, Washington, DC World Bank.

The New Entrepreneurs of Europe[1]

Elizabeth McPherson

To cope with industrial change, Europeans are trying desperately hard to become entrepreneurial. This involves more than changing the traditional Europan mindset that devalues commerce. Those working on the transformation confront a class system that is still relatively rigid, highly centralized political structures, an educational framework unsuited to entrepreneurial training, a lack of broad private-sector support, union skepticism, and governments that, no matter how supportive, are neophytes in this area.

Despite these obstacles, the entrepreneurial spirit is taking hold in Europe, born of economic decimation and the realization that the coal mines, steel mills, textile factories, and auto assembly lines will never again support the work force they once did. What chiefly distinguishes Europe's forces for enterprise development from those of the United States is the belief in Europe that the jobless and disadvantaged — those with low incomes, poor or outmoded skills, and little prospect for employment — have both the desire and the capacity to start their own enterprises.

Turning the Safety Net into a Ladder

Several European governments — both conservative and socialist — have adopted broad programs that permit the unemployed to use their jobless benefits to start new businesses. Since 1979, nearly 200,000 unemployed British and French citizens have taken advantage of such options. In the United Kingdom, the support comes in the form of a weekly government allowance. The French, on the other hand, are allowed to take six months of benefits in a lump sum to use as seed capital for a new business. Similar programs exist in Ireland, Belgium, the Netherlands, and Sweden.

Far from viewing income support solely as a way to 'maintain' people, these schemes actually invest in the unemployed to create jobs that otherwise would not exist. In so doing, they are transforming the safety net into a ladder. By contrast, US social-insurance entitlements, like social security and unemployment insurance, and the means-tested welfare programs, such as Aid to Families with Dependent Children, Medicaid, and Food Stamps, all currently operate quite outside the realm of economic development and job creation.

The United Kingdom's Enterprise Allowance Scheme is predicated on the belief that some unemployed people will be motivated to start their own businesses if not forced to relinquish their jobless benefits during the early uncertain months. Entrepreneurs who qualify for one of the 60,000 annual slots are paid £40 ($50) a week for up to a year while their new enterprises take root.

To be eligible, a would-be entrepreneur must have been unemployed for at least thirteen weeks, be able to raise £1000 ($1250) independently to invest in the business over the first year, and work full-time in the business. Interested applicants first attend a 'scaring-off' session, where they meet with job counselors, tax experts, accountants, and lawyers, and are informed of the risks and difficulties involved in starting a business. Those who want to go on fill out a simple form with little red tape.

The Manpower Services Commission — an independent government agency set up in 1974 — administers the program and offers free small-business counseling services through its seventy local job centers. Partnerships and cooperatives are eligible, but some kind of business are precluded — bars, gambling establishments, and clubs that promote political or religious views, for example. The enterprise must be new, independent, and small — under twenty employees during the first three months of operation.

Among 43,145 Britons drawing allowances as of last August, the majority were operating enterprise in the service sector, building trades, knitwear, or toy manufacturing. About one in five businesses is run from home, but some have grown quite large. Davisson and McNaughton Engineering, for example, started by two unemployed entrepreneurs, now has fifty workers in its sheet-metal fabrication works in Manchester. And the nation's largest independent crystal and glass shop was set up in Cambridge with the help of the scheme.

Of the firms begun during the program's 1982–83 pilot phase, more than 70 per cent were still trading eighteen months after start-up. Early surveys of the expanded program suggest each new enterprise is creating an average of one-and-a-half jobs. The majority of participants — 59 per cent — are between 25 and 44 years old. Those younger and those older are about equally represented. Half say they would not have started an enterprise without the government's initial help.

France introduced its Chomeur Createur (Unemployed Entrepreneur) program on an experimental basis in 1979 and extended it nationwide a year later. Unlike the British, the French now carefully screen business proposals. Originally the lump sum available to start a business was based on the participant's most recent salary, but this was changed after criticisms that the program unfairly favored unemployed executives. Now the maximum benefit is $4300 for all citizens entitled to unemployment compensation or welfare benefits, with bonuses for additional jobs created within six months. When a plant closes, workers in the same unit are encouraged to pool their benefits to start a new firm.

As of March 1984, 135,000 unemployed French workers had incorporated under the program. Their enterprises range from high-technology manufacturing to janitorial services. Service firms predominate, but nearly a third are manufacturing firms, as compared to 13 per cent under the British scheme. The government reports that 60 to 80 per cent of the enterprises survive the critical first year.

Job Creation Strategies of European Corporations

A different type of strategy to stimulate new enterprises is pursued by some large European corporations in communities where they must close plants or lay-off workers. American corporations faced with 'redundancy' — Europe's catch-all term to denote the factories and the workers whose products and skills are no longer economic — usually offer workers, at best, severance pay, relocation assistance, and possibly retraining and job counseling. Some European corporations have gone way beyond those traditional types of assistance.

The program begun nine years ago by the nationalized British Steel Corporation is Europe's showcase example. In the mid-1970s, the giant corporation began the process of closing down obsolete plants and laying off 150,000 employees. To cushion the blow and also to give asset-value to otherwise worthless plant and equipment, it spun off a subsidiary — BSC Industry — with a single mandate: to help create jobs in eight (eventually eighteen) steel closure areas in England, Scotland, and Wales.

After failing to recruit other large firms to these areas, BSC Industry decided to focus instead on smaller firms and would-be entrepreneurs. It began marketing the distressed communities as 'opportunity areas', both to improve the psychological climate for indigenous development and, where possible, to attract employers from elsewhere. The best of redundant facilities were converted into workspaces for enterpreneurs. New firms could avail themselves of comprehensive business assistance, including loans and seed financing.

As of March 1984, BSC Industry had helped 1500 companies create 20,000 jobs. New jobs are expected to reach 36,000 by 1986. The company's nine entrepreneurial workshops today house about 400 businesses, employing 1500. BSC Industry has also been active in helping local authorities and established businesses set up partnerships, known as enterprise agencies, to concentrate business expertise on the regeneration of industrially depressed communities. By the time it became independent of British Steel last year, the company had already turned over many of its business support responsibilities to these enterprise agencies.

Several other large British firms — United Biscuits, British American Tobacco, and the glassmaker Pilkington Brothers, for instance — also have moved to offer surplus premises, financing, and comprehensive business assistance to small firms in the wake of their plant closings. Sir Alastair Pilkington enlisted the help of several other leaders of industry and commerce in setting up Business in the Community, a national organization that quickly became the 'single front door' through which corporations could funnel cash-or-kind contributions to enterprise agencies in their communities.

In France, the central government has been the principal spur to corporate action. Large firms need government approval to close a plant and must offset jobs lost with persistent efforts to create new openings. The nationalized coal company, Charbonnages de France, was the first to create a subsidiary (SOFIREM) especially to entice other companies to redundant coal communities. Other firms in the midst of restructuring, including Elf Aquitaine, Saint Gobain, and Thomson, soon created their own subsidiaries to package equity, loans, and subsidies in an attractive way.

Increasingly, major corporations in Europe are hiring for-profit consulting firms to help them create jobs. Job Creation Ltd. (JCL), started by three former executives of BSC Industry, is one of the foremost firms. Its principal activity is to convert redundant facilities into attractive environments for new small business. Its clients — private firms and government, often in partnership — finance the acquisition and conversion of the property. JCL conducts feasibility studies, oversees renovation, and then manages the workshop. Its stake is a bonus for each job eventually created in the completed facility.

In Paisley, Scotland, near Glasgow, JCL is directing the conversion of a twelve-acre, nineteenth-century factory complex that once employed 1800 workers in the production of cotton thread. When completed in 1986, the new Abbey Mill Center could restore 500 jobs. A highly successful JCL workshop in The Hague was jointly financed by the municipality, the Dutch central government, and Philips Data Systems, a multinational electronics firm. Other conversions are under way in Ireland, Norway, Zimbabwe, the Federal Republic of Germany, and — in JCL's first US venture—Flint, Michigan.

The Incubator — A Hospitable Setting for New Businesses

'If you provide the environment — physical, psychological, and social — the entrepreneurs come from everywhere. The energy and resources exist in any community', said Paddy Naylor, JCL's Executive Director. The environments or workshops his firm and others create are often referred to as 'incubators', due to their function of nurturing young businesses and their neophyte owners. There, entrepreneurs can rent individualized space, varying from a few hundred to a few thousand square feet, within a complex where many other small firms are also operating. They share common facilities and services — parking, shipping, security, cleaning, bookkeeping, rest rooms, telephone switchboard, canteen, reception area, meeting rooms, exhibition areas. Leasing terms are attractive: tenants are usually committed only to short-term leases, often three months or less. There is generally an experienced manager on site and access to professionals who can offer free or low-cost technical assistance and psychological support.

Throughout the United Kingdom, old buildings are being reborn as business incubators. Antiquated schools and hospitals are fair game, along with redundant factories and warehouses. In the London borough of Hammersmith and Fulham, the development board has created two light-industrial workshops from an old army barracks and a former garage of the gas board. BSC Industry has made ingenious use of the ancillary buildings of steel works — general stores, administrative offices, canteen halls, inspection sheds, boiler shops, and even a clocking station. Only when no adaptable premises can be found are new buildings constructed.

Some of the more hopeful projects operate not in industrial or commercial settings but in depressed, primarily residential areas. A good example is Glasgow's massive public housing project Easterhouse, where 55,000 people live in 100 square blocks of five-storey, drab yellow brick buildings, cut off from transportation, stores, and services, There, in an area described as having 'no economy', where unemployment approaches 70 per cent and alcoholism, drugs, and vandalism are rampant, Provanhall Holdings Ltd., a local community corporation, has created a modest climate of regeneration. Its first project, begun in 1980, was the conversion of six vacant ground-floor flats into shop units. The enterprises that located there, including a laundromat, hairdresser, clothes shop, and solicitor's office, created about thirty jobs in the first two years. Next, Provanhall converted a school annex into seven workspaces. They now house a popcorn maker, a taxi service employing twenty-four, a cabinet maker, an upholsterer, a plumber, a roofer, a potato distributor, and a security service with sixty employees. The goal, community leaders say, is to legitimize the businesses of people in the underground economy and move them above ground.

Who can run workshops? The answer from Britain is almost anyone. Glasgow's Easterhouse is run by a local community corporation, London's Hammersmith and Fulham by a borough council. In Govan, Scotland, the sponsor is a community business. In several cities, enterprise agencies have created workshops. And of course there is JCL, which operates them as a profit-making business.

Some have criticized JCL for trying to make a profit on redundancy and unemployment. Others complain that because its reward depends in part on the number of jobs created, the firm 'creams' the best entrepreneurs and makes too little effort to help those who are 'less than ideal'. Paddy Naylor replies that JCL tries to include freelancers, people who work on a project-by-project basis, and even those trying to develop a hobby into an enterprise. 'We're trying to provide an environment where not only the more clever and brave can create their own jobs', he says, 'but also people who've got to go the long way round'.

An 'Aunt Agatha' for Every Entrepreneur

Despite the ballyhoo surrounding the venture capital industry in the United States, the majority of new US businesses start with capital drawn from the owner's personal savings or borrowed from friends, family, or associates. But, especially in poor communities where investable assets are scarce, entrepreneurs with worthy business ideas often cannot get enough seed capital.

The capital gap is even more pronounced in Europe. To compensate, the British and French have developed a variety of incentives and guarantees (in addition to the jobless-benefit reallocations already described, themselves a form of seed financing). 'We're going in to bridge the gaps for projects that are viable but the market won't respond', said John Dunbar, Director of BSC Industry, which has made some 800 seed-capital loans, the majority under $12,500. 'Our businesses don't have a lot of family dollars invested in them. We came in with the concept of being the "Aunt Agatha".'

A British tax incentive program encourages private citizens to make equity investments in small firms. Investors can write off up to $50,000 a year, provided that they hold the investments a minimum of five years.

Local government agencies often provide seed capital to cooperatives. The West Midlands County Council has given $375,000 in grants to forty-two cooperatives and helped capitalize a $250,000 revolving fund. In Scotland, the Highlands and Islands Development Board, describing itself as 'a merchant bank with a social purpose', has supplied small-scale financing to sixteen coops in its sparsely populated region.

The French government underwrites a series of premiums for the creation of new enterprise and new jobs. To encourage fledgling manufacturing firms, regional governments offer tax exemptions and cash grants of up to $16,000, depending on the industry, area, and amount of initial capitalization. Additional premiums, from $1100 to $5500 per job created, are allocated by regional councils to both existing and new enterprises. Other sources of seed capital in France are the widespread investment clubs and the non-profit France Initiative Fund, endowed by corporations, banks, and communities.

The Tools Needed to Survive and Grow

In their quest to be more entrepreneurial, Britain and France are relying heavily on a variety of initiatives offering entrepreneurs the tools they need to survive and grow. The goal is for them to become competent managers.

France's *boutiques de question*, or 'management shops', were initiated four years ago, when French officials realized that many new businesses were failing unnecessarily due to inadequate technical, psychological, and institutional support. Today, there are forty locally-based agencies, each serving a specific geographical area. They analyze the feasibility of business ideas, prepare business plans, conduct marketing studies, secure financing, and help bewildered clients negotiate the maze of central, regional, and local government requirements.

The clients are mostly what the French term the 'new population of business creators' — unemployed individuals, those seeking to develop cooperatives, activists promoting community enterprise development, and engineers and technicians with 'appropriate technologies' to market. Originally the focus was on the *économie sociale* (cooperatives and other forms of alternative ownership), but services are available today to anyone working at the local level to create economic activity and jobs.

The average agency's budget is modest, about $70,000 a year. About 40 per cent usually comes from fees charged for business assistance and training sessions, another 40 per cent from contracts with public agencies — largely for research and for economic planning assistance to local authorities — and the remainder from government and EEC grants.

A sampling of seventy-one *boutique*-aided firms throughout France showed that four-fifths had survived two years and were employing an average of six workers each. In Lille, historically an area with few new businesses, a network of seven agencies reported that it had helped create some 160 enterprises and 550 jobs by the end of 1984. One out of every ten enquiries eventually results in a business, according to the network's Director, Henri Le Marois.

Among other non-profit agencies offering entrepreneurial support and training in France, the Agency National pour la Création d'Entreprises (ANCE) is of particular interest. ANCE was begun in 1979 by the Giscard government and has been substantially expanded by the current administration. The agency uses a network of 1500 retired executives to assist entrepreneurs and can dispatch a 'swat team' of consultants to a struggling firm anywhere in France. It was instrumental in developing a new law that allows an employee to take a two-year leave while he or she gets a new venture underway.

Across the Channel, training for would-be entrepreneurs is largely handled by the Manpower Services Commission (MSC) at its centers throughout the United Kingdom. Its courses in basic business skills are geared to those who plan to start a one-person business. Entrepreneurs who intend eventually to employ a few others can enroll in a broader six to ten-week course, which will help them test their business ideas. Those whose ideas show real growth potential may undertake an MSC-sponsored sixteen-week course of study at a university business school. In most cases, MSC pays the full cost of training, and full-time trainees receive a weekly allowance.

Some heartening entrepreneurial-training benefits are flowing today from an unexpected source — the 200 Information Technology Centers (ITECs) that have sprung up across Britain since 1980 when two 'burnt out' school teachers opened the first such center in London's Notting Dale neighborhood. Far from dreaming of developing entrepreneurs, Anthony Hoskyns and Chris Webb hoped simply to improve the employability of disaffected, unskilled, non-academically inclined 16- to 18-year-olds who had been failing in the traditional education system. There are no educational prerequisites for their program of practical training in four high-technology skill areas: basic computing, microelectronics (including repair and maintenance), production, and office functions. 'We tell local career officers to send us the kids nobody else wants', says Hoskyns.

Today, as before, ITEC's main emphasis is on skills training and job placement — about 76 per cent of 'graduates' are placed in jobs — but the curriculum underscores the notion that normal training activities can yield viable products or self-employment potential. At the Notting Dale center, for example, young entrepreneurs function as independent, authorized repair agents for Apple, Commodore, and other microcomputers. They are also developing a computer touch-screen and special software for handicapped children.

Three Observable Hindrances to Further Growth

The level of British and French success with innovative methods for encouraging new businesses has been high enough to attract the attention of policymakers in several other countries, including the United States. However, three areas of weakness are to some degree hindering further achievement.

First, both countries need to do a better job involving women and minorities. More than four-fifths of those signing up for the United Kingdom's Enterprise Allowance Scheme are men; only 7 per cent of the entrepreneurs assisted by France's ANCE network are women. Groups like the Black Business Development Association in Hammersmith and Fulham — which promotes black entrepreneurism in a borough where minorities are 26 per cent of the population but own less than 1 per cent of the businesses — are few and far between. In fact, British government policy discourages 'positive' discrimination — the targeting of programs to specific disadvantaged groups. Neither Britain nor France appears to have accepted the concept that women and minorities, because of the history of discrimination they have faced, need specially designed, comprehensive programs and attention to bring them into full and equal participation in the economy.

Secondly, more loan guarantees and incentives are needed to encourage conservative, risk-averse lending institutions and investors to channel expansion funds to small and medium-sized firms. British and French banks are highly centralized; their focus is often national and even international. France, though, has begun trying to shake up its banks by encouraging 'proximity savings' — earmarking the savings of a community for area development. Alain de Romefort, a government official in the *économie sociale*, wants to renew the tradition of 'merchant banks' as investors in new enterprises. Efforts are even being made to tap some of the funds of the giant Caisse des Depots and Consignations, France's centralized savings institution with $108 billion in assets.

Finally, much more private-sector involvement seems essential, especially to support the entrepreneurial efforts of those on the margins of the economy. The private sector is virtually absent from the French *économie sociale*. Corporate support is more apparent in Britain, both in the enterprise agencies and in the loan of executives, or 'secondees', to assist in managing enterprise development programs. But, according to Robin Heal of British Petroleum, fewer than 300 of the 300,000 private firms in London are directly involved in assisting new enterprises. US corporations contribute an average of nearly 2 per cent of their annual profits for community philanthropy. British firms donate only one-tenth of a per cent, a fraction that is nonetheless ten times greater than the European average.

Enterprise Development is Efficient Public Policy

One feature alone makes a commitment to enterprise development sound and efficient public policy in both Europe and the United States. This is its potential to help achieve two important national objectives simultaneously: economic growth and assistance to communities in greatest need.

On both sides of the Atlantic, the democratic state has been built on two separate sets of policies — macroeconomic policies to protect the health of the mainstream economy and social policies to provide at least minimal support to those cut off from that economy. Industrial restructuring, rising unemployment, and higher welfare costs are calling into question the adequacy of this bifurcation. Social progress is being blocked by a faltering economy, while economic progress is limited by our inability to bring new people and products in the marketplace. Neither set of policies has successfully integrated women and minorities into the mainstream economy.

The juxtaposition of the social and the economic in entrepreneurial is central to its dynamism. People with ideas of how to do something better are the source of economic growth and adaptation. The best of Europe's enterprise-development programs are as good as they are because they cultivate the latent talent an ingenuity of people — often the very ones who are the great casualties of a stagnating economy. While these programs cannot be expected to have a dramatic impact on overarching problems, they are already reaping some valuable economic and social rewards.

Note

1   In October, 1984, the non-profit Washington, D.C.-based Corporation for Enterprise Development led a team of American economic-development policy-makers and practitioners on a study tour to England, Scotland, and France to find out more about their innovative enterprise-development strategies for the unemployed. The trip was sponsored by the German Marshall Fund of the United States. This chapter is reprinted with permission from *Transatlantic Perspectives*, a publication of the German Marshall Fund of the United States, and summarizes the study team's report on its findings.

Addresses of Contributors

Marc Bendick, Jr.,
4201 Massachusetts Avenue, NW.,
Suite 7031c
Washington, D.C. 20016
USA.

Lois-ellin Datta,
Program Evaluation and Methodology Division,
U.S. General Accounting Office,
441 G Street, N.W.,
Washington, D.C. 20548
USA.

Peter Dehnbostel,
Babelsberger Strasse 48,
1000 Berlin (West) 31,
Federal Republic of Germany.

Richard F. Elmore,
Graduate School of Education,
Michigan State University,
East Lansing,
Michigan, 48824,
USA.

Ken Inoue,
United Nations Development Program,
19 Keate Street,
Port-of-Spain,
Trinidad and Tobago.

Elizabeth McPherson,
The German Marshall Fund of the United States,
11 Dupont Circle, N.W.,
Washington, D.C. 20036
USA.

Ann Orr,
343 S. Ridgewood Road.
South Orange,
N.J. 07079
USA.

Paul Peterson,
The Brookings Institution,
1775 Massachusetts Ave., N.W.,
Washington, D.C. 20036,
USA.

Dudley Plunkett,
Department of Education,
University of Southampton,
Southampton,
SO9 5NH England.

Barry Rabe,
Department of Health Planning and Administration,
School of Public Health,
University of Michigan,
Ann Arbor,
Michigan 48109,
USA.

Einhard Rau,
Fredericiastrasse 29,
1000 Berlin (West) 19,
Federal Republic of Germany.

Ray C. Rist,
Program Evaluation and Methodology Division,
U.S. General Accounting Office,
Washington, D.C., 20548
USA.

Ralph E. Smith,
Congressional Budget Office,
U.S. Congress,
Washington, D.C. 20515
USA.

Søren Winter,
Institute of Political Science,
University of Aarhus,
Universitetsparken,
DK — 8000 Aarhus C,
Denmark.

Index